DISAFFECTED

Series editor: Elizabeth S. Anker, Cornell University

CORPUS JURIS: THE HUMANITIES IN POLITICS AND LAW PUBLISHES BOOKS AT THE INTERSECTIONS BETWEEN LAW, POLITICS, AND THE HUMANITIES—INCLUDING HISTORY, LITERARY CRITICISM, ANTHROPOLOGY, PHILOSOPHY, RELIGIOUS STUDIES, AND POLITICAL THEORY. BOOKS IN THIS SERIES TACKLE NEW OR UNDERANALYZED ISSUES IN POLITICS AND LAW AND DEVELOP INNOVATIVE METHODS TO UNDERTAKE THOSE INQUIRIES. THE GOAL OF THE SERIES IS TO MULTIPLY THE INTERDISCIPLINARY JUNCTURES AND CONVERSATIONS THAT SHAPE THE STUDY OF LAW.

DISAFFECTED

Emotion, Sedition, and Colonial Law in the Anglosphere

Tanya Agathocleous

CORNELL UNIVERSITY PRESS   ITHACA AND LONDON

Copyright © 2021 by Cornell University

All rights reserved. Except for brief quotations in a review, this book, or parts thereof, must not be reproduced in any form without permission in writing from the publisher. For information, address Cornell University Press, Sage House, 512 East State Street, Ithaca, New York 14850. Visit our website at cornellpress.cornell.edu.

First published 2021 by Cornell University Press

Library of Congress Cataloging-in-Publication Data

Names: Agathocleous, Tanya, 1970– author.
Title: Disaffected : emotion, sedition, and colonial law in the Anglosphere / Tanya Agathocleous.
Description: Ithaca [New York] : Cornell University Press, 2021. | Series: Corpus juris : the humanities in politics and law | Includes bibliographical references and index.
Identifiers: LCCN 2020040528 (print) | LCCN 2020040529 (ebook) | ISBN 9781501753879 (hardcover) | ISBN 9781501753886 (paperback) | ISBN 9781501753893 (epub) | ISBN 9781501753909 (pdf)
Subjects: LCSH: Political alienation—India—History—19th century. | Political alienation—India—History—20th century. | Sedition—Law and legislation—India. | Politics and culture—India—History—19th century. | Politics and culture—India—History—20th century. | Censorship—India—History—19th century. | Censorship—India—History—20th century.
Classification: LCC JA75.7 .A43 2021 (print) | LCC JA75.7 (ebook) | DDC 364.1/31—dc23
LC record available at https://lccn.loc.gov/2020040528
LC ebook record available at https://lccn.loc.gov/2020040529

CONTENTS

Preface: A Colonial Genealogy of a Political Emotion	vii
Acknowledgments	xv
Introduction	1

ONE
Affectation: The Aesthete and the Babu on Trial — 33

TWO
Parody: Colonial Mimicry, Colonial Parody, and the Multiplicity of *Punch* — 71

THREE
Review: Worlding White Supremacy and Indian Nationalism — 111

FOUR
Syncretism: From East and West to the Darker Nations — 145

Conclusion — 185

Bibliography — 193
Index — 207

PREFACE
A COLONIAL GENEALOGY OF A POLITICAL EMOTION

While I was writing this book, the global rise of populism and authoritarianism made some of its key terms freshly relevant and frighteningly quotidian: censorship, sedition, incivility, and—of particular interest to me—disaffection. On November 9, 2016, for instance, *Bloomberg News* ran an article with the headline "Trump's Unthinkable Victory Is a Tonic for Disaffected Americans." The article supplied a now-well-rehearsed explanation for the "unthinkable," analyzing the way Trump's cynical xenophobia and capitalist machismo appealed to "a white working class besieged by economic rip currents, terrorist threats and a rapid demographic shift to a nation with a majority made up of minorities" and how the election served as a referendum on the status quo candidacy of Hillary Clinton and the elite liberal establishment she was seen to represent.[1] The piece concludes, "Trump may not save America's disaffected white middle class. But for one election, at least, he gave it voice." The word "disaffected" neatly bookends the article, appearing both in the title and in the grudging uplift at the end, "At least, he gave it voice." But what exactly does disaffection mean in this context?

I used to associate disaffection more with political apathy than political anger, with people who don't vote rather than people who sweep an unlikely candidate into office. It is in fact used both ways: a quick search in the *New York Times* database reveals that the word appears in sociological studies of teens who cut classes and in articles about moody rock music, as well as ones about seemingly irreparable political schisms. The *OED* definition—"Alienated from or dissatisfied with a person or thing"—splits the difference between anger and apathy, implying a negative but inactivated stance.[2] My research on censorship in colonial India, however, taught me that the word first began to circulate widely in British and American print culture via journalistic coverage of sedition legislation.

---

1. Mike Dorning, "Trump's Unthinkable Victory Is a Tonic for Disaffected Americans." *Bloomberg News*, November 9, 2016.
2. *OED Online*, s.v. "disaffection, n.," accessed September 27, 2018, http://www.oed.com/view/Entry/53435?redirectedFrom=disaffection.

It was associated explicitly with political anger, and the height of its use in the colonial period coincided with the decline of the British Empire over the course of the twentieth century, as the colonial government struggled to curtail the rise of nationalism across its many territories.

Drawing on the history of Section 124a of the Indian Penal Code, a colonial law that made disaffection—defined as hatred of the government—the equivalent of sedition, this book maintains that the concept of disaffection lay at the heart of colonial rule in India: it shaped what could be said, how it could be said, and who could say it, and literalized the metaphoric paternalism, or coercive romance, of the colonial relationship by making affection for the government a mandate of colonial citizenship. (John Havard notes that "John Milton made reference to 'disaffection' in his published defenses of divorce, where the term referred to a breach within the marital state"—the term was thus from early on associated with romantic as well as political bonds).[3]

After the 1857 Rebellion, the British government began to closely monitor, and increasingly censor, the Indian press. In 1870 Section 124a was added to the Indian Penal Code to make disaffection a central yet loosely defined term in the government's arsenal against journalistic critique. Drawn from British sedition law but rarely used in British legal practice, the vagueness of what counted as disaffection broadened the possibilities for retaliation against verbal dissent. Because Section 124a made it interchangeable with incitement to violence, disaffection was punishable by censorship, fines, imprisonment, or transportation for life.

The effects of this strategy, crucial both to the shape of the colonial public sphere in South Asia and to the nationalist movement that grew out of it, continue to reverberate in India in this century, for the law prohibiting seditious speech has been used against journalists, student protesters, and activists such as Arundhati Roy to stifle dissent. Between 2017 and 2018, over ten thousand adivasis in the district of Jharkand were charged with sedition under Section 124a for invoking the constitution (via engravings on stone slabs) to protect their land rights.[4] In the wake of the 2019 Citizenship Amendment Act and subsequent protests, the government repeatedly weaponized it against demonstrators. Because

---

3. John Havard, *Disaffected Parties: Political Parties and the Making of English Literature, 1760–1830* (Oxford: Oxford University Press, 2019), 9.

4. "10,000 People Charged with Sedition in One Jharkhand District: What Does Democracy Mean Here?," *Scroll in*, November 19, 2019, https://scroll.in/article/944116/10000-people-charged-with-sedition-in-one-jharkhand-district-what-does-democracy-mean-here.

landmark judgments in the Supreme Court since independence have curtailed the effects of the law by ruling that seditious speech is only that which incites violence or disrupts law and order, most cases brought against dissenters are thrown out. But 124a is nonetheless brandished as a weapon against free speech by allowing for the arrest and trial—if not the conviction—of protestors because the language of affect still allows for broad application. Like many other aspects of colonial administration, then, 124a's antidemocratic effects reverberated long past the end of British rule.

Section 124a served imperial rule by encoding a stringent version of Enlightenment public sphere norms of rationality and impartiality into law, thus criminalizing negative affect and condemning writing that had the capacity to "excite" readers because it might *potentially* (rather than explicitly) incite violence or hatred of the government. Since disaffection was equated by the law with disloyalty, loyalty to the empire was necessarily connected to expressions of friendship and affection; the act thus made official the way that imperial power conflated coercion and consent.

If political discourse was racially fractured by sedition law, which created a different standard for the Indian and the British press, so was the legal sphere itself. In *Colonial Justice in British India*, Elizabeth Kolsky demonstrates how a preponderance of white violence against Indians instigated the development of laws against violent crime, even though in the colonial imagination it was Indians who were the criminal targets of these laws (and who were criminalized quite literally as well, by laws such as the Criminal Tribes Act of 1871 which identified a number of tribal groups with criminal tendencies). Much bodily violence on the ground, however, consisted of Anglo-Indians taking on "the state's monopoly of legitimate violence and pain-related power" to punish Indian workers.[5] Because of this, Anglo-Indians resisted efforts to make them subject to the rulings of Indian judges and juries, and were largely successful: by 1898, Kolsky writes, "no magistrate, unless he was a justice of the peace and a magistrate of the first class and a European British subject . . . had jurisdiction to inquire into or try any charge against a European British subject."[6] Racial discrimination was thus coded into law until the Criminal Law Removal of Racial Distinctions Act of 1949. An apartheid system—in speech and in fact—was the rule.

---

5. Elizabeth Kolsky, *Colonial Justice in British India: White Violence and the Rule of Law* (Cambridge: Cambridge University Press, 2010), 37. On the Criminal Trials Act, see Henry Schwarz, *Constructing the Criminal Tribe in Colonial India* (Chichester, UK: Wiley-Blackwell, 2010).

6. Kolsky, *Colonial Justice in British India*, 187.

How did the idea of disaffection and its criminalization shape conversations in the colonial public sphere? And how did the transportation of colonial conflict into the realm of affect influence the articulation of anticolonialism and its postcolonial aftermath? The color line within the law in British India is the context for my argument that disaffection is a vital term for understanding the centrality of affect to governance in the colonial period, as well as for recognizing and analyzing the varied forms that critique took in the Indian Anglosphere (a term I use to describe the English-language print culture generated by Indians, Britons, and Anglo-Indians that circulated across imperial space).[7]

In the debates about censorship that followed the 1857 Rebellion and raged on for several decades, British and Anglo-Indian journalism that circulated in India was upheld as a model of rational and judicious critique, and of intercultural dialogue and analysis; Indian writing was meant to model itself on this example, yet necessarily operated in a separate sphere from white writing, which was seldom policed by the government. Because this separate sphere was defined by the law as an affective one, Indian writing was repeatedly figured as a bad copy of white writing; as such it was dismissed as babu posturing derived from intemperate passions rather than analytic rigor, produced by base imitation rather than deliberate thought. In this way, the law against disaffection created a bifurcated public sphere in which British speech was associated with reason and detachment, and Indian speech with affect and atavism. The colonial public sphere, in other words, far from being a space of democratizing deliberation separate from the state (as the Habermasian model would suggest), was defined by the state and racialized. White writing was recognized as civil discourse while brown writing was seen as prone to irrationality and incivility and subject to exile from public debate.

The racialized double standard applied to Indian writing by the disaffection law meant that Indian imitation of the British press became a desirable and pragmatic journalistic style, or pose. Building on Homi Bhabha's concept of colonial mimicry, I use the term "print mimicry" to explore the way Indian writers and editors strategically reproduced and altered the forms and conventions of British periodicals in order to evade censorship. The dialectical relationship between periodicals and political discourse produced in Britain and in India helped shape both the imperial public sphere and colonial and postcolonial government. Each chapter of this book, then, explores different tactics of critique used by journalists

---

7. I thank Anjuli Raza Kolb for suggesting this formulation.

or editors in India that emerged in the context of censorship and in relation to the British press. I organize these tactics under four key terms that best describe how they work formally: *affectation, parody, review*, and *syncretism*.

Chapter 1 lays the groundwork for my exploration of disaffection and critique in India by examining the relationship between the Oscar Wilde trials and the trial of the *Bangavasi*: the first newspaper trial in India to introduce disaffection as a disciplinary strategy. I demonstrate how and why both trials were centrally concerned with sexuality, excessive affect, and the artifice of affectation, and show how the key terms operating in each trial circulated between Britain and India in the Anglophone press. In chapter 2, I analyze the overlap between colonial mimicry and colonial parody by exploring the ways that parody, inversion, and caricature, in both visual and verbal forms, played a central role in Indian responses to their representation in the British press. I focus in particular on *Hindi Punch*, an illustrated journal that was explicitly in dialogue with British *Punch* and the Anglo-Indian periodical the *Indian Charivari*. In its responses to racist cartoons in these journals, and in its counternarrative of contemporary political events, *Hindi Punch* used parody to reveal the ways that negative affect—in the form of distrust, paranoia, and racial contempt—far from being an external threat to the colonial public sphere, was in fact its guiding logic.

Chapter 3, on the literary review and the practice of reviewing as such, examines how attempts to subdivide the imperial public sphere along racial lines so as to undermine dissent led to the development of new mass media forms in which the racial divide was explicit. This affected both the ways audiences were addressed and the ways information was amassed and presented. Specifically, it investigates how an imperialist form of white supremacy influenced the emergence of two "reviews of reviews" at the turn of the twentieth century, within which the digestion and redaction of other periodicals was seen as a way to accelerate an imagined community into a lived reality. One was W. T. Stead's *Review of Reviews*, and the other was the *Indian World*, a Calcutta-based journal that was explicitly and cannily derivative of Stead's, and that radically adapted the global purview of his journal to the ends of Indian nationalism, changing Stead's own practice and his understanding of the relationship between empire and censorship along the way.

The final chapter shows how various forms and practices of modernist syncretism—the idea of East-West unity through cultural exchange and the melding of traditions—influenced Indian journals such as *East and West*, a modernist periodical published in Bombay, as well as famous British writers such as E. M. Forster and Rudyard Kipling. Syncretic works shared an interest in the redemptive potential of affection between colonizer and colonized and represented this idea via the romance of intercultural union: the ambivalence built into articulations of this romance, however, illuminates the dialectical tension between affection and disaffection that underwrote cultural exchange under imperialism. I demonstrate how this tension took literary form and how it influenced new anticolonial formations, such as those that took shape in London at the Universal Races Congress of 1911.

In the conclusion, I analyze Gandhi's trial for disaffection in 1922 to show how his canny appropriation of the term as a badge of honor helped galvanize the nationalist movement and reframe the terms of public discourse, bringing the critical subtext and covert nationalism of earlier journalism—its purported disaffection—to the fore and refashioning it as good rather than bad affect. I end with a brief account of the stakes of this research for the contemporary context. The colonial history of disaffection helps us understand why that term continues to be used to describe those who feel marginalized by politics and political debates today. While used in different, but related, ways from its colonial antecedents, the concept of disaffection is still valuable as a way of understanding the relationship between the content of politics and the form of publics. By exploring the dynamics of the imperial public sphere, I hope also to shed light on why publics continue to be shaped by feelings of exclusion and why exclusion is understood as a feeling. The law against disaffection made explicit the way the public sphere was divided into those who could and could not exercise free speech along racial lines and helps explain why censorship and free speech debates today so often coalesce around questions of identity and civility. Civility has always been identitarian or, to put it differently, we have never been civil.

Given our current political climate and the way public discourse has itself become a reliable source of disaffection, it is not surprising that scholarly studies of this hitherto understudied negative affect are beginning to emerge. Havard's *Disaffected Parties*, for example, traces the literary expression of political disaffection across the long eighteenth century. His understanding of disaffection in that period is similar to its usages today: in his treatment, disaffection encompasses "individual and collective expressions of feeling 'sick' of politics, grumbling . . . division and revolutionary agitation (as well as more elusive 'discontents')."[8] Martin F. Manalansan IV uses the term slightly differently, applying it in a contemporary context to describe the affect of Filipinx care workers, a kind of "composure . . . or an affective orientation that inclines towards a managed, if

---

8. Havard, *Disaffected Parties*, 46.

not studied, refusal to unleash or display emotional states publicly."⁹ For both these critics, disaffection suggests an act of repudiation and thus has dynamic potential. In Havard's view, it allows for both "estrangement and engagement, cynicism and critique," in Manalansan's for "emotions continuously moving across the borders of the domestic and the public, of the intimate and the distant."¹⁰ The colonial moment of disaffection upon which I focus falls roughly between the periods investigated by Havard and Manalansan but is also one defined by a dialectical dynamism in which a weapon of the state (Section 124a) creates the thing it was designed to suppress, shifting the grounds of power and possibility.

Disaffection is not only a compelling term for our contemporary political context but is also an important lens through which to reexamine the discipline of literary studies, which—this book suggests—uses interpretive practices first honed in colonial courtrooms. Fredric Jameson's 1986 article, "Third World Literature in the Era of Multinational Capitalism," which argued that postcolonial texts could be read as national allegories, was lambasted for its broad generalizations and seeming validation of a First World/Third World binary when it was first published, most famously by Aijaz Ahmad. Though now decades old, the essay occasionally resurfaces because of the amount of controversy it generated; Imre Szeman has attempted to offer the piece a more generous reading by recontextualizing some of its central terms.¹¹ Missing entirely from the conversation about the essay, however, is the context of censorship. As Sukeshi Kamra notes, "Allegory was the method by which the nationalist Indian press resolved the bind in which it found itself—to be nationalist ('seditious') on the one hand and evade the law on disaffection on the other."¹² This tactic did not escape the notice of the colonial government; in a debate about the 1911 Press Act, Sir Herbert Risley, describing the various "tricks" that journals employed to evade the censorship law, noted that "a frequent method, adopted by many journals, was to write in

---

9. Martin F. Manalansan IV, "Servicing the World: Flexible Filipinos and the Unsecured Life," in *Political Emotions*, ed. Janet Staiger, Ann Cvetkovich, and Ann Reynolds (New York: Routledge, 2010), 217.

10. Havard, *Disaffected Parties*, 8; Manalansan, "Servicing the World," 225.

11. Aijaz Ahmad, "Jameson's Rhetoric of Otherness and the 'National Allegory,'" *Social Text*, no. 17 (Autumn 1987): 3–25; Imre Szeman, "Who's Afraid of National Allegory? Jameson, Literary Criticism, Globalization," *South Atlantic Quarterly* 100, no. 3 (Summer 2001): 803–27.

12. Sukeshi Kamra, *The Indian Periodical Press and Nationalist Rhetoric* (New York: Palgrave Macmillan, 2011), 35.

allegories, the real meaning of which was manifest to everybody except the then law officers of the Crown."[13]

If, despite its flaws, we were to accept Jameson's argument that "national allegory" is a useful heuristic for postcolonial literature, it would not be because, as he starkly put it, "in third-world texts . . . the relationship between the libidinal and the political components of individual and social experience is radically different from what obtains in the west and what shapes our own cultural forms."[14] It would be because the use of national allegory under colonial governance—in India and across the empire—was the *precondition* of postcolonial literature, enabling early anticolonial writing and speech to reach its intended audience of those positioned to decode it. Allegory, then, was a tactic—and like the other tactics I examine here, its uses suggest that censorship, disaffection, and their interrelation are vital to our understanding of literary form and critical analysis, in past empires and present ones.

---

13. "The Indian Press Bill," *Times of London*, February 5, 1910, 9.
14. Fredric Jameson, "Third-World Literature in the Era of Multinational Capitalism," *Social Text* 15 (1986): 65–88, 71.

ACKNOWLEDGMENTS

I am lucky to have had Liz Anker as an editor; she has been unfailingly helpful and encouraging and I am proud to be a part of her exciting new series. Huge thanks to Camille Robcis for drawing my attention to it and being so supportive. Everyone at Cornell University Press has been an absolute pleasure to work with, in particular Diane Brown, whose calm intelligence has made the whole process seamless, and Jennifer Savran Kelly. Sukanya Banerjee and Seth Koven kindly revealed their identities as reviewers. I thank them for their rigorous, brilliant, and detailed readings and am indebted to them for their generosity and acuity.

For financial support and release time for research, I thank Hunter College and the PSC–CUNY research fund. A yearlong ACLS fellowship and a sabbatical allowed me to get the bulk of my research and writing done. I am also grateful for support and input from my department chairs over the years: Cristina Alfar, Sarah Chinn, and Angie Reyes.

When I first became an academic, I was drawn to Victorian studies because I was raised on British literature at the British schools I went to; I went to those schools because my parents are both from former colonies (Cyprus, India, and Kenya were all in the mix). This book is partly an effort to understand what it means to have received a colonial education and the particular type of double-consciousness that it produces—a question that required me to venture into fields I had little knowledge of at the outset, including the history of colonial India; colonial law; South Asian studies; periodical studies; and the history of print culture in India. Thanks are due to the many, many people who helped me figure out what I needed to know—I hope I've remembered all of them below but apologize to anyone I've missed.

A heartfelt thank you to those who read work that eventually became a part of this book, and helped make it better: Maeve Adams, Ayelet Ben-Yishai, Shoumik Bhattacharya, Annmarie Drury, Gloria Fisk, Ian Christopher Fletcher, Elaine Freedgood, Laura Frost, Toral Gajarawala, Lauren Goodlad, Hala Halim, Nathan Hensley, Isabel Hofmeyr, Sukeshi Kamra, Anjuli Raza Kolb, Anna Kornbluh, Lara Kriegel, Vince Lankewish, Wendy Lee, Caroline Levine, Tricia Lootens, Meredith Martin, James Mulholland, Janet Neary, Sonali Perera, Lloyd Pratt, Rajeswari

Sunder Rajan, Bruce Robbins, Camille Robcis, Jason Rudy, Purvi Shah, Katie Trumpener, Greg Vargo, Gauri Viswanathan, Dan White, and Sandy Young.

For encouragement, advice, helpful feedback, engaged discussion, speaking invitations, and/or searching questions along the way, I thank Rachel Ablow, Dohra Ahmad, Meena Alexander, Greg Allen, Ben Baer, Carolyn Betensky, Samia Bhutan, Shameem Black, Alexander Bubb, Supriya Chaudhari, Zahid Chaudhary, Joseph Chaves, Erik Dussere, Jill Ehnenn, Sarah Ellenzweig, David Eng, Jonathan Farina, Christine Ferguson, Ross Forman, Eileen Gillooly, Jeremy Glick, Abhijit Gupta, Robert Higney, Priti Joshi, Raji Kuar, Sebastian Lecourt, David Lelyveld, Ramesh Mallipedi, Amy Martin, Helena Michie, Benjamin Morgan, Ankhi Mukherjee, Mary Mullen, Stephanie Newell, Patrick O'Malley, Francesca Orsini, Achal Prabhala, Charlotte Priddle, Angie Reyes, Elda Rotor, Todd Shepard, Emily Sibley, Avery Slater, Neelam Srivastava, Faith Wilson Stein, Tyler Talbott, Mark Turner, Alan Vardy, Mike Vasquez, Gary Wilder, Siona Wilson, and Ken Wissoker. Particular thanks to Ross Forman, who offered all the above, read sections of the book, *and* gave me great restaurant recommendations in London.

Research assistants at the CUNY Graduate Center and Hunter College were immensely helpful at various stages of research and putting the manuscript together: thanks are due to Onur Ayaz, Filipa Calado, Michele Chinitz, Evelen Hough, Sylvia Scahill, Ryan Vera, and Mitchell Wilson. In addition, Zach Fruit and Kyle McCauley supplied meticulous and indispensable research at crucial moments when I couldn't get to the British Library and I am deeply grateful.

For personal and political reasons, I am attracted to collaborative work, and collaborations and collectivities of various forms were the most rewarding part of working on this project. Members of a New York–based Victorianist writing group (Tim Alborn, Carolyn Berman, Deborah Lutz, Adrienne Munich, Caroline Reitz, and Talia Schaffer) were instrumental in helping me figure out what the book was about in its early stages. My classes at Hunter College and the CUNY Graduate Center have been formative in my thinking at all stages of writing it, especially one on disaffection that I taught at the Graduate Center in Fall 2017—many thanks to the students in that class, both for their insights and their enthusiasm for the material.

Two international scholarly networks allowed me to meet people and learn about archives and research crucial to my work that I otherwise wouldn't have access to. One was the Commodities and Culture Network, whose conferences in Kolkata, Johannesburg, and New York I attended: a warm thank you to Supriya Chaudhury at the University of Jadavpur in Kolkata and Isabel Hofmeyr at the University of Witswatersand for being as generous and inspiring as hosts as they are as scholars. The second is the Postcolonial Print Cultures Network. I am grateful to Rajeswari Sunder Rajan for inviting me in, and to Elaine Freedgood for introducing me to her in the first place, getting me involved in the Commodities and Culture Network, and generously sharing resources of time and space, all while serving as the model of intellectual and political integrity that she is.

Participants at a series of panels at the ACLA and MLA annual meetings on Imperial Publics that I co-organized with James Mulholland were important to my thinking, as was the Working Group on the Universal Races Congress at the Center for Race and Ethnicity at Rutgers University, run by Mia Bay and Seth Koven. Thanks also to audiences at American University; George Washington University; New York University; Northwestern University; Oxford University; Princeton University; Rutgers University; University of Illinois at Chicago; University of Maryland; University of Northern Colorado; University of Warwick; University of Wisconsin–Madison; and, of course, Hunter College and the Graduate Center, City University of New York, who offered valuable feedback on various parts of the project.

For companionship, motivation, and solidarity, I am grateful to Gloria Fisk, Anjuli Raza Kolb, Meredith Martin, and Nicole Rice, each of whom worked alongside me at cafés and libraries for significant stretches of the writing of this book, and whose collective brilliance could power the sun. While, for geographic reasons, they seldom wrote alongside me, Jason Rudy and Janet Neary were there for me the whole time. I couldn't have finished this book without their unconditional support and unwavering good judgment, both emotional and intellectual; I feel incredibly lucky to be collaborating with them in writing and in life. I am also grateful for the ongoing support of Carolyn Williams, who was my dissertation director and is still the person I write for in my head. Sanda Lwin and Chris Barter entertained and accommodated me in London on my many trips to the British Library, where much of my primary research was conducted, and I appreciate their generosity and company. Karen Pittelman, writing coach extraordinaire and literal rock star, got me across the finish line. My brother, Alexis Agathocleous, and his work on criminal justice reform helped inspire my interest in colonial law. I am grateful to him, my parents, Chris O'Brien, and my daughter Zora for their love, support, and patience with my distraction as I completed this book. And thanks to Kevin Quirolo, who was there for all the hard parts. I'm so happy to have you in my world—for a day or a lifetime.

DISAFFECTED

INTRODUCTION

> Our critiques of literary studies ... must venture beyond the walls of the academy and analyze the spread of colonial law across the earth.
>
> —Siraj Ahmed, Archaeology of Babel

In 1855 James Long, an Anglo-Irish missionary who was active in schoolbook production and fascinated by Bengali literature, published *A Catalogue of Bengali Newspapers and Periodicals from 1818 to 1855*. As the author of this text he was in a good position to argue, two years later, that had the British paid more heed to the discontent on view in Indian periodicals, they might have prevented the 1857 Rebellion.[1] Colonialists had first become wary of the press before the Rebellion: as early as 1836, Christopher Bayly notes, "the expatriate newspaper, *The Friend of India*, remarked . . . 'our Indian Empire is one of opinion' and 'the progress of knowledge' would probably 'entail the separation of India from England.'"[2] After 1857 this concern metastasized into a full-fledged culture of surveillance. The Press and Registration of Books Act of 1867, an official acknowledgment of the power of the Indian press, decreed that all books and periodicals must be registered with the government and clearly display the name of their printer, publisher, and place of publication, so individuals could be held to account for what they published. This gave the government a panoptic view of the burgeoning Indian public sphere while simultaneously putting it on notice.[3]

---

1. Robert Darnton, "Book Production in British India, 1850–1900," *Book History* 5 (2002): 239–62, 241. Darnton notes that Long himself would eventually be prosecuted for libel against the colonial government because of his translation of *Nil Darpan*, a play about the exploitation of indigo farmworkers.

2. Christopher Bayly, *Empire and Information: Intelligence Gathering and Social Communication in India, 1780–1870* (Cambridge: Cambridge University Press, 1996), 2.

3. Walter Russell Donogh, *A Treatise on the Law of Sedition and Cognate Offences in British India* (Calcutta: Thacker, Spink, 1911), 241–44.

Along with the Press Act, the Native Newspaper Report (NNR) was a draconian policing tactic first used methodically in the post-Mutiny period. A survey of the vernacular press by government agents, the NNR was tasked with paying close attention to its "tone and influence"; it did this by producing translations and summaries of an astonishingly wide variety of Indian language newspapers and periodicals so they could be reviewed by the secretary of state.[4] Sukeshi Kamra's account of the NNR in her important book on Indian periodicals and the rise of nationalism argues that, because it sought to track political unrest through instances of emotional excess, individual reports numbering as many as a hundred pages a week "worked to consolidate a very particular image of Indian political and social psychology while allowing, even encouraging, its intended audience (government officials) to conclude that the Indian press and reading communities were hotbeds of simmering resentment at one end and volatility at the other."[5] Other governmental attempts to police the public sphere such as Section 153a, which penalized writing or speech that incited "class hatred," also relied on affect to serve as the canary in the coal mine of incipient rebellion.

Yet Section 124a, the law against disaffection, was perhaps the most overt attempt to use affect as a tool of governance. When it first became part of the Indian Penal Code in 1870, Section 124a read as follows:

> Whoever by words, either spoken or intended to be read, or by signs, or by visible representation or otherwise, *excites or attempts to excite feelings of disaffection* to the Government established by law in British India, shall be punished with transportation for life or for any term, to which fine may be added, or with imprisonment for a term which may extend to three years, to which fine may be added, or with fine [my emphasis].[6]

If Section 124a was designed to have a broad purview because it was potentially applicable to any form of speech in public circulation, it also sought to parcel out responsibility for disaffection as widely as possible. In his lengthy

---

4. Cited in Sukeshi Kamra, *The Indian Political Press and the Production of Nationalist Rhetoric* (New York: Palgrave Macmillan, 2011), 8.
5. Kamra, *Indian Political Press*, 9.
6. Donogh, *Treatise on the Law of Sedition*, 9. Those sentenced under the law were generally transported to a prison colony on the Andaman Islands.

interpretation of colonial sedition law, Walter Russell Donogh, barrister-at-law and advocate of the High Court at Calcutta, noted that the "whoever" at the beginning of the section could apply to "all persons who wittingly take part, whether actively or passively, in the dissemination of seditious matter."[7] And indeed, Section 124a was used to indict newspaper proprietors, editors, managers, printers, distributors, and even newsstand owners.[8]

Between its first use in the *Bangavasi* case trial in 1890 (discussed at length in chapter 1) and independence in 1947, Section 124a made every kind of text the government could think of subject to suppression, including "poetry, song lyrics, fiction, drama, essays, gramophone records, posters, broadsheets, and even garments, such as dhotis," as well as woodcuts and engravings (often used to create political cartoons and other visual forms of social satire and critique).[9] Though this book is concerned with the effect of the law on journalism—the form most frequently cited by the government as a source of civil unrest—other types of verbal performance were major targets as well; the theater, for instance, was deemed especially threatening because of its cross-class appeal.[10] In some cases, spoken words were treated as if they were more powerful than written ones because of their wider reach.[11]

---

7. Donogh, *Treatise on the Law of Sedition*, 84. Donogh's interpretive text is one of the best sources on sedition law in colonial India. Stephen Morton calls it "one of the most meticulous attempts to explain and clarify sedition legislation in the Indian Penal Code." Stephen Morton, *States of Emergency: Colonialism, Literature and Law* (Liverpool: Liverpool University Press, 2014), 68.

8. Donogh notes, however, that in cases where news-sellers were deemed to be unaware of the seditious libel they were disseminating, they were declared innocent, as were "the Trustees of the British Museum whose duty it was to receive copies of all publications for the Library, and to supply them to readers through their librarians." Though the libel case against the British Museum alluded to by Donogh (*Martin v. Trustees of the British Museum*) was unrelated to Section 124a, his reference to it demonstrates the degree to which the British and Indian legal systems were imagined as continuous and the ways in which the metropole was seen as potentially vulnerable to the excesses of government surveillance in the colonies. Donogh, *Treatise on the Law of Sedition*, 97.

9. Kamra, *Indian Political Press*, 99; Donogh, *Treatise on the Law of Sedition*, 76.

10. See, for example, Pushpa Sundar, *Patrons and Philistines: Arts and the State in British India, 1773–1947* (Delhi: Oxford University Press, 1995).

11. Robert Darnton provides a fascinating account of one such instance: Mukunda Lal Das was a nationalist singer-performer who traveled by boat through the Ganges Delta from one peasant village to another producing and starring in a play eventually deemed to be "a seditious allegory" by the British, not least because of the potency of "The White Rat Song," Mukunda's biggest hit. When the government finally caught up with him, Darnton notes, "Mukunda received twice as long a prison term for his singing as for the publication of his songs—testimony to the importance of oral communication in a society with a low rate of literacy." Robert Darnton, "Literary Surveillance in the British Raj: The Contradictions of Liberal Imperialism," *Book History* 4 (2001): 133–76, 167.

As Janaki Bakhle notes, surveillance and sedition law were "Britain's most powerful tools against nationalism," even after opposition to the government became more vocal and violent in the early twentieth century, because "the real terror was neither guns and bombs, nor anarchism or nihilism. It was Indian disaffection with colonial rule."[12] The irony of the disaffection law, though, was that rather than effectively propping up colonial rule, it ended up contributing to the rise and eventual success of the Indian nationalist movement.

It did this in a number of ways. First, by giving criticism of the government a distinct character—disaffection—it helped give shape to a practice of resistance and turn anticolonialism into an identity, as evidenced by Gandhi proudly calling himself a "disaffectionist" in his 1922 trial for sedition (see conclusion). Second, by associating anticolonial critique with affect—the lifeblood of nationalism, according to Benedict Anderson and many other influential theorists of the nation—the law enhanced critique's power.[13] The antidote to disaffection with the government was not affection for Britain but for India, at least according to nationalist rhetoric. As Sartre puts it in his introduction to Frantz Fanon's *Wretched of the Earth*, "Their feeling for each other is the reverse of the hatred they feel for you."[14]

If the disaffection law was meant to coercively court affection for British rule by suggesting that the realm of intimacy was the proper grounds of national belonging, then, it had exactly the opposite effect. For, as Partha Chatterjee has influentially demonstrated, it was the private sphere, the realm of feeling, that was imagined by Indians as the space of tradition, religion, and affective bonds—of Indian identity, in other words.[15] By officially making affect the cellular structure of political community in India, the disaffection law validated rather than inhibited the nationalist cause. Furthermore, as Kamra demonstrates, censorship and other forms of colonial repression helped create a melodramatic narrative of

---

12. Janaki Bakhle, "Savarkar (1883–1966), Sedition and Surveillance: The Rule of Law in a Colonial Situation," *Social History* 35, no. 1 (February 2010): 53.

13. See, for example, Benedict Anderson, *Imagined Communities: Reflections on the Origins and Spread of Nationalism* (New York: Verso, 1983); and Richard Rorty's arguments for the need for patriotic pride versus shame in progressive politics in *Achieving Our Country: Leftist Thought in Twentieth-Century America* (Cambridge, MA: Harvard University Press, 1999).

14. Jean-Paul Sartre, introduction to *The Wretched of the Earth*, by Frantz Fanon (New York: Grove Press, 1968), lvi.

15. See Partha Chatterjee, *The Nation and Its Fragments: Colonial and Postcolonial Histories* (Princeton, NJ: Princeton University Press, 1993); and Partha Chatterjee, *Nationalist Thought and the Colonial World: A Derivative Discourse* (Minneapolis: University of Minnesota Press, 1993).

Indian victimization and heroic resistance in which the law against disaffection was easily cast as one of the chief villains.[16]

Section 124a was also crucial to the rise of nationalism because it epitomized the hypocrisy of liberal-imperial governance and the racial double standard embedded in the structure and practice of colonial law. As Amitav Ghosh has eloquently put it, "Race is the unstated term through which the gradualism of liberalism reconciles itself to the permanence of Empire."[17] Unstated as it might have been, it was very much noticed by Indians: the nationalist leader Bal Gangadhar Tilak—who was tried for sedition on three separate occasions—stated in 1907 that "the goddess of British Justice, though blind, is able to distinguish unmistakably black from white." Sedition law and its uses thus became "a powerful rhetorical tool to criticise and contest the legitimacy of the British colonial government and the violence upon which that government is based."[18] The prohibition of critique, in other words, became the very grounds for critique because it served as irrefutable evidence of what Ranajit Guha terms the "unBritish character of British rule."[19]

The possibility of censorship generating considerable blowback occurred to a number of British politicians and commentators, who advocated against curtailments of free speech. In fact, there was no hegemonic consensus on how to deal with the Indian press, especially before the turn of the twentieth century. Gerald Barrier writes that, "caught between a tradition that favored a free press and anxiety over all but the most innocuous criticism, the British swung back and forth from strict controls to virtual freedom of expression."[20] Despite this political vacillation, sedition became an official concern of the government with the passing of Section 124a and its threat to empire became a self-fulfilling prophecy.

Tone Policing and the Politics of Affect

In putting Indian writers on trial for disaffection, the colonial government sought to make examples of them because of what Sianne Ngai might call their

---

16. Kamra, *Indian Political Press*, 124.
17. Amitav Ghosh and Dipesh Chakrabarty, "A Correspondence on Provincializing Europe," *Radical History Review* 83 (Spring 2002): 146–72, 152.
18. Morton, *States of Emergency*, 84.
19. Ranajit Guha, *Dominance without Hegemony* (Cambridge, MA: Harvard University Press, 1998), 57.
20. Norman Gerald Barrier, *Banned: Controversial Literature and Political Control in British India, 1907–47* (Columbia: University of Missouri Press, 1974), 4.

"tone." Ngai reclaims this term from its New Critical associations and expands it to mean "a literary text's affective bearing, orientation, or 'set toward' its audience and world."[21] The colonial government essentially meant it this way as well. In speaking about an amendment to Section 124a that sought to expand its applications, Lord Elgin said "he wished that the general tone of criticism of the newspapers of India were less unduly colored by prejudice."[22] In Tilak's 1897 trial for sedition, the judge told the jury that "the difference in tone and spirit and general drift between a writer who is trying to stir up ill-will and one who is not, is generally unmistakable."[23]

While it imported language from British sedition law, Section 124a gave disaffection prominence over the more concrete accusations of "sedition" and "seditious libel" in the original version: terms which refer to specific crimes rather than amorphous sentiments. According to Section 124a, however, all written or verbal critique of colonial rule was subject to legal action if it crossed an arbitrary line. While sedition was often imagined to be located in the text itself—the words that incited violence against the government—disaffection was associated with feelings, both those stirred up in the populace and those located in the person accused of it. Repressing and coercing emotion on either end of the affective scale, Section 124a established sovereignty over the colonial subject from within: a form of violence different from, but supplementary to, those used by the military, the police, and Anglo-Indian civilians.[24]

After Tilak's trial, Section 124a was revised to reflect a broader definition of disaffection.[25] The new version of 124a added the words "hatred and contempt" to the original phrasing—terms that had been used by the judge in the *Bangavasi* trial, the first newspaper trial to deploy the law (see chapter 1). In addition, a new explanation appeared beneath it: "The expression 'disaffection' includes disloyalty and all feelings of enmity." Here, the augmented definition drew from the proceedings of the Tilak trial, where the judge had highlighted the accused's

---

21. Sianne Ngai, *Ugly Feelings* (Cambridge, MA: Harvard University Press, 2007), 43.
22. "The Law of Sedition in India: Lord Elgin on the Proposed Amendment," *Glasgow Herald*, December 22, 1897.
23. Darnton, "Literary Surveillance," 162.
24. On the relation between quotidian and state-based colonial violence, see Kolsky, *Colonial Justice in British India*.
25. For a full analysis of the trial, see Sukeshi Kamra, "Law and Radical Rhetoric in British India: The 1897 Trial of Bal Gangadhar Tilak," *South Asia* 39, no. 3 (2016): 546–59.

"disloyalty."[26] Lord Elgin's rationale for the proposed amendment stated that "in preventing sedition . . . the Government acts for the public, whose interests will suffer if the *passions of the ignorant are excited* and the peace of the country imperiled by the action of a few persons *out of touch with the sentiments* of their fellows. The Government's aim is the establishment of an *impartial law*, not harsh in character but *prompt and firm*" (my emphasis).[27] Predictably, the justification for the law, like the law itself, describes Indians in affective terms ("passions," "excited," "sentiments") as opposed to the law-and-order terms used for the government ("impartial," "prompt," "firm"). This differentiation was increasingly necessary because the revised law, with its enhanced emphasis on affect, was increasingly distinct from British law.

In arguing for the passing of the new wording, the head of the select committee in charge of revision, Mr. Chalmers, appealed to the logic of civilizational difference: "No one in his senses would contend that because a given law is good and suitable in England, it is therefore good and suitable in India. . . . How much license of speech can be safely allowed is a question of time and place."[28] His rationale also shifted the discourse away from authorial intention to the overall effects of the speech in question, for what was really at stake was "not the apparent intention of the writers or speakers so much as the tendency of the writings or speeches . . . and the cumulative effect of depreciatory declamation on the minds of an ignorant and excitable population. . . . No Government, such as ours in India can afford to allow the minds of an ignorant and credulous oriental population to be gradually poisoned and embittered by persistent calumny."[29] In knowing how to generate affect among the masses, or, in Chalmers's phrasing, "how to appeal to their sympathies, credulity, and religious feelings," educated journalists were beginning to produce a "far more insidious" form of writing that therefore required more robust censorship.[30]

The government's response to the perceived threat of political emotion, then, was to inject *more* emotion into the law's application by expanding the ways it might be defined and identified. Even though James Fitzjames Stephen and other lawmakers were strategically reluctant to define disaffection, a host of affects

---

26. Donogh, *Treatise on the Law of Sedition*, 71.
27. "The Law of Sedition in India: Lord Elgin on the Proposed Amendment," *Glasgow Herald*, December 22, 1897.
28. Donogh, *Treatise on the Law of Sedition*, 64.
29. Donogh, *Treatise on the Law of Sedition*, 66–67.
30. Donogh, *Treatise on the Law of Sedition*, 67, 68.

would be evoked by judges and lawyers in their prosecution of sedition cases in the years following the *Bangavasi* trial, including

- hatred
- enmity
- dislike
- hostility
- contempt
- every form of ill will
- political discontent
- alienation of allegiance
- aversion
- insubordination
- animosity
- disloyalty
- "a disposition not to obey but to resist"
- "the repudiation of that spirit of acceptance of a particular government as ruler."[31]

The alarming proliferation of negative affects supposedly contained within the term "disaffection" suggests not only the difficulty of naming critique in a way that sufficiently discredited it, but also the government's increasing paranoia as the nationalist movement gathered strength. Fanon might say that the centrality of negative affect to the imperial power struggle is how "the white man's unconscious" justifies the aggression of the racialized subject and "gives it worth by turning it on himself, thus reproducing the classic schema of masochism."[32] From another psychoanalytic angle, the obsessive focus on negative affect reads as the repressed, projected, and ultimately circular logic of imperialism, wherein the violence of the colonizer is disavowed by its attribution to the colonized, which then serves as the justification for more violence. Instrumentally, however, it was the flexibility and expansiveness of disaffection as a way of naming dissent that attracted the government to the term.

But this vagueness of definition had its drawbacks as well. Some of the terms in the list above name interpersonal emotions (hate, enmity, hostility, contempt, aversion, ill will) while others are more specific to the ruler/subject relationship

---

31. Donogh, *Treatise on the Law of Sedition*, 74.
32. Frantz Fanon, *Black Skin, White Masks* (New York: Grove Press, 1967), 176.

(political discontent, insubordination, "a disposition not to obey," and the tortured formulation "repudiation of that spirit of acceptance"). The uneasy proximity of these different forms of feeling meant that the affect allegory that turned the colonial relationship into a form of intimacy was always poised on the brink of splintering apart to reveal the ruse of power. In his study of Section 124a, Donogh, exasperatedly trying to pin down a definition, explained that disaffection is "a state of mind or psychological disposition with well-defined characteristics. It is in fact the mental condition of being disaffected. To be disaffected is to be adversely affected towards, or turned against someone, e.g. the Government."[33] This tautological exegesis not only underscores the term's ambiguity but also enacts a telling slippage in the last sentence, where the awkwardness of "adversely affected *towards*" evokes the more common and grammatical usage, "adversely affected *by*," thus inadvertently switching the role of instigator to the government. Far from having "well-defined characteristics," disaffection is at once a state of mind, a feeling, and a political stance.

The way affect was used in the colonial context to understand power relations anticipates the way it has come to define them in today's fraught political landscape. In the last two decades, much has been written about the relationship between affects and/or emotions and their relation to politics. Theorists have analyzed the full range of political emotions (Hoggett and Thompson) and the way in which affect is leveraged by politicians (Berlant), and have argued for the importance of harnessing emotion to positive political ends (Nussbaum).[34] Sara Ahmed's and Lauren Berlant's accounts of the way affects shape political and cultural belonging and "attach us to the very conditions of our subordination" are particularly helpful in illuminating the politics of contemporary disaffection, such as that associated with the Trump voters in the article I cite in the preface.[35]

Yet this book is not about political affects as such: it is about how politics and affect became "officially" (legally) coupled at a crucial historical juncture, and the wide-ranging effects of this coupling on politics, literary culture, and ideas

---

33. Donogh, *Treatise on the Law of Sedition*, 74.
34. I have in mind Paul Hoggett and Simon Thompson, eds., *Politics and the Emotions: The Affective Turn in Contemporary Political Studies* (London: Bloomsbury, 2012); Lauren Berlant, "The Epistemology of State Emotion," in *Dissent in Dangerous Times*, ed. Austin Sarat (Ann Arbor: University of Michigan Press, 2003), 46–81; and Martha Nussbaum, *Political Emotions* (Cambridge, MA: Harvard University Press, 2013).
35. Sara Ahmed, *The Cultural Politics of Emotion*, 2nd ed. (Edinburgh: Edinburgh University Press, 2014), 12.

of criticism. Instead of looking at the actual affects of anticolonialism, then—and risk reproducing the mistranslation and essentialist logic that characterized colonial surveillance of Indian writing in the first place—I focus instead on what British administrators *thought* Indian affect was, how they sought to control it and the effects this had on print culture and the colonial public sphere. For this reason, I use the words affect and emotion interchangeably, reflecting the way they were used in colonial courtrooms, as prosecutors sought to find evidence and proof of disaffection. As opposed to being construed as prelinguistic—as a number of affect theorists understand affect to be—disaffection generally had to be recognizable as an emotion and discernible in language so that prosecutors could point to "hatred of the government" on paper and punish that apparent hatred.[37] On the other hand, some judges and lawmakers were also concerned about the unexpressed, spontaneous affects that disaffected language might stir up in the uneducated masses and descriptions of their impressionable volatility, susceptible to being shaped into hatred and violence, read more like contemporary understandings of affect.[36] My conflation of the "affect" in disaffection with recognizable emotions like hatred, then, recalls the conflation of affect and emotion in the period itself, as lawmakers simultaneously tried to decode how language produces feelings that have political effects, and figure out how to discipline this relationship.

Analyzing the way censorship influenced conceptions of the public sphere and of the politics of empire is crucial to our understanding of both. We have typically seen the Enlightenment valorization of reason over emotion as one of the central justifications of the civilizing mission: emotional self-regulation was seen as essential to self-control and thus "the possibility of a civil society comprised of self-governing individuals." Extended globally, this logic meant that only "the civilized nations, endowed with legitimate political authority, were deemed able to exert sovereignty."[38] This book shows what happens when this fantasy is reified in law, and when words, rather than subjects, become the target of the conversionary process. Bad emotions were to be suppressed and good (loyal) ones allowed to stand; in this way the civilizational narrative of emotion would

---

36. See the legal discussion of inflammatory language outlined in chapter 1.

37. This view of affect is most often associated with the work of Gilles Deleuze and Félix Guattari (*A Thousand Plateaus* [Minneapolis: University of Minnesota Press, 1987]) and their translator, Brian Massumi. See, in particular, his *Politics of Affect* (Cambridge: Polity Press, 2015).

38. Margrit Pernau and Helge Jornheim, introduction to *Civilizing Emotions: Concepts in Nineteenth Century Asia and Europe*, edited by Margrit Pernau and Helge Jornheim (Oxford: Oxford University Press, 2019), 1–26, 5.

be secured by legal statute. If, according to Jürgen Habermas, the public sphere names a field of communicative reason evacuated of political power so as to enable the free play of divergent ideas, the Anglo-Indian law against disaffection brought affect into this allegedly neutral field, turning reason into a thin veneer layered over volatile emotions that could erupt at any time, shattering the notion of shareable communicative norms and the legitimacy of the imperial project that sought to spread and uphold them. The public sphere in the age of colonial censorship was thus defined by good and bad affects rather than by reason, with loyalty to the government serving as the ultimate test of legitimate utterance.

In an essay on "The Epistemology of State Emotion" which examines the Bush-era "War on Terror" and "an emotional style linked to moral claims about truth and justice" that became prevalent in that moment, Berlant seeks to "contest the notion and norm of political rationality as the core practice of democracy in the United States by considering the national political sphere not as a real or ideal scene of abstraction-oriented deliberation, but as a scene for the orchestration of public feelings—of the public's feelings, of feelings in public, of politics as a scene of emotional contestation. The import of this shift from the notion of a rational critical public to an affective public is both conceptual and historical."[39] While her analysis focuses on the use of affect to cohere a public rather than police its boundaries, disaffection as deployed by colonial law had the effect of linking affect with political community and making feelings central to analyses of public discourse in precisely the ways described by Berlant. A *longue durée* view of disaffection that looks back to its efflorescence in the colonial period thus provides a crucial genealogy for contemporary debates about politics and affect. While much of the existing work on this nexus focuses on the present, this book traces a wide historical arc to show how affect first became explicitly connected to colonial discipline, and thus became an explanatory and structural feature of political life, in the late nineteenth century.

Theorists of the relation between politics and affect might be divided into those focusing predominantly on affect's relation to resistance and liberation (Sianne Ngai; Gilles Deleuze and Felix Guattari; Antonio Negri and Michael Hardt), and those who look more closely at its relation to toxic, debilitating nationalist fantasy (Lauren Berlant, Sara Ahmed).[40] My exploration of how

---

39. Berlant, "Epistemology of State Emotion," 47.
40. See Ngai, *Ugly Feelings*; Deleuze and Guattari, *Thousand Plateaus*; Antonio Negri and Michael Hardt, "Value and Affect," *boundary 2* 26, no. 2 (Summer 1999), 77–88; Lauren Berlant, *Cruel Optimism* (Durham, NC: Duke University Press, 2011); Berlant, "Epistemology of State Emotion";

affect was explicitly politicized in the colonial period via censorship law offers a new context for both emphases by showing how affect was produced both as an effect of governmentality *and* as the site of resistance to it. Gandhi's 1922 trial, discussed at length in the conclusion, exemplifies the ways in which the dialectic of colonial repression and anticolonial liberation politics coalesced around the idea of disaffection.

A number of important books have been written on colonial censorship and its relation to the rise of nationalism, including Kamra's aforementioned indispensable work on the topic.[41] This book, however, is less about the methodologies used to police dissent—the politicization of aesthetics—and more about the aesthetic effects of politicization. From babu English to the form of periodicals, from caricature to allegories of East and West, the policing of disaffection helped shape colonial politics, colonial literature, and their interrelation, by associating them with each other from the outset. Disaffection law is essential to our understanding of the operations of the public sphere in colonial India because the "sly civility" necessitated by government surveillance led to a range of creative modes of journalism that influenced the form as well as the content of anticolonial writing.[42] In analyzing how literary-political tactics were used to circumvent censorship, I focus in particular on the periodical, which brought literary and political writing into the same space and, because of its multivocality, functioned as a metonym for public opinion.

Dissensus, Disidentification, and the Indian Anglosphere

As well as examining the form and function of particular periodicals, I emphasize the import of their circulation in the Indian Anglosphere: the triangulated Anglophone public made up of British-educated Indians, the Anglo-Indian

---

Berlant, "Intimacy: A Special Issue," *Critical Inquiry* 24, no. 2 (Winter 1998): 281–88; and Sara Ahmed, *Cultural Politics of Emotion*.

41. See, in particular, Barrier, *Banned*; Robert Darnton, *Censors at Work: How States Shaped Literature* (New York: W. W. Norton, 2014); Graham Shaw, "On the Wrong End of the Raj: Some Aspects of Censorship in British India and Its Circumvention during the 1920s–1940s, Part 1," in *Moveable Type*, ed. Abhijit Gupta and Swapan Chakravorty (Delhi: Permanent Black, 2008), 94–172; and Kamra, *Indian Periodical Press*.

42. A term used by Homi Bhabha to describe the effects of colonial mimicry in *The Location of Culture* (New York: Routledge, 1994).

community, and Britain itself, that was addressed by Indians editing and writing in English-language periodicals.[43] In the first half of the nineteenth century, the Indian Anglosphere that emerged alongside Anglo-Indian governance was formed largely by Christian evangelicals and took shape around demands for a policy of religious neutrality on the part of the East India Company, which had initially sought to influence the region through the patronage of Hindu institutions. The aim of these evangelicals, Peter van der Veer argues, was "not to be hindered by the state in their efforts to convert people in the free market of opinion and [ideally] to have that aim supported by the state."[44] Ironically, then, the public sphere ideals of communicative reason derived from Enlightenment secularism were first put into circulation in India in the service of religious conversion. In publications such as the *Calcutta Review*, whose editorial boards "were largely staffed with clergymen," the transnational comparative mode central to these ideals was used to engage the educated Indian bourgeoisie in a rational debate about the relative merits of Hindu and Christian faith that inevitably identified Christianity with the public sphere ideals of rationality, modernity, and democracy, and Hinduism with their opposite.[45]

These missionary journals, however, quickly became only one small section of the Indian Anglosphere, as Indian editors founded their own publications, in part to contest their representation in British and Anglo-Indian ones. Anglophone Indian periodicals addressed a complicated assemblage of publics and counterpublics. While they most obviously spoke to the educated Indian elite who could read English, often in a local context (such as Bengal or Bombay, as opposed to all of India), periodicals projected an image of a broader Indian public as well, through appeals to the figure of Mother India, for example, and through innovative uses of periodical form that sought to represent a national totality. They also frequently "jumped scale" to address the British public, or an even larger body of global Anglophone public opinion, while bypassing,

---

43. The racial connotations of the term "Anglosphere," which—in the form of phrases like "the English-speaking world"—was first used in this period as a racial term meant to consolidate Anglo-American power and white supremacy, have been noted by critics such as Srdjan Vucetic; chapter 3 also explores the way W. T. Stead used this idea to racial ends. The idea of the "Indian Anglosphere" as developed here, by contrast, demonstrates that, while the Anglosphere was not restricted to white people, it was nonetheless racialized by laws such as Section 124a which treated nonwhite speech differently.

44. Peter van der Veer, *Imperial Encounters: Religion and Modernity in India and Britain* (Princeton, NJ: Princeton University Press, 2001), 22.

45. Henry Schwarz, "Aesthetic Imperialism: Literature and the Conquest of India," *Modern Language Quarterly* 61, no. 4 (December 2000): 579–80.

shunning, or shaming the Anglo-Indian public that was the implicit target of their critique. As Julia Stephens notes, "Newspapers in Calcutta were deeply sensitive to how local events played out on the broader imperial stage."[46]

The complex picture of colonial and postcolonial publics in South Asia that has emerged since the 1990s calls for plural and flexible understandings of the colonial public sphere that mediated between the British government, Anglo-India, and Indian public opinion. That the project of defining the public sphere in the South Asian context is a challenging and ongoing one is indicated by the two special issues of the journal *South Asia* dedicated to the subject, published almost fifteen years apart, one edited by Sandria Freitag (1991) and another by J. Barton Scott and Brannon D. Ingram (2015) that revisits the conversation initiated by Freitag. Along with these, a growing body of books and articles provide focused analyses of the kinds of publics specific to different South Asian regions and languages (such as Francesca Orsini's significant work, *The Hindi Public Sphere*).[47]

While some critics, like Partha Chatterjee, look at the way the British presence shaped public discourse in India, others—including Freitag, Christopher Bayly, and David Lelyveld—seek to depart from derivative models by showing how colonial publics were prefigured by earlier forms of political participation that helped shape them.[48] Alongside books, newspapers, and pamphlets, which increased in output and influence dramatically over the course of the nineteenth century, visual printed materials such as calendars and Kalighat caricatures helped shape political discourse, providing forms of commentary that could

---

46. Julia Stephens, "The Phantom Wahhabi: Liberalism and the Muslim Fanatic in Mid-Victorian India," *Modern Asian Studies* 47, no. 1 (2013): 22–52, 38.

47. See, for instance, Abhijit Gupta and Swapan Chakravorty, eds., *Moveable Type* (Delhi: Permanent Black, 2008; Gupta and Chakravorty, *Print Areas: Book History in India* (Delhi: Permanent Black, 2004); Gupta and Chakravorty, *Founts of Knowledge: Book History in India* (Hyderabad: Orient Blackswan, 2015); Anjali Nerlekar, *Bombay Modern: Arun Kolatkar and Bilingual Literary Culture* (Chicago: Northwestern University Press, 2016); Francesca Orsini, *Print and Pleasure: Popular Literature and Entertaining Fictions in Colonial North India* (Delhi: Permanent Black, 2010); Francesca Orsini, *The Hindi Public Sphere 1920–1940: Language and Literature in the Age of Nationalism* (Delhi: Oxford University Press, 2009); Ulrike Stark, *An Empire of Books* (Delhi: Permanent Black, 2007); A. R. Venkatachalapathy, *Scholars, Scribes and Scribblers in Colonial Tamilnadu* (Delhi: Permanent Black, 2011); and Baidik Bhattacharya and Sambudha Sen, eds., *Novel Formations: The Indian Beginnings of a European Genre* (Delhi: Permanent Black, 2018).

48. Chatterjee, *Nationalist Thought and the Colonial World*; Sandria Freitag, "Introduction: The Public and Its Meanings in Colonial South Asia," *South Asia* 14, no. 1 (1991): 1–13; Bayly, *Empire and Information*; David Lelyveld, "Sir Sayyid's Public Sphere: Urdu Print and Oratory in Nineteenth Century India," in *Islamicate Traditions in South Asia: Themes from Culture and History*, ed. Agnieszka Kuczkiewicz-Fraś (New Delhi: Manohar, 2009): 127–58.

reach both literate and nonliterate audiences.[49] At the same time, older forms of publicity, such as performances, assemblies, ceremonies, associations, and various kinds of petitioning, all helped inform, mediate, and transmit public opinion: oral and semiliterate forms of public culture thus coexisted alongside literate ones throughout the colonial period and beyond.[50]

Other arguments that challenge the relevance of the Habermasian model of the public sphere to the South Asia context cite the lack of bourgeois civic freedoms under colonialism (such as representative government and free speech); differences in South Asian religious and cultural practices from those in the European model (the widespread Indian practice of reading aloud to the illiterate, for example); the time line of print capitalism's emergence in India and its geographically differential spread; and the wider range of language cultures in colonial India than in its European contemporaries, where print languages included Bengali, Hindi, Gujarati, Tamil, Kannada, and Marathi, as well as English, and many publications contained two or more languages.[51]

Most scholarship on the public sphere in South Asia references Habermas, if only to depart from his ideas, but critics increasingly lean on the more historically and geographically capacious concepts of "the public," or "publics," and "counterpublics" in the vein of Nancy Fraser and Michael Warner.[52] In Warner's formulation, a public is an imagined audience given form by its address in texts and by "the social space created by the reflexive circulation of discourse."[53] Counterpublics are discursive spaces that "lack the power to transpose themselves to the generality of the state." Similar to "the linguistic fragmentation of many postcolonial settings," counterpublics create "resistance to the idea of a

---

49. See, for example, Kajri Jain, *Gods in the Bazaar: The Economies of Indian Calendar Art* (Durham, NC: Duke University Press, 2007); Partha Mitter, *Art and Nationalism in Colonial India, 1850–1922: Occidental Orientations* (Cambridge: Cambridge University Press, 1994); and Christopher Pinney, *Photos of the Gods: The Printed Image and Political Struggle in India* (London: Reaktion Books, 2004).
50. See Freitag, "Introduction," 1–13.
51. See the special issues of South Asia on the South Asian public sphere: *South Asia* 14, no. 1 (1991); *South Asia* 38, no. 3 (2015); as well as Orsini, *Hindi Public Sphere*. As Scott and Ingram caution in the introduction to their special issue, "In designating particular South Asian cultural forms as analogous to North Atlantic 'publics,' we need to be careful not to reify either set of materials or to abstract them from their complex and contested histories." J. Barton Scott and Brannon D. Ingram, "What Is a Public? Notes from South Asia," in "Imagining the Public in Modern South Asia," ed. Brannon D. Ingram, J. Barton Scott, and SherAli Tareen, special issue, *South Asia* 38, no. 3 (2015): 357–70, 359.
52. Freitag, "Introduction."
53. Michael Warner, *Publics and Counterpublics* (New York: Zone Books, 2002), 90.

sutured space of circulation" and point to fissures in the idea of the public, the space that supposedly influences state power through the production of rational-critical discourse.[54] The terms "public" and "counterpublic" influence my understanding of how the Indian Anglosphere worked—but what happens when the audience interpellated by a particular form of print culture was both bourgeois and oppositional, both public and counterpublic at once? What if the space that purportedly influences state power through the exercise of critical reason is racialized so that some speech counts as reason and some does not? What happens when different publics are addressed simultaneously at different registers—a practice Kumkum Sangari has called "double-coding"?[55]

Jacques Rancière's concept of "dissensus," like Sangari's "double-coding," is helpful to my analysis of how rhetoric and form functioned in the periodicals I examine, for unlike the opposition implied by publics and counterpublics, Rancière and Sangari allow for a space that contains both. In his writing on politics and aesthetics, Rancière states that "the essential work of politics is the configuration of its own space. It is to make the world of its subjects and its operations seen. The essence of politics is the manifestation of dissensus as the presence of two worlds in one."[56] Indian writers who attempted to intervene in colonial discourse and address its different factions did so by creating various effects of dissensus: a splitting of imperial space that addressed both British and Indian audiences, both the colonial government and a future Indian nation. This splitting also brought the fiction of a rational, homogeneous public sphere, and the freedom of expression that was meant to underpin it, dramatically into view by underscoring the "sly" as opposed to transparent civility necessitated by the policing of Indian writing.[57]

---

54. Warner, *Publics and Counterpublics*, 120. In Fraser's account, counterpublics arose at the same moment as Habermas's public sphere to contest "the exclusionary norms of the bourgeois public, elaborating alternative styles of political behavior and alternative norms of political speech." Nancy Fraser, "Rethinking the Public Sphere: A Contribution to the Critique of Actually Existing Democracy," *Social Text* 25/26 (1990): 56–80, 61.

55. Kumkum Sangari, "Politics of the Possible: Or the Perils of Reclassification," in *Politics of the Possible: Essays on Gender, History, Narratives, Colonial English* (London: Anthem Press, 2002), 19.

56. Jacques Rancière, *Dissensus: On Politics and Aesthetics* (New York: Bloomsbury, 2013), 37.

57. On reason and the Enlightenment public sphere, see Jürgen Habermas, *The Structural Transformation of the Public Sphere*, trans. Thomas Burger (Boston, MA: MIT Press, 1991). On counterpublics, see Warner, *Publics and Counterpublics*. On the public sphere in colonial India, see Sandria B. Freitag, introduction and "Enactments of Ram's Story and the Changing Nature of 'the Public' in British India," *South Asia* 14, no. 1 (1991): 1–13, 65–90, and "Aspects of 'the Public' in Colonial South Asia," the special issue of *South Asia* in which these essays appeared. See also Kamra, *Indian Political Press*, 29–35; Antoinette Burton and Isabel Hofmeyr on the "imperial commons,"

José Muñoz's approach to the intersection of politics and aesthetics in *Disidentifications* also illuminates the workings of the Indian Anglosphere. Muñoz identifies disidentification with "the survival strategies the minority subject practices in order to negotiate a phobic majoritarian public sphere that continuously elides or punishes the existence of subjects who do not conform to the phantasm of normative citizenship."[58] Focusing in particular on cultural texts, he argues that minority subjects both inhabit and reshape elements of the public sphere, using a given text "as raw material for representing a disempowered politics or positionality that has been rendered unthinkable by the dominant culture."[59] Though Muñoz's main subject—the performance practices of queers of color in the contemporary United States—seems distinct from mine, the chapters that follow demonstrate that the practices of Anglophone Indian writers and editors, whose sexuality and writing was regarded as aberrant because of their challenge to *imperial* citizenship, were structurally similar to those described in *Disidentifications*. Inhabiting print forms borrowed from British culture and speaking back to that culture while simultaneously, and circuitously, addressing an audience disenfranchised by it, Indian periodicals practiced disidentification in order to elude charges of disaffection.

While I use the term "Indian Anglosphere" when referencing English-language journalism in India, I also use "imperial public sphere" to indicate the larger imperial context in which some of the texts I reference also circulated: Gandhi's *Indian Opinion* could be found in South Africa, India, and Britain, for example, while W. T. Stead's *Review of Reviews* appeared in Britain, India, Australia, and the United States. In using these terms, my goal is to show how closely British and Indian print cultures were intermeshed, not only by the circulation of texts across the empire but by the ideological and legal pressure on Indian periodicals to model themselves on British ones—a practice I call "print mimicry." This practice, along with the censorship law that inspired it, influenced British print culture in turn. Since concerns about disaffection in India were inevitably related to concerns about fissures in the social contract in Britain, the criminalization of disaffection in India had concrete effects on British literary expression

---

"Introduction: The Spine of Empire? Books and the Making of an Imperial Commons," in Burton and Hofmeyer, *Ten Books*, 1–29; U. Kalpagam, "Colonial Governmentality and the Public Sphere in India," *Historical Sociology* 15, no. 1 (2002): 35–58; and Ankhi Mukherjee, "Introduction: Postcolonial Reading Publics," *Cambridge Journal of Postcolonial Literary Inquiry* 4, no. 1 (2017): 1–10.

58. José Muñoz, *Disidentifications: Queers of Color and the Performance of Politics* (Minneapolis: University of Minnesota Press, 1999), 4.

59. José Muñoz, *Disidentifications*, 31.

on the mainland. Graham Shaw's work, for example, takes stock of "the extent to which the India Office in London became embroiled in attempting to control the distribution of publications about or destined for India at the British end, and even to shape their content prior to publication," a phenomenon that impacted Leonard Woolf at the Hogarth Press, among others.[60] (Chapter 3 of this book unpacks a specific instance of this phenomenon in detail, demonstrating how an Indian periodical loosely based on W. T. Stead's *Review of Reviews* affected Stead's ideas as well as his publishing enterprise more broadly.)

The nation as a unit of analysis has remained stubbornly recalcitrant in literary studies of the nineteenth century despite the decades-old critique of this model by Edward Said, Gauri Viswanathan, Mrinalini Sinha, and numerous others. Yet scholars are increasingly looking at the transnational circulation of texts and ideas in imperial space as a way of transcending the national paradigm.[61] Mary Ellis Gibson's anthology and monograph on nineteenth-century Anglophone poetry, Elleke Boehmer's *Indian Arrivals*, Leela Gandhi's *Affective Communities*, and Jason Rudy's *Imagined Homelands* are notable examples of such work.[62] There has also been a move to more fully understand, in their local specificity and transnational ambit, the multiple, overlapping publics that made up what Antoinette Burton and Isabel Hofmeyr call "the imperial commons"—an imagined space which they figure as "a site of deterritorialized sovereignty in the textual economy of the British empire."[63]

While my work is influenced and inspired by these approaches, I seek not only to analyze what kinds of texts traversed the Indian Anglosphere, and how, but also the ways in which colonial governance restricted and shaped that circulation. The Indian Anglosphere was at once multiperspectival, productive, experimental, *and* deeply circumscribed by censorship and governmental

---

60. Shaw, "On the Wrong End of the Raj," 95.

61. See Edward Said, *Culture and Imperialism* (New York: Knopf, 1993); Gauri Viswanathan, *Masks of Conquest: Literary Study and British Rule in India* (New York: Columbia University Press, 1989); and Mrinalini Sinha, "Britishness, Clubbability, and the Colonial Public Sphere: The Genealogy of an Imperial Institution in Colonial India," *Journal of British Studies* 40, no. 4 (2001): 489–521, 495.

62. Mary Ellis Gibson, *Indian Angles: English Verse in Colonial India from Jones to Tagore* (Athens: Ohio University Press, 2011); Elleke Boehmer, *Indian Arrivals, 1870–1915: Networks of British Empire* (Oxford: Oxford University Press, 2015); Leela Gandhi, *Affective Communities: Anticolonial Thought, Fin-de-Siècle Radicalism, and the Politics of Friendship* (Durham, NC: Duke University Press, 2006); and Jason Rudy, *Imagined Homelands: British Poetry in the Colonies* (Baltimore: Johns Hopkins University Press, 2017).

63. Antoinette Burton and Isabel Hofmeyr, eds., *Ten Books That Shaped the British Empire: Creating an Imperial Commons* (Durham, NC: Duke University Press, 2014).

oversight.[64] In tracing its contours, I address the critical imperative to analyze how colonial publics took shape at specific historical junctures succinctly articulated by Veena Naregal: "If the field of colonial studies is to retain its political relevance, we need microhistorical studies that plot how the dissemination of modern discourses and cultural norms effectively structured the boundaries of inclusion and exclusion in different areas of the world."[65] This book provides one such microhistory, even as it links that local narrative to larger changes in the relationship of British authority to India at a crucial turning point in the global rise of anticolonialism.

The form of the Victorian periodical, with its emphasis on nonfiction, rational discourse, and the cross-cultural comparison of ideas, was presented to English-speaking Indians as exemplary of the modern, critical values that Britain was importing to India. As a result, the number and variety of the Anglophone periodicals that proliferated there during the colonial period is stunning, and makes up a significant portion of colonial literary culture.[66] The Indian writers who contributed to these periodicals were drawn to them partly because they were initially less scrutinized than their Indian-language counterparts. For instance, when instituting the Vernacular Press Act of 1878—which enforced a double standard whereby the Indian press was subject to special oversight and restrictions—Ashley Eden, then governor of Bengal, argued that "the papers published in this country in the English language are written by a class of writers for a class of readers whose education and interests would make them naturally intolerant of sedition; they are written under a sense of responsibility and under a restraint of public opinion which do not and cannot exist in the case of ordinary native newspapers."[67] If the English-language press was a space within which Indian writers might more easily evade charges of irrationality and disaffection, it also lent itself in certain ways to the articulation of nationalist and

---

64. On liberalism and the colonial public sphere, see U. Kalpagam, "Colonial Governmentality and the Public Sphere in India," *Journal of Historical Sociology* 14, no. 4 (December 2001): 418–40.

65. Veena Naregal, *Language Politics, Elites, and the Public Sphere: Western India under Colonialism* (Delhi: Permanent Black, 2014), 3.

66. Many of these periodicals have yet to be studied or digitized, but this is rapidly changing. Finishing this book in 2019, I was both thrilled and frustrated to find a new website, curated by Rahul Sagar, that presents an online index of 255 English-language journals from the period I examine, with a number of journals I had yet to come across in my research. An amazing resource for scholars of Anglophone Indian periodicals, this website not only lists a large number of journals but provides tables of contents and cover images for many of them. Ideas of India, The Periodicals, https://www.ideasofindia.org/#periodicals.

67. Quoted in Kalpagam, "Colonial Governmentality and the Public Sphere in India" (2001), 435.

cosmopolitan ideals, for English was leveraged by many nationalists as a language of pan-Indian cultural unity and a passport to world citizenship. Thus, an Indian writer in *East and West* associated "this great English language, this invaluable heritage of British history and British institutions" with "a craving for impartial justice, a sense of growing equality, nay, a glimmer of wide humanity which in its full light has an intensity and passion akin to that of religion itself."[68] As Timothy Brennan has argued in relation to postcolonial subjectivities, this dubious cosmopolitanism was attractive partly because it offered "a coming into 'modernity' as the global entrance into a common hybrid self-consciousness . . . without in the least disturbing the self-portraiture of the West."[69]

Naregal's book, *Language Politics, Elites, and the Public Sphere*, shows how the Anglophone Indian class was carefully cultivated through a bilingual educational strategy that positioned English as the gateway to political modernity and as a signifier of elite identity.[70] The cosmopolitanism of this elite class of writers was often as politically dubious as that in the contemporary situation Brennan discusses, though, because English-speaking Indians were meant, at least in theory, to shore up the colonial project by providing local knowledge in exchange for admission to positions of relative power and influence; from these positions, they were to mediate between the administration and the populace.[71] This book takes seriously the subversive, creative, and innovative work performed by these writers across a range of Anglophone periodicals.[72] But in emphasizing the

---

68. Quoted in Julie Codell, "Getting the Twain to Meet: Global Regionalism in *East and West: A Monthly Review*," *Victorian Periodicals Review* 37, no. 2 (Summer 2004): 214–32, 226.

69. Timothy Brennan, "Cosmopolitanism and Internationalism," in *Debating Cosmopolitics*, ed. Daniele Archibugi (New York: Verso, 2008), 45.

70. Naregal, *Language Politics, Elites*, 68.

71. Mrinalini Sinha sets up a useful analogy between the colonial public sphere and colonial clubs in terms of the effects of their simultaneous exclusivity and alluring permeability. As a crucial space for the shaping of influential Anglo-Indian opinion, the social club "functioned in an intermediate zone between both metropolitan and indigenous public spheres." Because they generally excluded Indians, non-elite Anglo-Indians, and women, these clubs helped create a limited yet highly visible version of "whiteness" that was raced, classed, and gendered. Yet the ideal of "clubbability" that the influential colonial clubs generated was nonetheless held out as an elite identity to which Anglophone Indians might aspire. As members of this class were begrudgingly admitted to clubs over time, the institution held out the promise of full admission—of Indian clubbability—in due course, an admission that would depend, as in the colonial Anglosphere, on successful adaptation to the norms of British "polite society." See Mrinalini Sinha, "Britishness, Clubbability, 492.

72. As Durba Ghosh and Dane Kennedy have argued of the case studies in their anthology *Decentring Empire: Britain, India, and the Transcolonial World*, "Some colonized subjects showed that they grasped strategies of wielding power very well and capitalized on the liberal promises of colonialism as a way of contesting British rule. . . . It should be possible to retain an analytic space for the strategic agency of colonial subjects while recognizing the context of coloniality and without resorting to

imbrication of British and Indian print cultures, I also seek to demonstrate how and why the proto-nationalism on view in Anglophone periodicals is impossible to fully disarticulate from the colonialism it seeks to critique, as well as from the chauvinistic Hindu nationalism that first took shape in this period and that currently dominates Indian politics (the case of the *Bangavasi* writers discussed in chapter 1 is especially illuminating in this regard).

Disaffection as State of Exception

This book focuses on the years between the first trial that used Section 124a in 1891 and Gandhi's trial for disaffection in 1922, a time when many journalists sought to avoid prosecution via the tactics of sly civility. Gandhi's embrace of the role of "disaffectionist" during the trial made disloyalty a framework for political resistance, however, signaling the transition into an overt and confrontational period of nationalism that was to last until independence in 1947. What follows is a brief history of the institution and application of the law against disaffection in the period leading up to Gandhi's trial that explains how it fit into colonial attempts to control the press and the populace more broadly.

Section 124a was first introduced into the Indian Penal Code (IPC) in 1870 by the governor-general's law administrator James Fitzjames Stephen. Stephen claimed that the fact that it had not been imported to the Indian context from British law when the code was first drafted in 1837 was merely an oversight, though the committee responsible for drafting it (headed by Thomas Babington Macaulay) may in fact have omitted it deliberately in order to sidestep the temptations of authoritarianism inherent to colonial rule.[73] Stephen had no such qualms, however. He was a vociferous critic of John Stuart Mill's more tolerant version of liberalism, against which he launched a book-length critique (*Liberty, Equality, Fraternity*). As an advocate for the curtailment of freedoms such as those of the press in the interests of morality and stability, he saw the codification, simplification, and standardization of aspects of British law in the IPC as an opportunity to make law the foundation of sovereignty in the colony.[74] The

---

crude notions of collaboration." Durba Ghosh and Dane Kennedy, eds., *Decentring Empire: Britain, India and the Transcolonial World* (Hyderabad: Orient Blackswan, 2006), 6–7.

73. See Nasser Hussain, *The Jurisprudence of Emergency: Colonialism and the Rule of Law* (Ann Arbor: University of Michigan Press, 2003).

74. See James Fitzjames Stephen, *Liberty, Equality, Fraternity*, ed. Stuart D. Warner (Indianapolis, IN: Liberty Fund Press, 1993).

streamlining of British law that took place in the shaping of Indian law, then, is an instructive instance of the way forms of modern governance not yet ironed out in the West—the British literary canon and fingerprinting, for instance—were to be tested in the colonies.[75] Stephen acknowledged as much when he declared that "to compare the Indian Penal Code to English criminal law is to compare cosmos with chaos."[76] In this telling analogy, the colony is the space in which the dark matter of Western democracy would resolve into a modern world-system.

The rule of law had a particular role to play in British imperialism because it served as the grounds of its moral legitimacy, as Nasser Hussain has argued. From Warren Hastings's governorship onward, the law was seen not only as "the preeminent form of a modern political rationality, but also as the central and distinguishing feature of *English* politics, morality, and civilization" in particular.[77] If ongoing questions of authority and legitimacy were endemic to colonial rule, law served as a sign of British fairness and enlightenment, as opposed to the Oriental despotism with which it was frequently juxtaposed. Because the colonial state had no electorate to sanction its existence, "legality became the preeminent signifier of state legitimacy and of 'civilization,' the term that united politics and morality."[78] Thus, Stephen said of British law that it is "in fact the sum and substance of what we have to teach them. It is, so to speak, the gospel of the English, and it is a compulsory gospel which admits of no dissent and no disobedience."[79]

Yet, imbedded within this system, which was purportedly fair because universally applicable, was a racial logic that imagined the law as both the sign and the "compulsory" weapon of colonial authority, both the proof of British superiority and the structure that would keep racial hierarchy in place through measures such as Section 124a, retrofitted from British law for the colonized subject.[80] Critics of colonial law have argued that its history illuminates how states of emergency and regimes of counterterrorism work today because it reveals

---

75. On the formation of British literary study in India, see Viswanathan, *Masks of Conquest*; on fingerprinting, see Chandak Sengoopta, *Imprint of the Raj: How Fingerprinting Was Born in Colonial India* (London: Macmillan, 2003).
76. Hussain, *Jurisprudence of Emergency*, 41.
77. Hussain, *Jurisprudence of Emergency*, 4.
78. Hussain, *Jurisprudence of Emergency*, 4.
79. Hussain, *Jurisprudence of Emergency*, 4.
80. My references to race here lean on Hussain's useful formulation in his analysis of Partha Chatterjee's work: "When Chatterjee speaks of race in the colonial realm, he is in fact utilizing a shorthand for the range of differences that runs from eighteenth-century conceptions of cultural

"the connection between racial and cultural conditions and forms of rule in general—and in doing so ... also makes explicit the relation between a rule of law and emergency, a relation that is as intimate as it is anxious."[81] Recalling Giorgio Agamben's definition of "the state of exception" as "the law that suspends the law," Stephen Morton notes that this formulation "bears an interesting conceptual resemblance to the colonial rule of law"—an area Agamben does not explore in depth even though its development of counterterrorist tactics and enactment of the state of exception prefigure, and continue to shape, our contemporary condition.[82] James Fitzjames Stephen's pronouncements on Section 124a demonstrate how adapting British law to the colonial state led directly to the form of paradoxical thinking where law suspends law.

Dismissing the idea of freedom of the press as a short phrase that contained "a surprising quantity of nonsense," Stephen argued that "liberty and law simply excluded each other: liberty extended to the point at which law stopped: liberty was what you might do and law was what you might not do."[83] In this contorted analysis, he ignores the way the law functions as a guarantee of freedoms and imagines it simply as a negation of them. The brother of Leslie Stephen and uncle of Virginia Woolf, Stephen is a case study in the ineluctable proximity of cultural to political power in turn-of-the-century Britain. He is also a fascinating figure in the history of British India, not only because his contributions to colonial law would be so influential on governance, but because of his Carl Schmittian frankness about his authoritarian views of the rights of rulers when exercised in the service of the greater good. If Schmitt emphasized the importance of a leader being able to transcend the law for the sake of expediency, though, Stephen sought to reimagine colonial law so that the exception was embedded within it.[84] In the colonial state, as in Agamben's modern state,

---

difference to nineteenth- and twentieth-century racial conceptions based on blood." Hussain, *Jurisprudence of Emergency*, 29.

81. Hussain, *Jurisprudence of Emergency*, 31. See also Morton, *States of Emergency*. Durba Ghosh's work on "gentlemanly terrorism" in Bengal traces in detail the ways that repression and revolutionary activity interacted in the lead-up to independence: "The colonial government rationalized the enactment of repressive legislation as a protection to the process of constitutional reform, which was intended to recruit Indians, but only those with moderate politics, into supporting the British government of India." Durba Ghosh, *Gentlemanly Terrorists: Political Violence and the Colonial State in India, 1919–1947* (Cambridge: Cambridge University Press, 2017), 3.

82. Morton, *States of Emergency*, 4.

83. Donogh, *Treatise on the Law of Sedition*, 6.

84. See Carl Schmitt, *Political Theology: Four Chapters on the Concept of Sovereignty* (Chicago: University of Chicago Press, 2005), originally published 1922.

the exception often *was* the rule—as was the case with Section 124a, which was applied almost exclusively to Indians.

This authoritarian twist on British liberalism worked in the colonies because of the persistent Orientalist idea of India's civilizational difference. When discussing sedition law one administrator argued that "the gravity of the situation demands that we take whatever is absolutely the most effective measure for controlling sedition in the press without regard to Western theories or sentiments, which are not applicable to the condition of this country."[85] As Uday Mehta has demonstrated, key theorists of liberalism such as John Locke and John Stuart Mill built an escape hatch into their concepts of political inclusion by making them contingent on the capacity to reason—and making the qualifications for that capacity contingent on certain kinds of education. Because of India's imagined infancy, "reminiscent of Locke's outlook toward children . . . projected onto a civilizational scale," education was positioned as an indefinitely long, uphill battle.[86] In supporting the passing of Section 124a, Stephen drew freely on this logic, stating that "if we wished the Indian Press to be what it ought to be; if we wished it to be conducted honestly, and to criticise the proceedings of Government fairly; we could not do worse than treat it like a spoiled child. . . . We should protect them so long as they did not commit crime, and punish them if they did."[87]

Outlawing disaffection proved to be harder than anticipated, however. When questioned about the vagueness of the term and the attendant problem of its applicability, Stephen's response presciently evoked the twentieth century cliché applied to both art and pornography: you would know it if you saw it.[88] The record of the proceedings at which the law was debated summarized his position as follows: "It was said that the language of the section was vague; that disaffection was a vague word. [Stephen] was perfectly willing to admit that that statement had some truth in it. But all human language was more or less vague. In a general way, everybody knew what disaffection was, but in that and every other word of that sort, there must be a good deal of vagueness from the imperfection

---

85. Darnton, "Literary Surveillance," 135.
86. Uday Mehta, *Liberalism and Empire: A Study in Nineteenth-Century British Liberal Thought* (Chicago: University of Chicago Press, 1999), 444.
87. Donogh, *Treatise on the Law of Sedition*, 6–7.
88. For example, the phrase was famously used by Supreme Court Justice Potter Stewart to describe his test for obscenity in *Jacobellis v. Ohio* (1964)—a case in which the manager of a movie theater in Ohio was convicted and fined for screening a Louis Malle film.

of the human mind itself."[89] Stephen's defense of the imprecision of the word "disaffection" is situated in the same amorphous realm of feeling the law was designed to critique, for according to the logic of his statement, disaffection is something one senses rather than grasps rationally. Both the accusation and its potential enforcement, then, were made strategically murkier by the evocation of affect.

Because of the way its recognition was ascribed to nebulous aesthetic judgment, and because it was seen as influential on the weak, disaffection functioned similarly to obscenity—a concept brought into legal prominence in the landmark British *Regina v. Hicklin* case of 1868, which defined obscene writing as that which could "deprave and corrupt those whose minds are open to such immoral influences."[90] This similarity was not coincidental. Early reports on Indian publishing, following those of James Long, dwelt more on "repulsion at Indian depictions of sex" than on political unrest but the two became complexly imbricated.[91] In an essay on sedition and seduction, Raminder Kuar and William Mazzarella demonstrate that obscenity, sedition, and blasphemy emerged alongside each other as "specific markers of excess": "The emergent publics of the latter half of the nineteenth century . . . saw a complex cross-cutting of nationalist, linguistic, communal, and moral-sexual concerns. . . . It is during this period that 'obscenity' formally emerged as a category of regulation, and as a category that was understood as implicated in 'sedition,' that is, in explicitly political forms of provocation."[92] The focus on disaffection, in its insistence on affect as the sacred bond of the colonial relationship, was thus from early on freighted with prurience and sexual anxiety. To be disaffected was not just to be disloyal but to be profane or, to use a properly imperial expression, beyond the pale.[93] (Chapter 1 explores at length the way this discursive nexus worked in the representation of so-called babu writers, who were sexually pathologized so as to simultaneously place them under political suspicion and discredit their politics.)

---

89. *Abstract of the Proceedings of the Council of the Governor General of India*, 9:446, 1870 (Calcutta: Office of the Superintendent of Government Printing, India, 1906).

90. See Colin Manchester, "A History of the Crime of Obscene Libel," *Journal of Legal History* 12, no. 1 (1991): 36–57.

91. Darnton, "Book Production," 246.

92. Raminder Kaur and William Mazzarella, "Between Sedition and Seduction: Thinking Censorship in South Asia," in *Censorship in South Asia: Cultural Regulation from Sedition to Seduction*, ed. Raminder Kaur and William Mazzarella (Bloomington: Indiana University Press, 2009), 14.

93. Though it has since turned into a metaphor for impropriety, this phrase is said to have emerged in the mid-seventeenth century as a reference to the area outside English territory in Ireland.

Both despite and because of the vagueness of its terminology, Section 124a was able to serve as an exemplarily racialized form of biopower. Kaur and Mazzarella argue, in a Foucauldian vein, that rather than shutting down discourse, censorship law tends to proliferate it, not only by generating "discourses on normative modes of desiring, of acting, of being in the world" but also by drawing attention to transgression and routinizing it: "There seems to be something of a correlation," they note, "between the regulation of cultural production and the proliferation of provocative forms."[94] If Section 124a helped proliferate transgression by outlawing it, it also contributed to the kinds of expression it sought to outlaw by generating a specific form of vicious cycle, wherein the law's racism and repression provoked dissidence, which then required the law to be expanded by an added emphasis on affect, which made it more racist because of the heightened pathologizing of Indians via their association with negative affect, thus producing more dissidence, and so on.[95]

Law functioned differently in the colony than in the metropole partly because in Britain the domain of the body was generally "made inviolable by habeas corpus and the individual's right to the security of his or her own person," while in the colony it was made available to exploitation and manipulation, as Ranajit Guha has argued.[96] The example he uses to make this point focuses on the way labor was forcibly extracted from the rural poor. But by allowing the government to use their writing to determine when Indian bodies were excessively agitated and punish them accordingly, Section 124a was another significant way in which discursive and disciplinary pressures were exerted on colonial bodies to transport them from political to bare life, outside the boundaries of citizenship; this transportation process was sometimes literalized by the exile of dissidents to a penal colony on the Andaman Islands, where harsh imprisonment conditions often led to death.[97]

---

94. Kaur and Mazzarella, "Between Sedition and Seduction," 4–5.

95. Once Section 124a had been saturated with affect in order to expand its applicability, a range of other acts were put into place to aid in the prosecution of sedition. In 1908 the Newspapers (Incitement to Offences) Act allowed the confiscation of printing presses from those accused of sedition, while the 1910 Press Act required not only that all publishers register with the government and provide copies of their publications but also that they make a deposit of 500–2,000 rupees, depending on what "the Magistrate may in each case think fit to require." This hefty sum would then be forfeited if the publication contained "any words, signs or visible representations which are likely or may have a tendency, directly or indirectly, whether by inference, suggestion, allusion, metaphor, implication or otherwise" to produce sedition (Donogh, *Treatise on the Law of Sedition*, 262).

96. Guha, *Dominance without Hegemony*, 26.

97. On bare life, see Giorgio Agamben, *Homo Sacer: Sovereign Power and Bare Life* (Palo Alto, CA: Stanford University Press, 1998).

In order that they could be targeted by the disaffection law, Indian bodies were imagined as inherently excitable. The groundwork for this imaginary had long been laid not only by post-Rebellion fearmongering but by the Orientalist philology that undergirded colonial law. In *Archaeology of Babel*, Siraj Ahmed demonstrates that the translations of Indian religious texts by philologists like William Jones served as source material for colonial law and thus made "cultural difference the central category of modern governance." Arguing that Persian poetry was the result of "violent passion," Jones subscribed to what we might today call a comparative Romanticist theory of literary production, in which poetry was the result of "diverse expressions of human desire."[98] But by identifying Indian poems with "violent passion," and putting them alongside the religious texts used to interpret shari'a law as sources of historical knowledge about India and the grounds of its colonial governance, Jones's work helped pave the way for the imagination of law as a tool for the disciplining of volatile emotions. Since vociferous critiques of the government or demands for citizenship could always be deemed excessive, colonial subjects were conveniently marked as ineligible for full citizenship precisely *because* of their demands for it, as these purportedly demonstrated that they were incapable of participating with decorum in the public sphere.

Print Mimicry and the Tactics of Sly Civility

Disaffection was thus at once a political, criminal, and peculiarly Indian emotion, hidden in words whose galvanizing power would be unleashed once it reached its target audience—unless it were intercepted along the way. In order to perform this interception, judge, jury and public had to become literary critics—analyzing tone, searching texts for hidden meanings, and producing plausible interpretations.[99] This rigid governmental oversight inevitably produced the practice of print mimicry, a phrase that I use to evoke Homi Bhabha's "colonial mimicry" while drawing attention to the crucial role of print culture, periodical form, and censorship in the production of mimic effects.

Bhabha's ideas about mimicry, first published in *October* in 1987, were immensely influential on postcolonial studies, in part because of their consonance

---

98. Siraj Ahmed, *Archaeology of Babel: The Colonial Foundation of the Humanities* (Stanford, CA: Stanford University Press, 2018), 42–43.
99. See Kamra, *Indian Political Press*, 88–98.

with important strains of deconstructive theory and psychoanalysis. Some of the arguments in *The Location of Culture*—the 1994 collection of essays in which "Of Mimicry and Man" was anthologized—have been challenged by postcolonial critics over the years for their inattention to materialism, their fetishization of ambivalence, and their privileging of discourse over politics, and have become less central to the field over time.[100] Bhabha's concepts of mimicry and sly civility are newly illuminating, however, when applied to the workings of print culture in the context of censorship and I draw on them to argue that the procedures of mimicry, irony, and destabilized assent had material effects in the moment of waning British power on the subcontinent.

Bhabha defines mimicry as "a complex strategy of reform, regulation and discipline, which 'appropriates' the Other as it visualizes power."[101] But by producing an Other that is "almost the same but not quite," colonial discourse calls its own primacy and legitimacy into question for "in 'normalizing' the colonial state or subject, the dream of post-Enlightenment civility alienates its own language of liberty and produces another knowledge of its norms."[102] The Indian Anglosphere, the space in which the colonizer encountered and produced his mimic man by enforcing public sphere norms, was rife with the hybridity, ambiguity, excess, splitting, and subversion Bhabha associates with colonial mimicry. But where he focuses on language as the source of mimic effects, this book emphasizes image, genre, and format—the way periodicals and their illustrations, as well as people and individual texts, functioned as agents and disseminators of mimicry.[103]

The concept of print mimicry can be applied to a number of journalistic strategies and periodical formats adopted by Indian writers and editors as they sought to avoid charges of sedition, but Bhabha's term "sly civility," which he borrows from an 1818 sermon describing the difficulty of converting Indians to Christianity, has salutary uses for this project as well. If "mimicry" is a term used to characterize the formulations of both colonizer and colonized—both the mimic man and the disciplines that produce him—sly civility, as used in the sermon,

---

100. See, for example, Neil Lazarus, *The Postcolonial Unconscious* (New York: Cambridge University Press, 2011); and Benita Parry, "Signs of Our Times: Discussion of Homi Bhabha's *The Location of Culture*," *Third Text* 8, nos. 28–29 (1994): 5–24.
101. Bhabha, *Location of Culture*, 122.
102. Bhabha, *Location of Culture*, 123.
103. Meredith McGill helpfully demonstrates the interrelation of forms and print formats in "What Is a Ballad? Reading for Genre, Format, and Medium," *Nineteenth Century Literature* 71, no. 2 (2016): 156–75.

refers more specifically to the response of the colonized to the efforts of the colonizer to convert him to Western norms.[104] In Bhabha's psychoanalytic formulation, the colonizer's "desire for 'authorization' in the face of a process of cultural differentiation . . . makes it problematic to fix the native objects of colonial power as the moralized 'others' of truth" and thus "the litigious, lying native became a central object of nineteenth-century colonial, legal, regulation."[105]

Colonial administrators were exasperated not only by the literary circumlocutions of sly civility but by the manipulations of publishing protocol that Indian periodicals used to evade press censorship. A 1910 article on "The Indian Press Bill" in the London *Times* quoted a parliamentarian saying that

> the ingenuity with which the conductors of these papers have in the past incessantly evaded the law is remarkable. . . . A favourite expedient had been to change printers frequently in order to evade inquiry. Another trick . . . was to appoint some obscure subordinate as nominal editor. Yet another device was to have a constant succession of sham editors. No one really knows how many persons "edited" *Bande Mataram* during its inglorious career. Mr. Tilak, now in confinement at Mandalay, practiced for years the astute plan of issuing two papers. The *Mahratta*, printed in English, dealt with government measures in comparative moderation; the *Kesari*, printed in Marathi, was often filled with inflammatory incitements on the very same subjects.[106]

As Bhabha's analysis of the splitting and difference produced by colonial mimicry would predict, this commentator is obsessed with duplicity and doubling: the changing of printers; the substitution of real for sham editors; the paper with two faces, one obedient and one rebellious.

My adaptation of Bhabha's insights to a historical-materialist view of the techniques and effects of colonial governance elucidates the ways that phenomena that fall under the heading of mimicry were direct and canny responses to censorship law. Indian journals that cited British ones, both in content and in form, were performing familial—or affective—bonds with British culture that served as claims to imperial citizenship and political modernity.[107] Texts defined

---

104. Bhabha, *Location of Culture*, 137.
105. Bhabha, *Location of Culture*, 142, 143.
106. "The Indian Press Bill," *London Times*, Saturday, February 5, 1910, 9.
107. On the way demands for imperial citizenship affected reform, and anticolonial and proto-nationalist discourse in the late nineteenth century and early twentieth century, see Sukanya

by the critical tactics I analyze here must thus be seen as part of a cross-cultural and triangulated conversation with the British and Anglo-Indian press, for they eluded censorship and manipulated public sphere norms by practicing dissensus and double-coding, speaking at different registers and to different audiences simultaneously. In the heyday of sedition trials, they made manifest the ways that interpretation depends on cultural location, intertextuality, and power.

The tactics of sly civility led to literary innovations in Anglophone Indian writing more commonly associated with British aestheticist and modernist writing of the same period: the subject of this book is not an alternative modernity, then, but an imperial one, for censorship in the colonies, as I have suggested, affected British culture as well.[108] As Sukanya Banerjee has argued, "*Systems* of colonial literary production . . . tend to get overlooked in ways that mark off the colony, casting it in all-too-familiar frames of lag or lacuna."[109] The "transimperial" perspective she calls for to counter this problem looks at the circulation of texts across imperial space and the different yet overlapping audiences addressed therein without glossing over the conflicts and disparities that defined the imperial public sphere. My chapters focus in particular on the self-conscious aesthetics of affectation; the duplicitous irreverence of parody and imitation; the comparatist approach of the literary review; and the utopian cosmopolitanism of East-West syncretism. Rather than being traceable to an origin in either Britain or India, this book shows how literary-critical forms that circulated between both spaces were shaped not just by exchanges between the like-minded dissidents that make up Leela Gandhi's "affective communities" or the poetic exchanges that Mary Ellis Gibson traces, but by the rhetorical play between affection and disaffection, resemblance and reversal, that colonial law provoked critique to perform.

The emphasis on words in disaffection trials reflected a recognition on the part of the government of the degree to which Indian writers were using creative forms of sly civility to evade the law, encrypting their message through literary devices such as "inference, suggestion, allusion, metaphor [and] implication" which required shrewd literary-critical interpretations. As a result, a whole host

---

Banerjee, *Becoming Imperial Citizens: Indians in the Late-Victorian Empire* (Durham, NC: Duke University Press, 2011).

108. On the concept of alternative modernities, see the essays in Dilip Parameshwar Gaonkar, ed. *Alternative Modernities* (Durham, NC: Duke University Press, 2001).

109. Sukanya Banerjee, "Marriage, Modernity, and the Transimperial," in *Replotting Marriage in Nineteenth-Century British Literature*, ed. Jill Galvan and Elsie Michie (Columbus: Ohio State University Press, 2018), 145–67, 162.

of literary terms and critical approaches were evoked during trials. As Robert Darnton puts it, "the courtroom turned into a hermeneutic battlefield, where each side acted out its interpretation of the other and imperialism appeared ... as a contest for symbolic dominance through textual exegesis."[110] Judge Stratchey's instructions to jurors in the Tilak case illustrate how they were urged to serve as literary critics: "You must be guided not only by your estimate of the effect of the articles upon the minds of their readers, but also by your common sense, your knowledge of the world, your understanding of the meaning of words, and your experience of the way in which a man writes when he is animated by a particular feeling.... It may not be easy to express the difference in words; but the difference in tone and spirit and general drift between a writer who is trying to stir up ill-will and one who is not, is generally unmistakable."[111] The number of contemporary literary-critical methodologies that Stratchey's directions conjure up is surprisingly wide-ranging: they include psychological interpretations ("your experience of the way in which a man writes when he is animated by a particular feeling"); intertextual readings (jurors were asked to interpret "allusion"); comparative literary readings (defense attorneys cited mistranslation and cultural misunderstanding in their arguments); attention to genre (the myths and religious narratives used in journalistic writing were often read as allegories for contemporary political situations); close reading (as well as paying attention to figurative language such as metaphor, jurors were told to look for disaffection in "the words themselves" since authorial intention was notoriously hard to prove); and, naturally, suspicious reading. In a statement exemplary of Eve Sedgwick's definition of paranoid reading—"the detection of hidden patterns of violence and their exposure"[112]—Stratchey informed his jurors that disaffection "may be excited in a thousand different ways. A poem, an allegory, a drama, a philosophical or historical discussion, may be used for the purpose of exciting disaffection just as much as direct attacks upon the Government. *You have to look through the form, and look to the real object: you have to consider whether the form of a poem or discussion is genuine, or whether it has been adopted merely to disguise the real seditious intention of the writer*" (my emphasis).[113] If censorship law generated creative forms of expression that sought to evade it, then, this in turn produced the need for an arsenal of interpretive strategies.

---

110. Darnton, "Literary Surveillance," 155.
111. Darnton, "Literary Surveillance," 163.
112. Eve Sedgwick, *Touching Feeling: Affect, Pedagogy, Performativity* (Durham, NC: Duke University Press, 2003), 143.
113. Donogh, *Treatise on the Law of Sedition*, 76.

Part of what this book aims to demonstrate is that views of critical and literary writing in the early twentieth century were shaped not just by the marketplace of ideas, or by the market itself, but by censorship, as were literary forms such as the periodical. The Indian periodical that resembled or referenced a British one (in title, organization, rhetoric, or layout) was also doing something strategically different and thus essentially new; by mimicking British journals but using form differently (often to critique the British original), editors were creating a type of criticism hard to detect on the sentence level. As Peter McDonald has argued in relation to South Africa under apartheid, censorship has cultural consequences: the imperial public sphere and the censorship that shaped it, then, are essential to our understanding of modern literary production.[114]

The critical tactic I look at in the first chapter of the book—affectation—focuses on the *Bangavasi* case, since this was the first moment when disaffection became a central term in the prosecution of sedition and was redefined specifically to address the colonial context. The last chapter examines the tactic of syncretism and ends with a reading of the modernist journal *East and West*, which ceased publication in 1921. This moment, just before Gandhi embraced the label of "disaffectionist" in his 1922 trial, is a suitable end point for the book's chronology because by this moment, in the wake of World War I, the nationalist movement was no longer clandestine or circumspect and thus was less likely to resort to the tactics of sly civility. Correspondingly, British attempts to quell dissent transitioned from amorphous measures like the disaffection law to more coercive maneuvers, such as the circulation of pro-government propaganda and the outright banning of a wide range of texts.[115] In the proto-nationalist period leading up to this moment, though, rhetorical and analytical tactics still with us today were shaped by the circulation of texts in the Indian Anglosphere and their scrutiny by censors, judges, and jurors. Between the 1890 trial of the *Bangavasi* and Gandhi's in 1922, colonial law and the tactics of sly civility brought British and Indian print cultures together in negative affective relation, shaping the expression of political and literary discourse across the empire.

---

114. See Peter McDonald, *The Literature Police: Apartheid Censorship and Its Cultural Consequences* (New York: Oxford University Press, 2009).

115. Barrier, *Banned*, 96. Barrier provides a thorough and still-indispensable account of the government's struggle to control information in India from the early twentieth century until independence, including a comprehensive and annotated list of banned texts arranged by topic.

1

AFFECTATION / The Aesthete and the Babu on Trial

The press, the law, and the courtroom were crucial to the form of the Indian public sphere in the nineteenth century, for the state legitimated its authority partly through court cases. As David Gilmartin argues, "The imagined intersection of law and sovereignty ... powerfully structured an emerging vision of an Indian 'public' located between the 'state' and 'society' and offering an ongoing critique of both."[1] The law and the press were also intimately connected by the prohibitions one placed on the other. In the 1890s, two sets of trials at opposite ends of the British Empire—one in London, one in Calcutta—subjected writers to criminal liability for improper affections. In both cases, the state attempted to wrest the role of literary critic from the actual critics on trial, for the prosecution relied on literary-critical evidence and worked to stabilize linguistic meaning in order to make that evidence credible.

One set of trials is well known to scholars of the Victorian period—Oscar Wilde's prosecution for "gross indecency," mobilized by his own libel suit against the Marquess of Queensbury in 1895. As many commentators have noted, what was at stake in the Wilde trials was not just the criminalization and punishment of homosexuality, but also Wilde's aestheticism, his literary-critical views of love and literature.[2] *The Picture of Dorian Gray* (1890) and Wilde's letters, among other texts, were used as evidence of the illegality and

---

1. David Gilmartin, "Rethinking the Public through the Lens of Sovereignty," *South Asia* 38, no. 3 (2015): 375.
2. See Stephen Arata, *Fictions of Loss at the Fin de Siècle* (Cambridge: Cambridge University Press, 1996). Other important and influential works on the Wilde trials relevant to my account include Ed Cohen, *Talk on the Wilde Side: Toward a Genealogy of a Discourse on Male Sexualities* (New York: Routledge, 1988); William Cohen, *Sex Scandal: The Private Parts of Victorian Fiction* (Durham, NC: Duke University Press, 1996); Linda Dowling, *Hellenism and Homosexuality in Victorian England* (Ithaca, NY: Cornell University Press, 1994); Michael S. Foldy, *The Trials of Oscar Wilde: Deviance, Morality, and Late-Victorian Society* (New Haven, CT: Yale University Press, 1997); Alan Sinfield, *The Wilde Century: Oscar Wilde, Effeminacy, and the Queer Moment* (New York: Columbia University Press,

immorality of Wilde's passion for men, even as he argued that his views of aesthetics and philosophy placed his writing in the realm of subjectivity, outside the jurisdiction of the law.

The other trial, less well known in literary studies but equally dependent on literature as evidence, was the 1891 trial of the *Bangavasi*, a conservative Hindu newspaper published in Calcutta. This trial is significant to the colonial history of sedition law because it was the first of a series of court actions whereby the colonial government sought to prosecute Indian newspapers for disaffection using Section 124a of the Indian Penal Code. As in Wilde's case, the *Bangavasi* trial was rooted in a sex scandal. In 1891 the proprietor, editor, printer, and manager of the *Bangavasi* were accused of attempting to "excite feelings of disaffection to the Government established by law in British India."[3] The conservative newspaper had published a series of articles protesting the government's imposition of a bill that raised the age of consent from ten to twelve and was seen by many as an affront to Hindu custom. Designed to protect child brides from their husband's conjugal rights, the bill sparked such a massive oppositional response that it came to be seen as a tactical error by many British commentators. More broadly at stake, though, was the right of Indians to criticize the government at all, and the terms of the criticism itself. The trial turned on the degree to which the paper's articles contained evidence of "disaffection"; comments might express "disapprobation" of the government only if they did so "without exciting or attempting to excite hatred, contempt or disaffection."[4] The fine line between disapprobation and disaffection, then—the moment when reasonable criticism became unreasonable because it was overly negative—was what the trial set out to define.

While the queer affect policed at the Wilde trials may seem unrelated to the purportedly seditious affect being scrutinized in the 1891 newspaper trial in India, I suggest in what follows that both trials show how new regulations about gender and sexuality and the policing of subversive speech were related, and how literature was used as evidence of the wrong kind of feeling. In her introduction to a special issue of *South Asia* on sedition in the contemporary context, Svati Shah argues that "gender and sexuality are categorically, affectively,

---

1994); and David Schulz, "Redressing Oscar: Performance and the Trials of Oscar Wilde," *Drama Review* 40, no. 2 (Summer 1996): 37–59.

3. "Section 124a (Inserted by Act 27 of 1870)," in *The Indian Penal Code, 1860* (Mumbai: Amit Nanda for Current Publications, 2016), 79.

4. "Section 124a," 79.

aesthetically, and juridically rendered in relation to governance in general and in relation to the ways in which speech and dissent are under specific forms of attack across the region today."[5] If the Wilde trials seem to be more about sexuality and the *Bangavasi* trial more about speech, looking at them together, with their resonances and shared historical context in mind, helps us see the confluence identified by Shah taking recognizable shape at the end of the nineteenth century. From one perspective, this is a contrapuntal reading that emphasizes the interconnected but unacknowledged structures of governance and dependency linking events in Britain and India during this period. But my approach also emphasizes the material consequences of the circulation of ideas and news in the imperial public sphere and is thus a "transimperial" reading as well. In Sukanya Banerjee's useful formulation, a transimperial frame allows us to place colony and metropole together on an "interrelated plane of modernity without flattening the difference between [them] or suggesting equivalence between the two." Instead, the transimperial assumes "a proximate commonality that is underwritten by the shared, fraught, and evolving relation with modernity in *both* sites."[6] The trials of Wilde and the *Bangavasi* were linked not by causality but by continuity—by the ways that acts of legislation, ideas about masculinity, and fears of the power of writing traveled not unidirectionally from Britain to India, or vice versa, but formed a complex network of influence between the two spaces.

Wilde and the *Bangavasi* writers both evoked stereotypical and suspect figures—the aesthete and the babu respectively. But these in turn evoked each other within the imperial public sphere because of what Sara Ahmed calls "metonymic slide," whereby the representations of different reviled figures seen as a threat to the nation are related to one another: "What makes them 'alike' may be their 'unlikeness' from 'us.' . . . Hate cannot be found in one figure, but works to create the outline of different figures or objects of hate, a creation that crucially aligns the figures together."[7] Though the prosecution in both London and Calcutta struggled to affix evidence of crime to the writers' actual words, the words were largely beside the point. Wilde and the *Bangavasi* were being tried for the impudence of hiding in plain sight, for skirting the boundaries of the permissible and

---

5. Svati P. Shah, "Sedition, Sexuality, Gender, and Gender Identity in South Asia," *South Asia* 20 (2019): 1–23, 3.
6. Sukanya Banerjee, "Marriage, Modernity, and the Transimperial," 162–63.
7. Sara Ahmed, *The Cultural Politics of Emotion*, 2nd ed. (Edinburgh: Edinburgh University Press, 2014), 44.

expecting to get away with it. In both cases, the improper affection of the men on trial (homosexual love in Wilde's case and seditious hatred in the *Bangavasi* case) was at issue, but also their improper *affectation*, the slyness and insolence with which they used rhetoric to fly under the radar. The trials were designed to tackle these evasive strategies head-on by showing how improper affection and affectation go hand in hand, the latter enabling the former and allowing it to exist, in semivisible ways, in public. The prosecution in both cases sought to blow the cover off an affect-saturated type—the aesthete or the babu—and expose it to censure and discipline.

If the Wilde trials made homosexuality visible in new ways, the trial of the *Bangavasi* and subsequent newspaper trials were similarly a turning point in the visibility of the Indian nationalist movement.[8] The Wilde and *Bangavasi* trials illuminate each other, then, in their shared desire to articulate the proper relationships among masculinity, law and order, and the function of the critic. Far from being coincidental, their resemblance had to do with the necessity of imagining empire from center to margin and back as a cohesive and orderly space, containable within a British political imaginary. In marking the difference between legitimate and criminal affect, the trials attempted to sanitize the imperial public sphere by corralling its increasingly audacious provocateurs.

The Trials of Empire

Since the Wilde trials have already been analyzed extensively by scholars in Victorian studies and queer theory, I focus more closely here on the *Bangavasi* case, a turning point in colonial legal history carefully chronicled in Sukeshi Kamra's *The Indian Periodical Press and Nationalist Rhetoric* (2011), but otherwise analyzed mainly in relation to the Age of Consent Act controversy in which the *Bangavasi* was embroiled. Before turning to the fin-de-siècle moment of that trial, however, a short detour to an earlier moment in imperial history is necessary, for, as Nicholas B. Dirks argues in *The Scandal of Empire* (2008), the impeachment of Warren Hastings at the end of the eighteenth

---

8. This is one of Kamra's central arguments in *The Indian Periodical Press and Nationalist Rhetoric*.

century laid the groundwork for the use of the law as a disciplinary spectacle. The scandal of power abuse in India and in Britain, Dirks contends, was connected by show trials that helped legitimate and consolidate imperial power by containing its excesses.

Between 1788 and 1795, Hastings, then governor-general of India, was on trial for presiding over the pillaging of India by the East India Company, whose corrupt practices he had been commissioned to reform. Turning the indictment of his rule, and of Company exploits in general, into a dramatic and long-running national spectacle, the trial effectively purged empire of the scandal of its violence and greed by decrying Hastings's methods while simultaneously allowing Britain to profit from his work.[9] Though Hastings was eventually acquitted, the trial, famously prosecuted with grim determination by Edmund Burke, helped change the way imperialism was justified and actualized. The nabobs (a word originally used for Muslim administrators in the Mughal Empire) who returned to Britain with vast wealth derived from waging war, conquering territories, monopolizing trade, and extorting payments from their inhabitants, were widely reviled in the metropole.[10] But as their name suggested, their venality was associated from the start with Eastern corruption, particularly that of the local Indian rulers with whom the Company dealt and fought. After the trial, the burden of scandal and corruption was shifted back to the East, not only because Britain had ostensibly demonstrated its commitment to weeding out dishonesty via a mesmerizing legal drama, but also because the rhetoric of the trial worked to displace the scandal onto India. While purportedly sympathetic to India, Burke influentially characterized the subcontinent as both victim and victimizer; for instance, he compared the nawab of Arcot (who had colluded with Company employees to exploit his dependents) to a "gorgeous Eastern harlot."[11] In Dirks's reading, the nawab became "a symbol of how India was corrupting the callow youth of the Company service not only with its immense wealth but with its irrevocable, and deeply sexualized, alterity."[12] Burke also instrumentalized the

---

9. Kamra, *Indian Periodical Press*.
10. For a comprehensive study of metropolitan perspectives on the nabobs, see Tillman Nechtman, *Nabobs: Empire and Identity in Eighteenth-Century Britain* (Cambridge: Cambridge University Press, 2010).
11. Quoted in Nicholas B. Dirks, *The Scandal of Empire: India and the Creation of Imperial Britain* (Cambridge, MA: Belknap Press, 2008), 79.
12. Dirks, *Scandal of Empire*, 78.

alleged rape and torture of women by the Indian agents of a revenue collector to enhance the trial's drama. Thus, the scandal of British behavior in India was transformed into the scandal of India's endemic political and sexual corruption, and scandal "became the principal justification for empire rather than the unfortunate means of empire's creation."[13]

The Great Wahhabi Case is another important context for the *Bangavasi* trial. In 1869 two Calcutta businessmen, Amir and Hashmadad Khan, were arrested and kept for fourteen months without charges on suspicion of funding Wahhabi rebels on the northwest frontier.[14] Like Hastings's trial, the Khans' ordeal dragged on for years. In 1871 Hashmadad was finally acquitted while Amir was convicted—but then pardoned again in 1877, suggesting the government's lack of faith in its own case. The Wahhabi case was a significant precursor of the newspaper sedition trials that began with the *Bangavasi*'s in 1891 because it was a glaring example of liberal principles being undermined by "state of emergency" politics and became a subject of combative public debate for that reason. One major legal outcome of the case was that the government gained the right to suspend habeas corpus in India; another was that the case helped instigate the passing of Section 124a, for "official correspondence on Section 124a cited the threat of Wahhabi fanaticism to justify greater powers to punish anyone believed to be spreading disaffection."[15] Julia Stephens's close analysis of the case emphasizes the way it represented a growing paranoia about conspiracy and sedition post-1857 and a consequent shift from liberal governance to "ideas of colonial difference and authoritarian strategies."[16] At the same time, its long-running melodrama generated an ongoing conversation in the Anglo-Indian and Indian press about government overreach and the betrayal of liberal ideals, and helped establish the role of public opinion in influencing policies and decisions.[17]

The *Bangavasi* trial—like Hastings's and that of the Khan brothers—was another imperial show trial followed closely by the press and debated avidly

---

13. Dirks, *Scandal of Empire*, xii.
14. The term "Wahhabi" refers to a specific Islamic sect but was applied broadly by the British to describe a range of Islamic reform movements and associate them with political sedition.
15. Stephens, "Phantom Wahhabi," 41.
16. Stephens, "Phantom Wahhabi," 34.
17. Stephens notes that "officials privately acknowledged the role of public opinion in shaping their decision to release Amir Khan" ("Phantom Wahhabi," 47).

by colonial publics.[18] While it was no more a triumph for the government than Hastings's trial, it too staged India as a land of excess in order to reestablish British sovereignty in India at a moment of imperial misstep.[19] It accomplished this by turning British transgression (namely, breaking the vow of noninterference in Indian religious practices by raising the age of consent) into a spectacle of Indian transgression instead (of the new journalistic double standard the trial was designed to enforce). If Indian corruption became the subtext of Hastings's trial, India's political immaturity was the more prominent justification of empire ushered into its place by sedition trials such as that of the *Bangavasi*. Empire's new alibi was that the Indian ruling class was too irrational, effeminate, and sexually excessive to lead a modern nation.

The disaffection law and its application were, in effect, designed to perpetuate empire by making explicit calls to Indian nationalism—now labeled "disaffection"—the very sign that Indians, in their callow emotionalism, were not yet ready to form a nation (the endless "not yet" that Dipesh Chakrabarty puts at the center of Western historicist consciousness).[20] If the scandal of colonial governance and its excesses and the scandal of sex were connected and rewritten as the scandal of Indian backwardness in the Hastings trial at the end of the eighteenth century, these two types of scandals came together again at the end of the nineteenth, to similar effect.

The Trials in the Press

Wilde's trials obviously had more to do with sex scandal than the excesses of government. One contention of this chapter, however, is that the events of the trials—both the courtroom drama and the sensationalist coverage of it by the press—were inspired partly by a new investment in policing any kind of criticism, whether literary or political, because of a growing sense of imperial fragility.

---

18. For a reading of the *Bangavasi* trial's impact focused specifically on its use of dramatic convention, see Julie Stone Peters, "Theatricality, Legalism, and the Scenography of Suffering: The Trial of Warren Hastings and Richard Brinsley Sheridan's *Pizzaro*," *Law and Literature* 18, no. 1 (2006): 15–45.

19. Sara Suleri's reading of the *Bangavasi* trial also suggests that the prosecution's rhetorical excesses had the effect of turning India into a scene of the sublime and of suffering, and thus had a lasting effect on the figuration of India in the British imagination. Sara Suleri, *The Rhetoric of English India* (Chicago: University of Chicago Press, 1992).

20. Dipesh Chakrabarty, *Provincializing Europe: Postcolonial Thought and Historical Difference* (Princeton, NJ: Princeton University Press, 2008), 8.

The intersection of the public sphere in Britain and the English-language sphere in India meant that the two were continually in tacit dialogue and were mutually influential. While discourses of gender and sexuality, as well as the sense of embattled British values that underlay them, circulated between Britain and India in the late nineteenth century, news of the *Bangavasi* and Wilde trials did too.[21] From the coverage of sensational events such as the trials of Oscar Wilde to the development of new periodical forms such as W. T. Stead's *Review of Reviews* (see chapter 3), public debates in Britain were formed partly in reaction to colonial disaffection as expressed and penalized in colonial newspapers, some of which circulated in Britain or were extracted in British newspapers. The term "disaffection" appeared frequently in the British press, usually in connection with anticolonial uprisings or sedition cases, while both Indian discontent with British rule and the illiberalism of censorship law in India were debated in the press and in Parliament.

The Wilde trials, meanwhile, were profiled by Indian English-language newspapers in India, as well as in the many British newspapers distributed there. The *Times of India*, for instance, ran a series of articles on the *Bangavasi* trial that reported on the accusations, the events of the trial, and its outcome in considerable detail, while the *Friend of India and Statesman* also published a lengthy account. In Britain, the *Times* chronicled the *Bangavasi* case from start to finish, drawing attention to the newly defined legal concept of disaffection as hatred of the government, and noting that the disaffection in question was inspired by the Age of Consent Act. Follow-up articles reported on the trial's outcome and the implication of the government's victory.

The *Times* also paid close attention to the prosecution of B. G. Tilak for sedition in 1897. While the *Bangavasi* case was noteworthy because it was the first time Section 124a was used to criminalize the press in India, Tilak's case was a high-profile one because the disaffection supposedly incited by his writing was by then associated not only with hatred, but with organized political radicalism. The *Times*'s reporting on both of these trials, as well as on revisions made to Section 124a in 1898, and later on Gandhi's trials, underscored the importance of the disaffection law to the maintenance of colonial rule. Following the logic of imperialist punditry of the time, the paper argued that the Indian press must be prosecuted because of the possible breadth of its influence: "Though appeals

---

21. Mrinalini Sinha, *Colonial Masculinity: The 'Manly Englishman' and the 'Effeminate Bengali' in the Late Nineteenth Century* (Manchester: Manchester University Press, 1995).

through the newspapers affect immediately only a very small proportion of the people who live under British rule in India, the fraction that is so influenced may carry the seeds of sedition among the Indian masses."[22] Wilde's perceived threat to the nation was imagined in similarly feverish terms: an outlaw minority, he might spread his disease, "seed[ing]" his homosexuality among callow and impressionable working-class men.

From the 1890s onward, regional publications such as the *Standard*, the *Glasgow Herald*, the *Northern Echo*, and the *Liverpool Mercury*, as well as the Irish *Freeman's Journal and Daily Commercial Advertiser*, also reported on the new applications of sedition law in India, and on signs of native discontent more generally. Unlike the *Times*, whose articles on disaffection seemed designed to reinforce the disciplinary function of the trials, these papers printed letters and articles about growing disaffection that were more critical of imperial rule, or at least of its shortsightedness. A letter to the editor of the *Northern Echo* in 1897, for example, attributed the "recent disaffection" in India to the fact that British doctors and other European "physiologists and bacteriologists" had turned the colony into a testing ground for experimental cholera and plague vaccines; to make matters worse, the writer noted, these scientists were injecting Indians with animal excreta, thereby "offending ... religious sensibilities."[23] The British author of this letter depicts disaffection as a logical outcome of colonial practices rather than an intemperate response to reasonable governance—something that Indians were forcibly infected with rather than a disease they were spreading themselves.

The *Freeman's Journal and Daily Commercial Advertiser*, published in Ireland, also took a sympathetic view of Indian disaffection. In a letter entitled "The Disaffection in India" addressed to the paper's editor, the nationalist journalist and politician F. Hugh O'Donnell insisted on the importance of "a sympathetic treatment

---

22. "Editorial," *London Times*, December 23, 1897, 7.
23. Sidney G. Trist, "Disaffection in India," *Northern Echo* (Darlington, England), July 16, 1897. While doctors, scientists, and the military did perform egregious experiments on colonial subjects (for example, the Porton Down experiments, in which mustard gas was tested on hundreds of Indian solders), many false rumors about the spread of disease in India and its relation to colonial activities circulated in the press and elsewhere, so it is hard to judge the veracity of this particular claim. See Anita Guerrini, "The Human Experimental Subject," in *A Companion to the History of Science*, ed. Bernard Lightman (Hoboken, NJ: John Wiley, 2016), 126–39; and David Arnold, *Colonizing the Body: State Medicine and Epidemic Disease in Nineteenth-Century India* (Berkeley: University of California Press, 1993), 218–40.

of the Indian question" to Irish nationalism.[24] India, he contended, was being impoverished by British rule, which had brought with it famine, disease, and the mistreatment of women by colonial men, just as it had in Ireland. As Amy Martin's work has demonstrated, this article was hardly anomalous; from the 1857 Indian Mutiny into the twentieth century, a number of Irish nationalists engaged in rigorous comparisons between India and Ireland, creating "a remarkably compelling vision of a world dominated by empire and capital, of violence in the process of decolonization, and the problem of writing the history of the colonized and of the non-modern."[25] Wilde himself was not known for his anticolonialism, but in 1882 he gave a lecture in San Francisco in which he proudly identified himself as an Irish writer and hailed his mother as a poet and Irish nationalist. Lady Jane Wilde had written for the radical Irish periodical the *Nation* in the 1840s, and her articles calling for armed rebellion against the British had contributed to its suppression for sedition. Tinged with this legacy of political subversion, Wilde's cultural subversion was all the more threatening.

The Aesthete and the Babu

In both Wilde's trials for gross indecency and the newspaper trials for disaffection, the focus of the law shifted from the unlawful act (sodomy in one case, sedition in the other) to unlawful affect. In each instance, forms of criticism were interpreted as evidence of excessive affects (sexual love and political hatred) and a new literary-criminal other was created (the aesthete-pervert and the babu-traitor) and cast out of the body politic—a space defined by this casting out as one of restrained affect. While much has been written about the figures of the aesthete and the babu separately, I seek to demonstrate how they are historically and representationally connected and to argue for the significance of these connections to the shaping of British imperial identity, Indian national identity, and the tensions between them, as well as to the policing of speech and affect that is the subject of this book.

Both figures were late-Victorian literary types associated with effeminacy and posing. The word "babu"—sometimes spelled as I have spelled it here, and

---

24. F. Hugh O'Donnell, "The Disaffection in India," *Freeman's Journal and Daily Commercial Advertiser* (Dublin), July 6, 1897.

25. Amy Martin, "Representing the 'Indian Revolution' of 1857: Towards a Genealogy of Irish Internationalist Anticolonialism," *Field Day Review* 8 (2012): 126–47, 132.

sometimes as "baboo," like the frequent British spelling of "Hindoo"—was initially used by administrators as a polite title for an Indian clerk. In Indian languages, the meaning varies; in Hindi it functions as an honorific but is also a term of endearment, as it is in Telugu. In modern Bengali, Nasia Anam notes, it is "simultaneously used as a term of affection for small children and as a diminutive of *baba*, meaning father, as well as to mean a person of consequence, a governmental clerk, or an effete intellectual."[26]

In the early nineteenth century, "baboo" and "baboo English" were terms often associated with petition writers: scribes who recorded grievances on behalf of colonial subjects who wished to address them to the government. A petition was a letter of supplication to a British administrator and under Company rule was "the most ubiquitous means to appeal for redress, resolve disputes, or stake claims to resources."[27] Due to the emphasis on writing and recording that Bhavani Raman dubs "document raj" (a useful shorthand for the way British power depended on the bureaucratization and inscription of colonial knowledge), the written petition was the only officially sanctioned method of presenting a grievance. Yet, as Raman's analysis of this practice demonstrates, the formalization of petitions did not make them readily legible. Indeed, the fact that they were "a quintessentially hierarchical form of address" based on older forms of supplication and thus "often expressed intense forms of praise" made them suspicious to their British addressees, as did their mediated quality as documents produced by scribes for pay, rather than firsthand accounts by the petitioners themselves.[28]

As a result, Raman argues, petitions were judged based on a principle of "sincerity," a quality that was reflected by their "linguistic register": "Petition writers wrote in an ornate bureaucratic prose that translated somewhat awkwardly into 'Babu English.' They used an idiom of civil or respectful language that not only marked hierarchy but also evoked an emotive devotional praise. . . . The Committee on Petitions declared this sort of language to be excessive. All petitions, they believed, were written too theatrically, as though the petitioner were

---

26. Nasia Anam, "Can the Babu Speak (to the Dandy): A Study of the Nineteenth Century Literary Phenomenon of the Babu" (unpublished essay, cited with permission of the author). Anam's work importantly stresses the differences as well as continuities between the dandy and the babu, arguing that dandyism was chosen, often in defiance of normativity, while the label "baboo" was not: "To be a Babu was to never be granted, in representation, this self-acknowledgement of transcendental and transformative power that Dandyism was. Equally reviled in both their respective historical and geographical contexts, the Babu and the Dandy were never on equal footing . . . the Babu always lagging behind and never earning the celebratory afterlife of the Dandy."
27. Bhavani Raman, *Document Raj* (Chicago: University of Chicago Press, 2012), 161.
28. B. Raman, *Document Raj*, 161, 163.

seriously maltreated."²⁹ In response to their distrust of petition rhetoric, the Company attempted various methods of standardizing petitions (such as stamps and signatures) in order to render them more legible.

The use of petitions by the colonial state is significant because of the way it corralled dissent by grounding "ideas of correct behavior in peaceable civil writing rather than disorderly conduct," while at the same time subjecting that writing to constant scrutiny and suspicion.³⁰ Babu English and the idea of the babu writer as a dubious, affected, and theatrical mediator between colonizer and colonized were thus by-products of the early administrative strategies of "document raj" that would help shape the ways in which critique was staged in the press and interpreted by law.

This also helps explain the growing historical baggage of the term "babu," which by the turn of the century was most often used derogatively as a label for politically engaged, bourgeois Indian intellectuals, particularly those in Bengal. *Hobson-Jobson* (1886) noted of the word that, "in Bengal and elsewhere, among Anglo-Indians, it is often used with a slight savour of disparagement, as characterizing a superficially cultivated, but too often effeminate, Bengali."³¹ (Stephanie Newell's research on the representation of educated colonial subjects in British West Africa demonstrates that the term had some transimperial currency as well).³²

The babu figure was most obviously an outgrowth of the way British masculinity was opposed to Hindu, and particularly Bengali, effeminacy in the service of imperial rule—as in Thomas Babington Macaulay's notorious claim that "the physical organization of the Bengalee is feeble even to effeminacy.... During many ages he has been trampled upon by men of bolder and more hardy breeds."³³ But the derogatory connotations of the term were multilayered, derived also from its growing association over time with pretension, elitism, and professionalism—an

---

29. B. Raman, *Document Raj*, 171.
30. B. Raman, *Document Raj*, 191.
31. "Baboo, s. Beng. and H.," in *Hobson-Jobson: The Definitive Glossary of British India*, by Henry Yule and A. C. Burnell, ed. Kate Teltscher (Oxford: Oxford University Press, 2016), 72.
32. Stephanie Newell, "Local Cosmopolitans in Colonial West Africa," *Journal of Commonwealth Literature* 46, no. 1 (2011): 103–17.
33. Thomas Babington Macaulay, "Warren Hastings," *Edinburgh Review*, October 1841. For more on the uses of effeminacy in colonial discourse, see Sinha, *Colonial Masculinity*; Abhik Roy and Michele L. Hammers, "Swami Vivekananda's Rhetoric of Spiritual Masculinity: Transforming Effeminate Bengalis into Virile Men," *Western Journal of Communication* 78, no. 4 (July–September 2014): 545–62; and Sikata Banerjee, *Make Me a Man! Masculinity, Hinduism, and Nationalism in India* (Albany: State University of New York Press, 2005).

outgrowth of the mediating role of scribal culture and its relationship to dissent. Sukanya Banerjee's work on the Indian civil service is another important context for this figure, for it shows how men (both British and Indian) who earned their place in government through competitive examinations were seen as unmanly "competition wallahs," similar to and intersecting with the babu.[34] The stereotype of the competition wallah, together with that of the effeminate Bengali writer, helped identify professionalism with masculine weakness—a conjunction used against moderates in the nationalist movement, who were often seen as allies of the bureaucratic state, or politically ineffectual, or both (the word "cuck," used by the alt-right to denounce political moderates in the United States today, works similarly). Anticolonial leaders such as Swami Vivekananda thus explicitly tackled the stereotype of the effeminate Indian in their writing and self-fashioning. Arguing for the importance of physical culture Vivekananda wrote, "You will understand the Gita better with your biceps, your muscles, a little stronger. . . . You will understand the Upanishads better and the glory of the Atman when your body stands firm upon your feet, and you feel yourselves as men."[35]

Visual and verbal stereotypes of the babu were employed by Indian writers and artists as well as English and Anglo-Indian ones. While British versions of the caricature tried to defang the babu's criticism of the government by making him weak and comical, Indian versions used him to opposite ends by making him metonymic of an emergent Anglicized comprador class. Bankim Chandra Chattopadhyay, the famous Bengali writer who composed the Indian nationalist song "Vande Mataram," ridiculed babus in his writing for their aping of English manners, as did Rabindranath Tagore. Hurree Chunder Mookerjee in Rudyard Kipling's *Kim* (1901) efficiently combines both versions of this type. Referred to as "Hurree Babu" or "the Babu" throughout the text, he is an educated gentleman depicted as "superficially cultivated" and comically effeminate, but also as a canny operative deploying that stereotype to spy for the British.[36] The visual stereotype of the babu, complementing his son's verbal one, is captured in one of the nine

---

34. See Sukanya Banerjee, *Becoming Imperial Citizens*, chap. 5.
35. Swami Vivekananda, "Vedanta in Its Application to Indian Life," in *The Complete Works of Swami Vivekananda* (New York, Discovery, 2018), 3:117.
36. Newell's astute reading notes that Hurree plays up his "babu" role as part of his work as a government agent. For instances of Hurree's babuness, see Rudyard Kipling, *Kim*, ed. Paula M. Krebs and Tricia Lootens (1901; New York: Pearson, 2011), 149, where Kim, conspiring with Hurree, tells him they should avoid English in order not to draw attention to themselves and Hurree answers in full mimic-man mode, "flinging his shoulder-cloth jauntily": "That is all raight. I am only Babu showing off my English to you. All we Babus talk English to show off."

bas-relief illustrations that Kipling's father, John Lockwood Kipling, provided for an edition of the novel (Figure 1.1).

Visual caricatures of babus by Indians were common too, especially in Kalighat paintings.[37] Krishna Dutta describes the recurrent type in these paintings as follows: "Their dandyism is strongly satirized: the babu is seen as a spendthrift and fake gentleman. His oiled hair is nattily parted in Prince Albert style and his mustache glued symmetrically to his cheeks. . . . A pair of shiny pumps adorns his feet. In his hands he holds a hookah or a fragrant flower such as a rose, or a fancy walking stick."[38]

The opposition between British masculinity and Indian (or colonial) effeminacy in the imperial public sphere helped generate further, internal oppositions. In the British context, we see it in the juxtaposition between the action-oriented imperialist and the overcultivated aesthete (epitomized by Sir Henry Curtis and Captain Good in *King Solomon's Mines* (1885), and still visible decades later when Flory, the passive critic of colonialism in *Burmese Days* (1934), finds himself unable to identify with either the "manly man" imperialist or the "nancy boy" pacifist). While retaining civility as a crucial British value, this dichotomy suggests that the civilizing process can go too far, "cultivating too much urbanity, too much empathy, too much civility."[39] In the Indian context, the virile nationalist figure that Vivekananda sought to embody was juxtaposed with the many iterations of the servile babu: comprador, poseur, bureaucrat. The caricatures of the babu and of the aesthete overlapped, then, in their evocations of vanity, effeminacy, and pretension, and the threats these posed to imperial discipline and the masculinity that ideally embodied it. The "metonymic slide" at play here is captured in a photograph of Swami Vivekananda taken in San Francisco in 1900 that departed from the tendency of his portraits to depict him in Indian clothing with a strong "masculine" stance that conveyed his interest in a robust physicality, such as the widely circulated one taken in Chicago in 1893 (Figure 1.2).

The American portrait reverses the terms of this depiction; in this photograph, he wears Western clothing but adopts the languid, artistic pose associated with one of Wilde's famous portraits and with aesthetic dandyism more generally (Figure 1.3).

---

37. Kalighat paintings were small, colorful paintings sold to visitors to the Kalighat temple by local artists throughout the nineteenth century and into the early twentieth. They generally depicted animals, Hindu gods and goddesses, and caricatures of contemporary life, such as the babu figure. See Krishna Dutta, *Calcutta: A Cultural History* (Northampton, MA: Interlink Books, 2008), 35–36.

38. Dutta, *Calcutta*, 38.

39. Pernau and Jornheim, introduction, 12.

FIGURE 1.1 / Illustration of Hurree Chunder Mookerjee by John Lockwood Kipling from *Kim* (New York: Doubleday, 1901), 278. Internet Archive, https://archive.org/details/kim_____00kipl.

FIGURE 1.2 / Portrait of Swami Vivekananda in Chicago, September 1893. Wikimedia Commons, https://commons.wikimedia.org/wiki/File:Swami_Vivekananda-1893-09-signed.jpg.

FIGURE 1.3 / Portrait of Swami Vivekananda in San Francisco, ca. 1900. Wikimedia Commons, https://commons.wikimedia.org/wiki/File:Swami_vivekanand_old_archive.jpg.

FIGURE 1.4 / Portrait of Oscar Wilde in New York by Napoleon Sarony, 1882. British Library. Shelfmark MSS 81785, © British Library Board.

Possibly Vivekananda's emphasis on celibacy and his monkish asceticism seemed as eccentric to the photographer as Wilde's self-conscious aestheticism and an implicit parallel was set up in the posing process. But whether the studio or Vivekananda himself suggested the pose, and whether or not it consciously echoed Wilde's portrait, one can see it as further evidence of a semiotic connection between the figure of the British outsider-aesthete and that of the Indian nationalist as seen through Western eyes.

If the aesthete was considered a poseur because he drew attention to the artifice of art and the performance of identity, the babu was considered one because of his presumptuous mimicry—his ability to navigate the imperial system and the world of letters on their own terms.[40] In his work on Wilde, Patrick Mullen draws on Eve Sedgwick's *Epistemology of the Closet* (1990) to describe the structure of homoerotic affect as "connotation and suggestiveness, denial and evasion."[41] This succinct formulation works just as well to describe the rhetoric of anticolonialism at the turn of the century, in response to press surveillance and censorship.

The Age of Consent Controversy

Like the figures of the aesthete and the babu, the Age of Consent Act controversy that led up to the trial of the *Bangavasi* makes the most sense when seen through the lens of the imperial public sphere, for the gender and sexuality reform initiatives of which it was part took shape contemporaneously in Britain and India and influenced each other's articulations. The passing of the Age of Consent Act in India had much to do with the passionate advocacy of Behramji Malabari, a Parsi reformer and newspaper editor from Bombay who campaigned for widows rights and against child marriage. Later to become the editor of the innovative modernist periodical *East and West* (analyzed in chapter 4), he had significant political and journalistic ties both in India and Britain, and first circulated a public note aimed at the protection of widows and children in 1884.[42] In 1885

---

40. On the relation between Wilde's alleged criminality and his "insincerity" or affectation, see Arata, *Fictions of Loss at the Fin de Siècle*, 59–66.

41. Patrick Mullen, *The Poor Bugger's Tool: Irish Modernism, Queer Labor, and Postcolonial History* (Oxford: Oxford University Press, 2012), 30.

42. On the connections between the Age of Consent debate in Britain and India, see Richard Phillips, *Sex, Politics and Empire: A Postcolonial Geography* (Manchester: Manchester University Press, 2006); Antoinette Burton, *At the Heart of the Empire: Indians and the Colonial Encounter in*

W. T. Stead, a British journalist and social purity campaigner—whose journalism Malabari followed closely and with whom he was in touch—performed a similar public intervention by publishing "The Maiden Tribute of Modern Babylon," a sensationalistic series of articles condemning the prevalence of child prostitution that is thought to have helped instigate the passing of Britain's Criminal Law Amendment Act later that year (more on this in chapter 3). The act raised the age of consent from thirteen to sixteen, but also produced new legislation criminalizing prostitution and homosexuality—most notoriously, it was the act's Labouchere Amendment, outlawing "acts of gross indecency," that led to Wilde's prosecution.

In 1890, inspired by Stead's success in using journalism and publicity to advance his cause, Malabari circulated another note on his reform proposals, this time addressed to a British audience, and persuaded influential figures such as Max Müller to lend their voices to his campaign (he also got a boost from Stead, who covered his campaign in the *Review of Reviews*).[43] Prompted by Malabari's advocacy and the public opinion he had successfully stirred up in Britain, the colonial government, which had initially resisted the reform because of prescient fears of the opposition it would stir up, introduced the Indian Age of Consent Act in 1891.

As the government predicted, the act was immediately seen as an outrageous transgression of Queen Victoria's 1858 Proclamation, which promised to respect Indian religious and cultural beliefs: "We declare it to be Our Royal Will and Pleasure that none be in any wise favored, none molested or disquieted by reason of their Religious Faith or Observances; but that all shall alike enjoy the equal and impartial protection of the Law."[44] Because of the sanctity of the private (religious, cultural) sphere to nationalists as the realm reserved for Indian rather than Western values, as Partha Chatterjee has influentially demonstrated, the act was seen as an outrageous intrusion on the sanctity of that sphere and on Indian male privilege—in this case, the sacred right and duty of a man to have sex with

---

Late-Victorian Britain (Berkeley: University of California Press, 1998); Meera Kosambi, "Girl-Brides and Socio-Legal Change: Age of Consent Bill (1891) Controversy," *Economic and Political Weekly* 26, nos. 31/32 (August 3–10, 1991): 1857–68; Tanika Sarkar, *Hindu Wife, Hindu Nation: Community, Religion, and Cultural Nationalism* (Delhi: Permanent Black, 2003); and Sinha, *Colonial Masculinity*.

43. Kosami, "Girl-Brides and Socio-Legal Change," 1858.

44. "Proclamation by the Queen in Council to the Princes, Chiefs, and People of India (published by the Governor-General of Allahabad, November 1st, 1858)."

his wife.⁴⁵ Since the act did not change marital law, a man could marry and share a room with his underage bride, but was forbidden from consummating the marriage, an emasculating scenario that made the policing of male sexuality explicit. While conservative newspapers like the *Bangavasi* protested the bill on orthodox religious grounds, even some prominent feminist reformers who spoke out against child marriage were loath to support a measure that so glaringly symbolized colonial interference in the private sphere and sought to contest the bill on other grounds instead, such as the lack of a marital rape clause in British law.⁴⁶ Tilak, the nationalist leader soon to undergo his own sedition trials, also came out against the act. Then a member of the Indian National Congress, later an important leader of the Swadeshi movement, and eventually a nationalist icon—after he was found guilty of seditious writing at his second trial for disaffection in 1908 and exiled to Mandalay for six years under Section 124a—Tilak was against child marriage. But he believed that reform should be initiated by Indians, and that the community alone should be responsible for protecting underage girls; his vehement opposition to the bill helped galvanize protests against it. At the peak of the controversy, a rally in Calcutta against the act drew a crowd of two hundred thousand.

Arguments against the act focused on the difference between Hindu culture and religion and Western norms, or at least a certain brahmanical patriarchal interpretation of Hinduism championed by those most offended by the act.⁴⁷ These arguments suggested it was the female *body* that gave consent rather than the individual, for a girl who had begun menstruation was thought to be prepared for sex, and religious law stated that intercourse must occur two weeks after menstruation to promote procreation. The passing of the Age of Consent law meant that if a girl menstruated before the age of twelve, the religious duty of husband and wife to have sex with the goal of reproduction would go unfulfilled.⁴⁸ The law thus infringed on patriarchal privilege in every sense—it could prevent a husband from having sex with his wife, from starting a family, and from having control over his home (for, theoretically, the government could invade or surveil it to protect an underage girl). For these reasons, the *Bangavasi*'s vehement criticism of the law attracted a huge following: it became "the leading Bengali daily,

---

45. Partha Chatterjee, *The Nation and Its Fragments: Colonial and Postcolonial Histories* (Princeton, NJ: Princeton University Press, 1993).
46. See Sinha, *Colonial Masculinity*, 141.
47. Laws were extrapolated as applying across caste when historically they did not. Sarkar, *Hindu Wife, Hindu Nation*, 209.
48. Kosami, "Girl-Brides and Socio-Legal Change," 1858.

changing over from its weekly status, and pulling a whole lot of erstwhile reformist papers into its orbit for some time."[49]

Feminist scholars have argued that the Age of Consent Act controversy, while initiating a conversation about the rights of women and girls, had the effect of consolidating a conservative Hindu patriarchal view of Indian culture still influential today.[50] For one thing, it sidelined women's voices; both Indian and British women, especially doctors, had spoken out against child marriage but the debate was framed as a male contest in which both the British government and the Hindu opposition to the act spoke for female consent. It also forestalled the progress of women's rights because the nationalist fervor it provoked turned gender reform into a third-rail issue for the government—while it continued to crack down on the press's response from the *Bangavasi* trial onward, it refrained from passing any similar reformist legislation for almost three decades afterward.[51] Ideologically, moreover, the controversy put "ideas about Hindu conjugality at the very heart of militant nationalism in Bengal" and contributed to the nationalist trope of Mother India as a saintly and self-sacrificing figure (see chapter 2 for more on the insidious effects of this trope).[52]

Thus, a debate about the rights of women was displaced by one about the rights of the (Hindu) collective, which women were to represent symbolically, rather than agentially. As Tanika Sarkar argues, "The forced surrender and real dispossession of the [colonized Hindu male] was counterposed to the allegedly loving, willed surrender and ultimate self-fulfillment of [his wife]";[53] "the Hindu woman's submission to community discipline" was made vital because it preserved the "last remnants of authenticity wherein also lay the promise of future nationhood."[54] It is fitting that the outrage inspired by the Age of Consent Bill triggered the deployment of Section 124a, with its focus on affect, because both the outrage and the sedition law used to quell it were attempts to adjudicate desire and intent by locating it in the body. If menstruation was understood as the desire (of the body) to engage in reproduction in the case of women, negative affect was understood as the desire to undermine the government in the case of writers.

---

49. Sarkar, *Hindu Wife, Hindu Nation*, 222.
50. On the relationship of gender, sexuality, nationalism, and normative masculinity today, see Shah, "Sedition, Sexuality, Gender, and Gender Identity in South Asia," 10.
51. Sarkar, *Hindu Wife, Hindu Nation*, 244.
52. Sarkar, *Hindu Wife, Hindu Nation*, 191, 250.
53. Sarkar, *Hindu Wife, Hindu Nation*, 198.
54. Sarkar, *Hindu Wife, Hindu Nation*, 228.

The Two Trials

While the *Bangavasi*'s critique of the bill was not strikingly different from those of many other newspapers, the newspaper's trial was clearly symbolic—an attempt to stem the rising tide of antigovernment sentiment by using Section 124a to target affect rather than seditious language. The prosecution drew attention to affect by accusing the newspaper of appealing to people's superstitions, of comparing the government to "revolting characters in the Hindu mythology," and of shunning "reasonable discussion of the Age of Consent Bill" in favor of "vituperation and invective."[55] One of the articles in question, for example, "The Revealed Form of the English Ruler," compares the Englishman's new guise as guardian of Indian women to "the sudden transformation of the great Tapaswi . . . into the ten-headed, twenty-eyed, monarch of the Rakhansas."[56] The writer apostrophizes him thus: "Oh! Englishman! You, who call yourself civilized in consequence of the pride (arising) from the strength of your arms, you who slander the Hindus by reason of the strength of your rifle, you who are utterly indifferent as regards the improvement of your own self, (you who) are eager to improve others. . . . For the sake of mercy—your 'humanity,'—hide (from us) this universally frightful, dismal, revealed form of yours. We cannot bear it."[57] Despite the classical references in the article (written partially in Sanskrit), obviously designed to encode some of its meaning for insiders, the writers' irony-laden critique of the government was hard to miss.

The writing in the *Bangavasi*, like Wilde's, was vexing to the prosecution because it was filled with paradox: on the one hand, articles declared loyalty to the government, and on the other, their critique was searing. One of the charged articles disguised critique as self-reproach and submission: "We are wanting in strength, downtrodden, without process, without power, and without courage. We cannot say nay to your wishes or oppose them."[58] The aforementioned article on "The Revealed Form of the English Ruler" used this self-proclaimed weakness to revile the figure of the English leader in terms that cast his masculinity as grotesque: "In enacting the Consent Act, the English, being drawn into the revolutions of the wheel of circumstances, have cast off both the mask and the

---

55. Quoted in Kamra, *Indian Periodical Press*, 113.
56. "The Revealed Form of the English Ruler," *Bangavasi* (Calcutta), March 28, 1891, in *Proceedings of the Home Department*, P/3880, October 1891, 1577.
57. "Revealed Form of the English Ruler," *Bangavasi* (Calcutta), March 28, 1891.
58. "Our Condition," *Bangavasi* (Calcutta), March 28, 1891, in *Proceedings of the Home Department*, P/3880, October 1891, 1576.

slough. There stands before us now the dreadful, monstrous, disgusting, naked form of the Englishman; our heart trembles at the sight of this form."[59] Among the many ways in which Indian writers protested the Age of Consent Bill, this statement no doubt seemed particularly provocative and devious in its manipulation of the terms of colonial discourse, for it recasts the rape scene conjured up by the bill. Here, the male writer rather than the underage girl is the victim of a "monstrous" naked body, and the aberrant body is that of the colonizer rather than the colonized.

The trial took place in an atmosphere fraught with frustration on the part of British administrators and lawmakers who had struggled, over the course of the century, with various strategies of adapting British law to the peculiar needs of colonial governance.[60] Wendie Ellen Schneider, for example, writing on perjury and the various strategies for producing veracity that emerged during the Victorian era, notes that India proved to be a particular challenge: "Perjury loomed large in the colonial imagination because of the British conviction of its prevalence."[61] At one point during Company administration in the eighteenth century, a penalty for perjury was to have the words "I am a perjurer" tattooed on one's forehead. This strategy, Schneider argues, "responded to specifically colonial anxieties by attempting to make the lie visible."[62] The *Bangavasi* trial, in attempting to prove that babu journalists were traitorous despite their declarations of loyalty, demonstrates a similar logic, in which affect, rather than a tattoo, would provide the visceral evidence of wrongdoing.

Letters in the trial files from Sir John Edgar, the chief secretary to the governor of Bengal, to C. J. Lyall, the secretary of the governor of India that discuss the "growing license of the newspaper press" reflect their attempts to draw out the disciplinary potential of Section 124a by focusing on its reference to disaffection.[63] In this and other correspondence related to the trial, the British administrators practice the discursive shift that they hope the act might generate on a larger scale by focusing on the bad affects of the periodical. Citing a "large and

---

59. "Revealed Form of the English Ruler," *Bangavasi* (Calcutta), March 28, 1891.

60. See, for example, Bernard Cohn, *Colonialism and Its Forms of Knowledge: The British in India* (Princeton, NJ: Princeton University Press, 1994); Kolsky, *Colonial Justice in British India*; Wendie Ellen Schneider, *Engines of Truth: Producing Veracity in the Victorian Courtroom* (New Haven, CT: Yale University Press, 2016); and Henry Schwarz, *Constructing the Criminal Tribe in Colonial India* (Chichester, West Sussex: Wiley-Blackwell, 2010).

61. Schneider, *Engines of Truth*, 104.

62. Schneider, *Engines of Truth*, 117.

63. John Edgar, chief secretary to the Government of Bengal, to C. J. Lyall, secretary to the Government of India, April 20, 1891, in *Proceedings of the Home Department*, P/3880, October 1891, 1501.

Particulars of Vernacular Newspapers published in the Lower Provinces and in Assam, in the year 1890, with brief notes of their Editors, Proprietors, &c.

No.	Name of paper.	Place and press at which published.	Language and character in which published.		Period of publication.	Circulation.	Name, profession, or status, &c., of the Proprietor.	Name, profession, or status, &c., of the Editor.	Tone, politics, &c., of the paper.
			Language.	Character.					
1	"Ahmadi"	The Ahmadi Press, Debidar, Tangail, Mymensingh.	Bengali	Bengali	Fortnightly	600	Moulvie Abdul Hamed Khan Eusofzai.	The same as proprietor	A well-written paper. The professed object of the conductors is to promote social union between Hindus and Musulmans. Displays no religious bigotry.
2	"Hitakari"	Kushtea	Ditto	Ditto	Ditto	800	Mir Mossaref Hossein	Ditto ditto	An indifferent paper, written from the Brahmo standpoint, and treating of local matters. Not a political paper.
3	"Kasipore Nibasi"	The Kasipore Press, Barisal.	Ditto	Ditto	Ditto	280	Protap Chandra Mukerjea	Ditto ditto	
4	"Savamihir"	Printed at the Basanti press, Mymensingh, and published at Gkatail, Mymensingh.	Ditto	Ditto	Ditto	500	Durga Churn Roy	Ditto ditto.	
5	"Sahayogi"	The Hitaishi Press, Barisal.	Ditto	Ditto	Ditto	342	Monoranjan Guha	Ditto ditto.	
6	"Uluberia Darpan"	Printed at the Somprakash Samiti Press, Calcutta, and published at Uluberia.	Ditto	Ditto	Ditto	700	Monimohan Ghosh, Pleader and Surendranath Roy, Medical Practitioner.	Surendranath Roy	Gives much attention to local matters and discusses social questions from the orthodox standpoint.
7	"Arya Darpan"	11, Simla Street, Calcutta.	Ditto	Ditto	Weekly	102	Jaya Govinda Shom, M.A., B.L., Vakeel, High Court, a Native Christian convert.	Ditto ditto.	
8	"Bangavasi"	The Bangavasi Machine Press, Calcutta.	Ditto	Ditto	Ditto	20,000	Jogendra Chandra Bose, formerly Sub-Editor of the Sadharani newspaper; a tenure-holder.	Indra Nath Banerjee, B.A., B.L., a distinguished Bengali writer, and a successful pleader of the Burdwan Judge's Court.	Tone less sensational than before cynical and not quite liberal in politics, extremely orthodox in its views on social and religious questions. Advocate of the ryots and tenure-holders. Its columns often contain humorous sketches and poetry, and are at times illustrated by cartoons.
9	"Bangabibasi"	The Commercial Steam Machine Press, Calcutta.	Ditto	Ditto	Ditto	8,000	Mahesh Chandra Pal, a publisher of Sanskrit philosophical works.	Ram Deb Dutt	An orthodox paper, exceptionally violent in tone.
10	"Burdwan Saijivani"	The Burdwan Press, Burdwan.	Ditto	Ditto	Ditto	335	Jogesh Chandra Sarkar	The same as proprietor	Moderate in tone and liberal in politics. Treats often of local matters.

FIGURE 1.5 / Chunder Nath Bose, Bengali translator to Government of India, report on the vernacular newspapers published in the Lower Provinces and in Assam in 1890, March 9, 1891. India Office Records, British Library. Shelfmark IOR/P/3880, p. 1545 © British Library Board.

Ab6. CLASSIFICATION OF VERNACULAR NEWSPAPERS IN BENGAL. No 262.

I.—Brahmo papers.

No.	Name of Paper.	Attitude to Government.	Attitude to Congress.	Attitude on the subject of social reform by legislation.
1	Dacca Gazette ..	Rather hostile ..	Pro-Congress ..	For social reform.
2	Gramvasi	Ditto ..	Ditto ..	Ditto.
3	Sanjivani	Ditto ..	Ditto ..	Ditto.
4	Sansodhini	Indifferent ..	Ditto ..	Ditto.

II.—Hindu papers.

1	Banganivasi ..	Very hostile ..	Pro-Congress ..	Opposed to social reform.
2	Bangavasi ..	Ditto ..	Anti-Congress ..	Ditto.
3	Behar Bandhu ..	Indifferent ..	Pro-Congress ..	Ditto.
4	Bengal Exchange Gazette ..	Very hostile ..	Ditto ..	Ditto.
5	Burdwan Sanjivani ..	Rather hostile ..	Ditto ..	Opposed to social reform.
6	Dacca Prakash ..	Ditto ..	Anti-Congress ..	Opposed to social reform.
7	Dainik-o-Samachar Chandrika.	Very hostile ..	Ditto ..	Ditto.
8	Education Gazette ..	Friendly ..	Cautious supporter of the Congress.	Not opposed to social reform.
9	Hindi Bangavasi ..	Hostile ..	Anti-Congress ..	Opposed to social reform.
10	Hindu Ranjika ..	Rather hostile ..	Pro-Congress ..	Ditto.
11	Navayuga ..	Hostile ..	Sceptical ..	Ditto.
12	Pratikar ..	Rather hostile ..	Pro-Congress ..	Ditto.
13	Rungpore Dik Prakash ..	Indifferent ..	Ditto ..	Ditto.
14	Sahachar ..	Friendly ..	Ditto ..	For social reform.
15	Sakti ..	Hostile ..	Ditto ..	Opposed to social reform.
16	Samaj-o-Sahitya ..	Indifferent ..	Anti-Congress ..	Ditto.
17	Samvad Prabhakar ..	Rather hostile ..	Pro-Congress ..	Ditto.
18	Saraswat Patra ..	Ditto ..	Ditto ..	Ditto.
19	Som Prakash ..	Ditto ..	Ditto ..	Ditto.

III.—Indifferent in religion.

1	Charuvarta	Rather hostile ..	Pro-Congress ..	For social reform.
2	Samay	Ditto ..	Ditto ..	Ditto.
3	Surabhi-o-Pataka ..	Ditto ..	Ditto ..	Against social reform.

IV.—Mussulman papers.

1	Ahmadi	Rather hostile ..	Pro-Congress ..	Against social reform.
2	Gauhar	Ditto ..	Anti-Congress ..	Ditto.
3	Sudhakar	Very hostile ..	Ditto ..	Ditto.
4	Urdu Guide and Darussaltanat.	Rather hostile ..	Ditto ..	Supported Consent Bill.

H. P.—Reg. No. 138T—31—13-6-91.

FIGURE 1.6 / John Edgar, chief secretary to the Government of Bengal, classification of vernacular newspapers in Bengal, June 1891. India Office Records, British Library. Shelfmark IOR/P/3880, p. 1513 © British Library Board.

growing section of the educated population who crave for malicious and high-spiced attacks, breathing hatred and contempt for government," Edgar noted that the *Bangavasi* would be a good target for prosecution because of its rhetorical tone: "It entertains a *mean* opinion of England, her people and her civilization, and takes every opportunity of instilling an *active dislike* of both into its readers. This dislike, *deepening often into hatred and contempt*, has been expressed in an *extremely aggravated* form in connexion with the Consent Bill agitation" (my emphasis).[64]

The attempt of the British administrators instigating the trial to reimagine the colonial public sphere in affective terms is made explicit in two reports on the "vernacular press" that were generated in this period. The first of these reports was produced by Chunder Nath Bose, Bengali translator to the Government of India, and the second is an abbreviated classification of the information Bose provided put together by Edgar or his office (Figures 1.5 and 1.6). Bose's report focuses on tone more than affect, using the language of aesthetic rather than psychological judgment. He notes, for example, that the *Ahmadi* is a "well-written paper" and that the *Charuvarta* is "diffuse in style and declamatory in tone."[65] Clearly practicing a neutral tone in his own writing, Bose is also blandly descriptive in his reporting on the periodicals' subject matter, saying of the *Uluberis Darpan*, for example, that it "gives much attention to local matters and discusses social issues from the orthodox standpoint."[66] Edgar, commenting on this report, praised it for being "full and impartial" and wrote that "the general effect is of a Press ... in fair and honest opposition."[67]

But this, of course, was precisely why it was inadequate: the structure of Bose's report did not do enough to highlight the growing hostility that Edgar sought to quell and thus, he went on to say, it "gives, and cannot but give, a very inadequate picture of the Native Press."[68] Edgar's alternative taxonomic redaction of Bose's report reclassifies newspapers according to the degree of positive or negative affect they displayed. Papers are deemed "friendly," "indifferent," "rather hostile," "hostile," or "very hostile," and their political stance is determined strictly in relational terms, through a definitive (pro- or anti-) assessment of their attitudes toward Congress and governmental reform measures.

---

64. *Proceedings of the Home Department*, P/3880, October 1891, 1507.
65. *Proceedings of the Home Department*, P/3880, October 1891, 1513 and 1546.
66. *Proceedings of the Home Department*, P/3880, October 1891, 1513.
67. John Edgar, chief secretary to the Government of Bengal, to C. J. Lyall, secretary to the Government of India, June 13, 1891, in *Proceedings of the Home Department*, P/3880, October 1891, 1507.
68. *Proceedings of the Home Department*, P/3880, October 1891, 1505.

The *Bangavasi* trial was an opportunity to make these psychologizing judgments actionable in a legal arena, and thus to control not only the public sphere but also the *feeling* of colonial subjecthood. (In the similarly important show trial of Tilak in 1897, the judge's statements demonstrated the degree to which the government had reified this logic by this point: "The test was whether the writer intended to excite feelings of disaffection [defined as want of affection] towards the Government in any way by anything he wrote, whether an editorial article, a poem, or a disquisition concerning some hero").[69] As the *Bangavasi* case files suggest, another goal of the trial was to make sure that charges of disaffection would stick, despite the slipperiness of the term. In British law, sedition was linked to incitement to violence and was notoriously hard to prove. Much of the correspondence between Edgar and Lyall thus centers on how to use disaffection to shift the focus from violent acts to violent affects.

One of Edgar's letters on the subject, for example, spoke of it as a way to "remove from the law the necessity of proving intention and to provide that punishment should follow on the proving of the simple fact that words have been used whose natural effect is to hold up the Government to hatred and contempt, or to stir up enmity and ill-feeling between different classes of the population."[70] In the trial itself, the meaning of the word "disaffection" was questioned, as the administrators feared it would be. But the judge appealed to a broad dictionary definition rather than the standard legal designation, claiming that disaffection meant the opposite of affection and not merely incitement to violence. As well as being vaguer than "sedition" from the start, then, "disaffection" was reshaped in the trial so as to cover wider territory. Edgar and Lyall's gambit, in putting "disaffection" to the test as a tool of governmentality, had paid off.

Nonetheless, the government ultimately failed to successfully prosecute the *Bangavasi*. The defense argued that the newspaper's statements fell within the boundary of legitimate criticism, especially given the numerous professions of loyalty to the government that accompanied its critique; because Section 124a allowed for critique in the context of loyalty, insincerity, or at least paradox, was a constitutive feature of articles that sought to critique the Raj, as they simultaneously had to praise it. Since the articles in question were translated from Bengali, the defense also contended that the specific context of the native (as opposed to

---

69. Cited in Janaki Bakhle, "Sarvarkar (1883–1966), Sedition and Surveillance: The Rule of Law in a Colonial Situation," *Social History* 35, no. 1 (February 2010): 51–75, 69.

70. John Edgar, chief secretary to the Government of Bengal, to C. J. Lyall, secretary to the Government of India, April 20, 1891, in *Proceedings of the Home Department*, P/3880, October 1891, 1502.

the English) press had not been adequately considered. At the end of the first session, the judge called for a unanimous vote, but the verdict was split seven to two in favor of the prosecution. Before the next session, the accused submitted a petition in which they professed loyalty to the government in suitably affective terms, declaring their "deep and heartfelt sorrow" for their transgressions, and the charges against them were dropped.[71]

In his correspondence with Lyall, however, Edgar states that the verdict had been close enough to prove that disaffection *could* be prosecuted. Moreover, in accepting the *Bangavasi*'s apology, the government could "take the opportunity of shewing that it is not influenced by vindictive feelings" by modeling the restrained affect that the trial as a whole was attempting to enforce.[72] The *Bangavasi*'s apology and the government's leniency were thus widely publicized after the trial. In publishing government documents about the trial, newspapers like the *Times of India* stayed on the leading edge of an important story; by circulating the cautionary tale of what became of newspapers that transgressed, they also turned themselves into spectacles of self-discipline.

Despite its anticlimactic outcome, the *Bangavasi* trial played a defining role in imperial policy, as well as in the growing nationalist response to it. The case created an interpretive framework in which both writers' and readers' intentions were purportedly legible to the government, notwithstanding language barriers and the ambiguity that inevitably characterized articles that sought simultaneously to criticize government policy and to express loyalty. According to the prosecution's arguments, the newspaper was deliberately inciting hatred of the government, and a susceptible population was likely to act on that hatred. By identifying affect as a potential site of government action, the *Bangavasi* trial laid the groundwork for future trials in which newspapers and nationalist leaders would be successfully prosecuted on similar terms. It also helped make official the counterpublic sphere of anticolonial critique, now delimited from the larger colonial public sphere of which it was once a part by the criminal law to which it was uniquely subject.[73]

---

71. Petitions to Charles A. Elliott, Lieutenant-Governor of Bengal, from *Bangavasi* editors and publishers, September 4, 1891, in *Proceedings of the Home Department*, P/3880, October 1891, 1617.

72. John Edgar, chief secretary to the Government of Bengal, to C. J. Lyall, secretary to the Government of India, September 9, 1891, in *Proceedings of the Home Department*, P/3880, October 1891, 1615.

73. See Kamra, *Indian Periodical Press*, 27–35, on public sphere theory and Indian periodicals during this period. Citing Nancy Fraser, she argues that "it would be more correct to say that this public sphere developed as a counterpublic sphere" (29).

The shift from the criminalization of an action (sedition) to that of an affect (disaffection) that took shape around the deployment of Section 124a was patently strategic. But it also reinforced the central place of Indian emotionalism in the imperial imaginary; arguments against Indian self-government and Indians' right to self-expression, as suggested earlier, repeatedly referred to their labile, heightened, and feminine emotions. In the *Bangavasi* trial, the prosecution claimed that the articles in question were written with the intention of "inflam[ing] the prejudices of people of the lower classes by appealing to their superstitious feelings."[74] A similar anxiety about inflammatory speech also motivated an article in the *Fortnightly Review* written a few months after the trial by the imperial administrator Lepel Griffin. Echoing Macaulay, he argued that,

> when men, as the Bengalis, are disqualified for political enfranchisement by the possession of essentially feminine characteristics, they must expect to be held in contempt by stronger and braver races ... to our undeveloped civilization in India the Baboo is necessary. His fluent English—a sesquipedalian compound of Dr. Johnson and Mrs. Malaprop; his arithmetical facility, his pedantic accuracy, and want of originality, make him an ideal clerk in positions where no responsibility or courage, moral or physical is required. But the Baboo, though necessary, is still an evil. He arrives in an unsophisticated province with his seditious commonplaces ... and distils his slow poison into the ears of the simple listeners, who were ignorant that they had a grievance.[75]

This passage rehearses the standard babu stereotype, evoking and connecting his effeminacy with political immaturity and affectation (his fluent but flawed English and "want of originality"). But it also makes clear that what was at issue was the babu's "sly civility" and the effect it might have on a volatile populace: in Griffin's fantasy, the "simple" and "ignorant" listeners would be affected by the babu's toxic seditious language no matter how uninspired ("commonplace") it might be. A hybrid figure, Indian in blood and color and not quite English enough in taste, opinions, morals, and intellect, Griffin's babu is both a dull functionary and a dangerous subversive.

While Wilde was ultimately prosecuted for sex acts, the trial's focus indicated that his critical and fictional writing were also feared in terms of their capacity to

---

74. Cited in Karma, *Indian Periodical Press*, 115.
75. Lepel Griffin, "The Place of the Bengáli in Politics," *Fortnightly Review* 51, no. 306 (June 1892): 811–19, 811–12.

spread his sins around Britain.⁷⁶ Like Wilde, the "Baboo" conjured up by Griffin is not literally traveling from province to province spreading sedition—it is his words that travel, via print and its various forms of dissemination. If the trials turned Wilde and babu critics into contagious bodies, they also turned their bodies into texts-in-circulation—ones that personified the subversive discourses of aesthetic homoeroticism and nationalist anticolonialism respectively.

The trials were also similar, as I suggested earlier, in focusing on improper affections rather than improper acts. While acts of sedition and sodomy would historically have been the grounds for prosecution, both the newspaper trial and Wilde's trials, in lieu of being able to prove conclusively that such acts had occurred, sought to broaden the scope of criminality to include desire, intention, and affect—an untoward structure of feeling that could serve, by negative example, as a model of what proper citizenship looked like. Prosecutors in the *Bangavasi* trial, in an attempt to affix disaffection to the paper itself rather than to the effect it had on others (which was harder to prove), asked the jury to consider whether the articles in question had the intention of stirring up hatred of the government. The *Bangavasi* staff, in the strategic apology that procured their pardon, also evoked intention. While conceding that the language of their articles was "intemperate, disrespectful and unjustifiable," they acknowledged that their work could be construed as evidence of disaffection but pledged that they had not "intended" it to be read as such.⁷⁷ But by making this pledge, they demonstrated the degree to which British law was now condemned to produce the very thing its designers feared—the insincere, linguistically subversive babu.

Ironically, the wounding of Indian masculinity by the babu typology, and its increasingly insulting applications over the course of the nineteenth century, contributed to the irruption of resistance to the Age of Consent Bill of which the *Bangavasi* commentary was a part. But if Indian writers used "claims of native masculinity" to galvanize nationalist energies, these claims were also used that way in Britain.⁷⁸ Mrinalini Sinha argues there was a parallel "'crisis' in British masculinity arising from, among other things, the feminist challenges of the

---

76. More broadly, the 1880s and 1890s were a time of suspicion toward any literature considered to be immoral, such as penny dreadfuls, because of the spread of literacy among the working class and ideas about their impressibility. On the Wilde trials and the discourse of national degeneration, see Arata, *Fictions of Loss at the Fin de Siècle*.

77. Petitions to Charles A. Elliott, lieutenant-governor of Bengal, from *Bangavasi* editors and publishers, September 4, 1891, in *Proceedings of the Home Department*, P/3880, October 1891, 1617.

78. Sinha, *Colonial Masculinity*, 139.

1880s."⁷⁹ Thus, while Anglo-Indians had to stand their ground once the bill was in place and could only attempt to control its disastrous effects through existing legislation such as Section 124a, the discourse surrounding the bill in Britain was much more sympathetic to the negative Indian response. Sinha notes that "antifeminist backlash in Britain . . . produced greater tolerance for patriarchal institutions in India."⁸⁰ In the wake of the repeal of the Contagious Diseases Acts and the feminist and purity crusades for the passage of the Criminal Law Amendment Act of 1885 (to which Stead's articles had contributed), commentators in Britain wrote articles that were uncharacteristically supportive of Indian opposition to the government. The *Saint James Gazette*, for example, stated that "it is perfectly clear that the strongest and best native opinion is against the Age of Consent Bill," and suggested that the British might learn from the Indian example in terms of domestic arrangements.⁸¹ Even while the interests of British and Indian masculinity were ostensibly opposed to each other in the period, then, they were subject to realignment in the face of threats to male prerogative on the home front.

This sense of embattled masculinity, of course, also influenced the Wilde trials. Wilde was tried three times in 1895. The first trial occurred after he sued his lover's father—the Marquis of Queensbury—for libel after the marquis left a card at his club calling him a "posing somdomite [*sic*]." During the trial, an interrogation of his literary work for its homosexual and "immoral" content put him on the defensive. With his case looking weaker than he had expected, and the defense threatening to call as witnesses a series of young working-class men whom he had hired for sex, Wilde was advised by his lawyer to drop the suit; proof of sex acts could lead to a criminal charge of "gross indecency" (thanks to the aforementioned Criminal Law Amendment Act). Dropping charges against the marquis did not help, however, for Wilde was brought to trial again, this time accused by the government of gross indecency. Once again, his work was cited, and he defended "the love that dare not speak its name" on aesthetic grounds, but the evidence supplied by the men called as witnesses undermined his case. Because the jury did not immediately reach a verdict, Wilde was released on bail. In a third trial, however, he was found guilty of gross indecency and given the maximum sentence—two years of hard labor in prison. Upon his release, he went into exile in France and died three years later of meningitis, thought by some to be a secondary effect of an unhealed prison injury he sustained to his ear.

---

79. Sinha, *Colonial Masculinity*, 140.
80. Sinha, *Colonial Masculinity*, 152.
81. Quoted in Sinha, *Colonial Masculinity*, 154.

As with the *Bangavasi* trial, Wilde's first trial hinged on literary-critical evidence. The prosecution sought to stabilize the meanings of Wilde's texts, in the face of his famous paradoxes and linguistic play, in order to solicit from them evidence of his desires and proof that "his sexual practices were relevant public knowledge."[82] Here, as in the *Bangavasi* trial, it was important to the trial's outcome and its symbolic value that the writing of the accused should have a clear intention and that this intention be defined in affective terms, located in the body of the accused, and made legible to the public by the trial process.

In their evocation of unruly bodies, his trials shared with the colonial sedition trials a concern about contagion and the way aberrant masculinity might create new circuits of affect between the educated elite and the working classes. Scholars of the trials such as Ed Cohen have pointed to the ways in which contemporary fears of diseases traveling from working-class to middle-class bodies enhanced the scandal of Wilde's use of male prostitutes, particularly in the wake of the Contagious Diseases Acts of the 1860s.[83] But contagion flowed the other way as well. Wilde's affect might be infectious too, to the detriment of supposedly healthy affects and national productivity. Thus, the *Evening News*'s report on the trial's conclusion stated of Wilde that "to him and such as him we owe the spread of moral degeneration amongst young men with abilities sufficient to make them a credit to their country. At the feet of Wilde they have learned to gain notoriety by blatant conceit, by despising the affects of healthy humanity and the achievements of wholesome talent."[84] These fears of contagious degenerative affect were fueled mainly by Wilde's sexual identity, but they might also have had to do with the subversive political identities he briefly took up and put on—socialism (in his 1891 essay, "The Soul of Man under Socialism") and Irish nationalism (in his American lecture).

What was most unsettling to his critics, though—most notably the Marquess of Queensbury, for whom his "posing" and his "somdomite" status were inseparable—was his commitment to identity as performance. Refusing to respect the boundaries of either sexual or political norms, at a time when Britain's imperial power rested symbolically on the former and instrumentally on the latter, made Wilde an outlaw in all senses. As Moe Meyer argues, "Wilde's

---

82. E. Cohen, *Talk on the Wilde Side*, 128.
83. See E. Cohen, *Talk on the Wilde Side*. For a broad overview of the relationships among ideology, sexuality, and the state in Victorian Britain, see Jeffrey Weeks, *Sex, Politics and Society: The Regulation of Sexuality since 1800* (New York: Routledge, 2014).
84. Cited in H. Montgomery Hyde, *The Trials of Oscar Wilde* (New York: Dover, 1962), 18.

parodic posing suggested that the order of things was far from inevitable, that the 'natural' was, perhaps the unnatural.... Oscar Wilde, posing somdomite [sic]: a black hole in the fabric of the white man's universe."[85] If Wilde's trial symbolically reestablished order and marked his defeat, forcing him to wear his sexuality as a fixed label of criminality, it also served as the occasion to stress the importance of proper affect as opposed to affectation. The *Illustrated Police Budget*'s report on Wilde's reaction to his verdict thus focused on his emotions and their visibility on the surface of his body: "He clutched convulsively at the front rail of the dock... *his eyes glared and twitched from an unseen excitement within, and his body practically shook with nervous protestation, whilst a soft tear found a place in his eye.* ... At this point there is no doubt whatever that the man felt his position keenly.... Yes, Wilde was indeed affected, and at the last seemed to realize he was in great danger of not seeing the light of freedom for some time to come" (my emphasis).[86] The article underscores Wilde's guilt through references to his physical loss of control over his performance. Wilde's "soft," effeminate tear—simultaneously evidence of his guilt, of his true homosexual identity, and of the punishment permanently affixed to it—is used to suggest to the newspaper's audience that affect (Wilde's anguish) has been successfully realigned with morality.

Sodomy and Sedition

While sodomy was Wilde's chief contagious disease, sedition was the babu's, spread (according to Griffin and others) by his subversive whispering into the ears of impressionable peasants. In his letters to Lyall about prosecuting the *Bangavasi*, Edgar cites the spread of Bengalis across India, and their persistent attempts to "stir up race feeling," as one reason to nip disaffection in the bud.[87] Sodomy is not irrelevant to British concerns about the babu, however. As Robert Aldrich and others have demonstrated, homosexuality was considered, in the late nineteenth century, to be a widespread pathology of the non-European world.[88] In India, the sexuality of the educated Bengali—the most politically threatening

---

85. Moe Meyer, "Under the Sign of Wilde: An Archaeology of Posing," in *The Politics and Poetics of Camp*, ed. Moe Meyer (London: Routledge, 1994), 75–110, 99.
86. Cited in Schulz, "Redressing Oscar," 45.
87. John Edgar, chief secretary to the Government of Bengal, to C. J. Lyall, secretary to the Government of India, April 20, 1891, in *Proceedings of the Home Department*, P/3880, October 1891, 1502.
88. On imperial views of non-Western male sexuality, see Robert Aldrich, *Colonialism and Homosexuality* (New York: Routledge, 2002); Ronald Hyam, *Empire and Sexuality* (Manchester:

masculine figure—came under particular scrutiny, contributing to the development of the babu stereotype: "The debilitating sexuality of the Bengali male intersected ... with the elaboration of a distinct homosexual personality in contemporary medical and scientific discourses in Britain."[89] Both figures were seen as depraved and excessive and contributed to the passing of the sex-reform legislation that underlay Wilde's trial and that of the *Bangavasi*.

This is not to say that effeminacy and homosexuality have the same connotations, then or now. Before Wilde, the effeminate dandy, like the babu, could be associated with an excess of heterosexual desire rather than homosexuality.[90] Alan Sinfield notes that "effeminacy preceded the category of the homosexual [and] overlapped with and influenced the period of its development.... To run the two together is to miss the specificity of their relations, both in historical sequence and as they overlap."[91] But these trials, and the press that surrounded them, illustrate the ways in which these two categories overlapped in India as well as in Britain, and the degree to which this overlap was related to the needs of imperial governance. It is suggestive, in light of these connections, that sodomy and sedition are metaphorically connected in the British Incitement to Mutiny Act of 1797, and an updated version of it, the Incitement to Disaffection Act of 1934, both of which made it a criminal act to "seduce" members of H.M. Forces from their duties and allegiance. The association of political conspiracy with homoerotic seduction was a thinly veiled subtext of British law throughout the imperial period.

If, as the Foucauldian story goes, biopolitical discourses and their contribution to the Wilde trials helped produce the homosexual as a type in the 1890s, the *Bangavasi* trial and the series of newspaper trials that followed produced a newly visible type as well—the disaffectionist. By 1922, as nationalist protest became more overt, disaffection was appropriated as a key term in Gandhi's pathbreaking form of nonviolent anticolonialism. In the face of his own trial under Section 124a for seditious articles in his newspaper *Young India*, Gandhi stated: "I have become an uncompromising disaffectionist and non-cooperator.... Affection

---

Manchester University Press, 1991); and Joseph Boone, *The Homoerotics of Orientalism* (New York: Columbia University Press, 2014).

89. Sinha, *Colonial Masculinity*, 19.

90. See Denis Denisoff, *Aestheticism and Sexual Parody, 1840–1940* (Cambridge: Cambridge University Press, 2001), 16.

91. Sinfield, *Wilde Century*, 78.

cannot be manufactured or regulated by law."[92] In embracing the category of outcast, Gandhi radically reconfigured it. Accepting his sentence as a form of "voluntary submission to the penalty for non-cooperation with evil," he effectively undermined the association of disaffection with political violence and hatred and allied it with *ahimsa* (nonviolence) and spiritual values instead.[93] In doing so, he revealed the extent to which Section 124a had helped label, make visible, and galvanize the anticolonial nationalism it sought to foreclose (see conclusion for more on this trial and its effects).

But Gandhi also demonstrated the degree to which ideals of masculinity and anticolonialism had become mutually constitutive, thanks to the gendering of the colonial relationship through figures such as the babu. In *The Intimate Enemy* (1983), Ashis Nandy notes that Gandhi's approach to nationalism at the height of his leadership departed from the muscular version advocated by figures such as Vivekananda in its willingness to challenge Western concepts of masculinity and femininity.[94] Drawing on Indian philosophies that abjured gender binaries, Gandhi's writings and religious practices asserted that "manliness and womanliness are equal but the ability to transcend the man-woman dichotomy is superior to both, being an indicator of godly and saintly qualities" and that "the essence of femininity is superior to that of masculinity, which in turn is better than cowardice or, as the Sanskrit expression would have it, failure of masculinity."[95] As part of his 1922 trial statement, however, Gandhi asserted, "I hold it to be a virtue to be disaffected towards a Government which . . . has done more harm to India than any previous system. India is *less manly* under the British rule than she ever was before. Holding such a belief I consider it to be a sin to have affection for the system" (my emphasis).[96]

Though masculinity was not a prominent feature of Gandhi's nationalism as it was for many other leaders, in this declaration disaffection is figured as the opposite of unmanliness, which is equated in turn with sinfulness. To remain in an affectionate relationship with one's colonial rulers is, in effect, to be an unmanly man dominated by a masculine conqueror and thus disgraced both in religious

---

92. A. G. Noorani, *Indian Political Trials, 1775–1947* (New Delhi: Oxford University Press, 2005), 235.
93. Noorani, *Indian Political Trials*, 235.
94. See Ashis Nandy, *The Intimate Enemy: Loss and Recovery of Self under Colonialism* (Delhi, India: Oxford India Paperbacks, 2009), 48–55.
95. Quoted in Nandy, *Intimate Enemy*, 53.
96. M. K. Gandhi, "Trial Statement," in *Collected Works of Mahatma Gandhi* (New Delhi: Ministry of Information and Broadcasting, Government of India, 1958), 26:384.

and secular terms. In the same speech, Gandhi declared that "a subtle but effective system of terrorism and an organized display of force on the one hand, and the deprivation of all powers of retaliation or self-defense on the other, have emasculated the people and induced in them the habit of simulation."[97] Here, the simulating babu and emasculation are correlated once again and juxtaposed to the righteousness of self-defense and retaliation. If homosexuality as such was a construct still in the making in the wake of the Wilde trials, colonial sedition law contributed to its formation by generating alignments between effeminacy, excess, and threats to political consensus (both that of British imperialism and of anticolonial nationalism).[98]

This comparative analysis of the prosecution of sodomy and sedition in two specific cases demonstrates how intimately Britain and India were connected by the imperial public sphere, as well as by discourses of gender, sexuality, and national belonging that circulated within it. It also illustrates how incomplete our understanding of these discourses is when their histories are artificially segregated into distinct national narratives or versions of the metropole/colony binary. Together, the Wilde trials and the *Bangavasi* trial allow us to see the dialectics of imperial power in fine-grained detail—the crucial moments when the law brought into view the very thing it was attempting to suppress, and deemed it contagious.

---

97. Gandhi, "Trial Statement," 384.
98. For more on the criminalization of sodomy in India and its complex relationship to British law, see Anjali Arondekar's *For the Record: On Sexuality and the Colonial Archive in India* (Durham, NC: Duke University Press, 2009), which emphasizes the ways in which "the incoherencies of colonial rule are scripted as law" (76).

2

PARODY / Colonial Mimicry, Colonial Parody, and the Multiplicity of *Punch*

In September 2012, the Indian cartoonist Assem Trivedi was arrested for sedition under Section 124a and his website, Cartoons against Corruption, was taken down. A year earlier, as part of an anticorruption movement, Trivedi had launched an internet campaign to disseminate and popularize cartoon-based critiques of the Indian government through social media in order to send "a strong message to the masses."[1] One of the cartoons that prompted the government crackdown was "Gang Rape of Mother India."

The cartoon's use of gang rape as a metaphor for corruption at a time when Indian feminists were calling for more sensitive media treatment of its quotidian and widespread nature is lamentable, not least because the gendering of the nation through figures like "Mother India" contributes to the use of rape as a tool of political struggle and a way of flexing patriarchal privilege, especially in the face of other forms of disenfranchisement.[2]

Yet Trivedi drew negative attention mainly because of his alleged disrespect for his harshest critic, the government. In this way his arrest is part of the living history of colonial censorship, rooted in a time when Indian critics and their British rulers were engaged in a struggle for control over the representation of

---

1. Preetika Rana, "Cartoonist Faces Ban on Right to Poke Fun," *Wall Street Journal*, January 4, 2012, https://blogs.wsj.com/indiarealtime/2012/01/04/cartoonist-faces-ban-on-right-to-poke-fun/. Trivedi's charges were eventually dropped and he continues to publish cartoons and to organize against censorship and human rights violations.

2. See, for example Reetinder Kaur, "Representation of Crime against Women in Print Media: A Case Study of Delhi Gang Rape," *Anthropology* 2, no. 1 (2013), https://doi.org/10.4172/2332-0915.1000115. Much has been written on the relationship between gender, nationalism, and sexual violence, but Nira Yuval-Davis, *Gender and Nation* (London: Sage, 1997), provides a good overview of the relationship between these concepts. In relation to both the contemporary and colonial context in India, see Geetika Raman, "The 'Avenging Angel' and the 'Nurturing Mother': Women and Hindu Nationalism," *South Asianist* 4, no. 2 (2016): 165–71. See also Jenny Sharpe, *Allegories of Empire: The Figure of Woman in the Colonial Text* (Minneapolis: University of Minnesota Press, 1993), for an analysis of how these relations—and related anxieties about rape—are figured in literature about empire, post-Mutiny.

FIGURE 2.1 / "Gang Rape of Mother India," 2012. https://cartoonsagainstcorruption.blogspot.com/search/label/dirty.

political power. Because this struggle was metaphorized in affective terms via the law against disaffection, it often took on gendered dimensions. If disaffection meant hatred of the government (or even just "want of affection," according to a Bombay judge), then the ideal colonized subject loved their ruler—an ideologeme that played into the notion of the colony as female, and thus to its frequent depiction in Indian periodicals as Mother India under assault.

The struggle for control of the public sphere was racialized, as we have seen, not only through the use of censorship law but also via racist writing and images, particularly caricatures.[3] Racialization was chiefly used to discredit Indian critics in two ways: (1) by characterizing them as mentally inferior mimic men, incapable of original or rational thought, and (2) by depicting their critiques of Brit-

---

3. On caricature as a global phenomenon, see Todd Porterfield, ed., *The Efflorescence of Caricature, 1759–1838* (New York: Routledge, 2011).

ish rule as racially motivated and inherently disaffected because they were driven by passion rather than reason.

In a speech delivered to his constituency in Arbroath on October 21, 1907, John Morley, then secretary of state for India, defended himself against accusations of illiberalism for his policies in India by arguing that "the root of the unrest, discontent, and sedition . . . is racial and not political. Now, that being so, it is of the kind that is the very hardest to reach. You can reach political sentiment. Racial dislike, perhaps some would call it in some cases hatred—it is a dislike not of political domination, but of our racial domination."[4] He had attempted to counter this dislike, he goes on to say, by adding Indian membership to the Council of India (which served his office in an advisory capacity)—an action that contradicts his claim about the irrelevance of politics to Indian dissent. But the most noteworthy aspect of this speech is the way it places sedition, discontent, and racial animosity side by side, thus making legitimate political critique impossible because of its equivalence to sedition and racism. While the word "race" in this period could mean cultural, hemispheric, biological or phenotypical difference, or a combination of these, the significance here is the way political domination and material exploitation is displaced onto difference and affect, or "racial dislike."

Like the *Charlie Hebdo* killings in France in 2015, Trivedi's work and his arrest demonstrate how the enduring inflammatory potential of political cartoons is rooted in the colonial history of visual caricature.[5] In what follows, I will show how the connections between cartoons, racism, and debates about freedom of the press—and the constructs of affect through which these debates are articulated—are illuminated by the history of imperial censorship that this book traces. Here and in subsequent chapters, I demonstrate how attempts to evade censorship affected the formal tactics used by critics in the Indian Anglosphere. Practices of mimicry, parody, and inversion had particular purchase in the English-language press because imitative form allowed Indian writers and editors to potentially evade censorship while addressing a British audience in terms both familiar and familial (Indian journals based on British ones could position themselves as their siblings or offspring and were referred

---

4. In John Morley, *Sedition or no Sedition: The Situation in India; Official and Non-Official Views* (Madras: G. A. Natesan, 1907), 1–21.

5. On this question in relation to the *Charlie Hebdo* bombings, see Sandrine Sanos, "The Sex and Race of Satire: *Charlie Hebdo* and the Politics of Representation in Contemporary France," *Jewish History* 32, no. 1 (2018): 33–63.

to as such—British *Punch* described Indian versions of *Punch* as its "cousins," for example).⁶ Since British journalism was upheld as the exemplum of public discourse that Indian writing should imitate in order to avoid accusations of intemperance, many Indian English-language periodicals echoed the form of popular British periodicals, but with a parodic difference. The widespread practice of print mimicry helped define the limits of empire as a viable public, a political entity, and a form of affiliation.

In this chapter, I focus on the relationship between three journals that circulated within the imperial public sphere which united Britain with its colonies: *Punch*, the *Indian Charivari*, a British-run magazine based in Calcutta, and *Hindi Punch*, a Indian journal based in Bombay and published in Gujarati and English. Imitation is crucial to their relationship to each other; the *Indian Charivari* and *Hindi Punch* were based on the form of British *Punch*, while all three employed parody, a form of satire that involves critical imitation of the text being parodied.

Parody—and visual caricature in particular—was a particularly successful and widely traveled transnational mode in the colonial context, and one that sheds light on the relationship between literary form and historical transformation. In making this claim, I draw upon Homi Bhabha's influential account of colonial mimicry but use the concept of parody to rethink his theory about the function of colonial discourse. Rather than evacuating the political implications of Bhabha's analysis, I suggest that a sharper formal focus on the specific iterations of mimicry in print culture—of which parody was one—draws out questions of agency and history that remain submerged in his account.

Parody vs. Mimicry

To date, imitation in the colonial context has most often been understood through the lens of Bhabha's work, though it was also central to the work of Ashis Nandy. Both critics theorize colonial imitation through psychological and psychoanalytic paradigms. By focusing in this chapter on colonial *parody* rather than mimicry, I argue that an analysis of imitation that foregrounds form (how

---

6. Hans Harder, "Prologue: Late Nineteenth and Twentieth Century Asian *Punch* Versions and Related Satirical Journals," in Harder and Mittler, *Asian Punches*, 4. For those interested in *Punch* and/or cartoons and caricature as a global phenomenon, this is a crucial and extensive study of the *Punch* phenomenon.

parody works) and material circulation (how parodic texts circulated) helps us understand the ways in which the colonial discourse these critics so influentially diagnosed was reshaped by it. If theories of colonial mimicry unpack contradictions and tensions in the colonizer/colonized relationship, the theory of colonial parody offered here demonstrates how parodic forms create change over time by shifting the power relation between colonial and anticolonial representation. As others have argued, parody both incorporates its object and displaces it, positioning it in the past.[7] At the same time, I suggest, its analytical stance points toward a future in which its critique has weakened the purchase of the original, while reiteration has diluted its originality and impact—a powerful effect, particularly in the face of virulent racist caricature. Viewed in this light, colonial parody has a temporal logic that distinguishes it from colonial mimicry and accounts more fully for the transformative power of imitative form, while also helping to explain the popularity of parody as an anticolonial mode.

In *The Intimate Enemy*, Nandy chiefly explores the idea of colonial imitation via the colonized's emulation of the colonizer: "In the colonial culture, identification with the aggressor bound the rulers and the ruled in an unbreakable dyadic relationship. . . . Many Indians . . . saw their salvation in becoming more like the British, in friendship or in enmity."[8] For Bhabha, however, mimicry is "one of the most elusive and effective strategies of colonial power and knowledge."[9] It is both "reform, regulation and discipline" and a "difference or recalcitrance" within that regime of discipline that "coheres the dominant strategic function of colonial power, intensifies surveillance and poses an immanent threat to both 'normalized' knowledges and disciplinary powers."[10] Mimicry, Bhabha contends, "necessarily raises the question of the authorization of colonial representations" because "in 'normalizing' the colonial state or subject, the dream of post-Enlightenment civility alienates its own language of liberty and produces another knowledge of its norms." In Bhabha's account, then, mimicry is the logic of colonial power and also a way of naming the contradictions therein.

In its desire for "a reformed, recognizable Other," mimicry is intrinsically ambivalent because the colonial subject has to be both an other but also know-

---

7. See Linda Hutcheon, "Parody without Ridicule: Observations on Modern Literary Parody," *Canadian Review of Comparative Literature* 5, no. 8 (Spring 1978): 201–11; and Carolyn Williams, *Gilbert and Sullivan: Gender, Genre and Parody* (New York: Columbia University Press, 2011).
8. Nandy, *Intimate Enemy*, 7.
9. Homi Bhabha, *The Location of Culture* (New York: Routledge, 1994), 122.
10. Bhabha, *Location of Culture*, 122.

able and visible: "*a subject of a difference that is almost the same but not quite.*"¹¹ Thus, Thomas Babington Macaulay infamously called for the creation of "a class of persons, Indian in blood and colour, but English in taste, in opinions, in morals, and in intellect."¹² Symbolizing this "class of persons," the figure of the babu explored in chapter 1 is a loaded and vexing one precisely because he epitomizes this ambivalence. While caricatures of the babu were particularly prevalent in India in Kalighat paintings, they also circulated between Britain and India via British *Punch*, the *Indian Charivari*, and other forms of illustrations such as the one from *Kim* reproduced in chapter 1.

An example is this image from British *Punch* that appeared in the magazine in 1895 as part of a serialized novel about the exploits of Baboo Jabberjee (Figure 2.2). As the lady's snigger indicates, the babu figure here is a comic one, presumably because he dresses like an English gentleman. But since mimicry is always ambivalent, Bhabha argues, it can easily slide into menace: a turn from what he calls "a difference that is almost nothing but not quite" to "a difference that is almost total but not quite."¹³

A cartoon from the *Indian Charivari*, the Anglo-Indian version of *Punch*, illustrates a more menacing version of the babu in which he is, at the risk of redundancy, both a parrot and a monkey—a hybrid creature at once comical *and* monstrous (Figure 2.3). In this image, the "jabber" commonly associated with the babu figure is represented by the doggerel that accompanies the image, which lampoons the Indian press for its grievances against the government by emphasizing its linguistic pretentiousness. As opposed to the sartorial pretentiousness of Baboo Jabberjee, the babu's critical writings are more immediately threatening, and thus the doggerel and cartoon, despite their comic tenor, more fully register the ambivalence Bhabha describes.

For Bhabha, though, mimicry is not merely the work of power; it also offers opportunities for subversion at those moments when, as he puts it, "the look of surveillance returns as the displacing gaze of the disciplined."¹⁴ In his writing on hybridity, he contends that "the words of the master become the site of hybridity—the warlike, subaltern sign of the native . . . the repetition of the 'same' can in fact be its own displacement, can turn the authority of culture

---

11. Bhabha, *Location of Culture*, 122 (italics in original).
12. Thomas Babington Macaulay, "Minute on Indian Education," speech, February 2, 1835, in *Selected Writings*, ed. John Clive and Thomas Pinney (Chicago: University of Chicago Press, 1972), 243.
13. Bhabha, *Location of Culture*, 131.
14. Bhabha, *Location of Culture*, 126.

"IT WAS HERE," I SAID, REVERENTLY, "THAT THE SWAN OF AVON WAS HATCHED!"

FIGURE 2.2 / Illustration of Baboo Jabberjee by F. Anstey, *Baboo Jabberjee*, B.A., 1895, 129. General Reference Collection, British Library. Shelfmark 012206.i.1/51, © British Library Board.

FIGURE 2.3 / "Patriotic Baboo" from *Indian Charivari*, February 20, 1874, 39. Asia Pacific and Africa Holdings, British Library. Shelfmark SW 238, © British Library Board.

into its own nonsense precisely in the moment of enunciation."[15] As this quote, and his chief examples in "Of Mimicry and Man" demonstrate, Bhabha understands mimicry as something that happens at the level of language or other sign systems, such as images or clothing.

But in cases where Indian editors *chose* to use parody and its affordances, the process of repetition was a conscious one.[16] In this case, visual and literary *forms* of parody specifically, rather than language more broadly, do the work of generating difference and subversion. The following exploration of *Punch* variants in the Indian Anglosphere examines the workings and circulation of these forms to understand the way parody produces political effects and, correspondingly, how the potentialities of representation—both visual-verbal and political—change over time. Building on Bhabha's theory of mimicry, this chapter offers a theory of colonial parody based on a study of its workings in the triangulated relationship between British, Anglo-Indian, and Indian versions of *Punch*.

---

15. Bhabha, *Location of Culture*, 195.

16. In *Forms: Whole, Rhythm, Hierarchy, Network* (Princeton, NJ: Princeton University Press, 2015), Caroline Levine adapts the term "affordances" from design to literary theory: thinking about what characteristics of forms help them to do "allows us to grasp both the specificity and the generality of forms—both the particular constraints and possibilities that different forms afford, and the fact that those patterns and arrangements carry their affordances with them as they move across time and space" (6).

Colonial Parody

You'll be back
Soon you'll see
You'll remember you belong to me
You'll be back
Time will tell
You'll remember that I served you well
Oceans rise, empires fall
We have seen each other through it all
And when push comes to shove,
I will send a fully armed battalion to remind you of my love ...
... And, no, don't change the subject
'Cause you're my favorite subject
My sweet, submissive subject
My loyal, royal subject
Forever and ever and ever and ever and ever
—Lin Manuel-Miranda, *Hamilton* (2015)

While it has been explored and defined by critics from a range of literary fields and academic disciplines, there is a general consensus that parody involves, in the words of Seymour Chatman, "stylistic imitation for satirical effect."[17] In these *Hamilton* lyrics, parody works at two different levels—the song of a jilted lover parodies his petty delusions through exaggeration and incongruously jaunty rhythms, while both of these devices are used to parody the affection allegory that structured colonial relationships and the logic that underpinned Section 124a: the idea that colonial exploitation might be understood instead as mutual affection and dependence.

If parody is a "subspecies of satire," it differs from satire in that its meaning relies on the object it satirizes.[18] The parodic text plays off the original with some degree of repetition but also with a difference, either in form or content, that highlights and satirizes some aspect of the prior text. Critics differ, however, as to what parodic element of the text they consider most determining of its satirical effect. Chatman, for example, contends that good parody should be "informative about the features that characterize individual styles."[19] Pierre Bourdieu, in *The*

---

17. Seymour Chatman, "Parody and Style," *Poetics Today* 22, no. 1 (Spring 2001): 25–39, 30.
18. Chatman, "Parody and Style," 30.
19. Chatman, "Parody and Style," 25.

Field of Cultural Production, locates the change not as much in the form as in the context of the work, arguing from a materialist-sociological perspective that

> the meaning of a work . . . changes automatically with each change in the field within which it is situated for the spectator or reader. . . . Breaks with the most orthodox works of the past . . . often take the form of *parody* . . . which presupposes and confirms *emancipation* . . . the newcomers 'get beyond' ['dépassent'] the dominant mode of thought and expression not by explicitly denouncing it but by repeating and reproducing it in a sociologically non-congruent context, which has the effect of rendering it incongruous or even absurd, simply by making it perceptible as the arbitrary convention it is. . . . Pastiche or parody [is] the indispensable means of objectifying, and thereby appropriating, the form of thought and expression by which they were formerly possessed.[20]

Margaret Rose, in her transhistorical analysis of "ancient, modern, and postmodern" parody, sees parody as "the comic refunctioning of preformed linguistic or artistic material." More than Chatman or Bourdieu, she emphasizes the importance of the reader in the proper functioning of parody. Though it can imitate both the form and content of the "preformed" material, it usually changes one or both of these so as to create a critical relationship to the original. For this reason, "the reception of the parody by its external reader will depend upon the latter's reading of the 'signals' given in the parody text which relate to or indicate the relationship between the parody and the parodied text and its associations."[21]

Like mimicry, parodic discourse is hybrid and ambiguous. In Mikhail Bakhtin's terms, it is hybrid because it involves two languages "crossed with each other, as well as two styles, two linguistic points of view, and in the final analysis two speaking subjects."[22] It is ambiguous because parodists can be sympathetic or critical toward their objects, or both (Chatman argues that parody is best defined as "at once ridicule and homage").[23] Pointing out that the term "para" in Greek can mean both nearness and opposition, Rose notes that the parodic text simultaneously inhabits and identifies with its object and reifies it, holding it up for

---

20. Pierre Bourdieu, *The Field of Cultural Production: Essays on Art and Literature* (New York: Columbia University Press, 1993), 31.

21. Margaret Rose, *Parody: Ancient, Modern, and Postmodern* (Cambridge: Cambridge University Press, 1993), 41.

22. Mikhail Bakhtin, *The Dialogic Imagination: Four Essays*, ed. Michael Holquist (Austin: University of Texas Press, 1982), 76.

23. Chatman, "Parody and Style," 33.

scrutiny. Even the explicitly critical text is ambivalent because, while it makes "the comic discrepancy between the parodist's style and that of the target text into a weapon against the latter," it is "refunction[ing] the target's work for a new and positive purpose."[24] The parodied text is thus both a bad and good object—at least to the extent that it provides fodder for the new, positive purpose.

Colonial parody was a key tactic of disaffection. Instances of colonial parody offered an image of a British or Anglo-Indian public (addressed by the original text) and an Indian counterpublic (addressed by the critique of the original text), and in doing so provided a critique of their object while drawing attention to the contours and limits of imperial citizenship. As well as changes in form and content that contribute to the parody, the shift from public to counterpublic—in Bourdieu's terms, from the perspective of the "dominant mode of thought and expression" to that of the "newcomers"—is a change in field that alters the meaning of the object being parodied.

A short satirical fictional piece by the Bengali humorist Rajshekhar Basu (best known by his pen name Parashuram), entitled "The Scripture Read Backward," exemplifies and metaphorizes this change in field by imagining a shift in the space of empire itself: the action takes place in a Britain that has been colonized by India and reverses the logic and dictums of colonial discourse to comic and critical effect. The piece might loosely be described as a play, but one clearly not designed for performance. Far from observing Aristotelian unities of time, it shifts rapidly from one site to another to highlight the different scales empire works at—a kind of sped-up version of the "meanwhile" that Benedict Anderson associates with the novel and newspaper.[25] It begins in a local school, where students are being taught "official" history: "The condition of the Europeans is gradually improving. Their greed has been curbed, their barbaric love of luxury dispelled; they look less toward this world and more toward the next. The children of India have crossed the seven seas and thirteen rivers to selflessly spread peace, order, and civilization through these wild and remote lands."[26] At the same time, in a "women's quarters," British girls attempt to learn Bengali manners; in Hyde Park, a speaker tries to rally the crowd against the government before being bribed into preaching compliance; and in Germany a local prince describes to

---

24. Rose, *Parody*, 51.
25. See Anderson, *Imagined Communities*.
26. Parashuram, "The Scripture Read Backward," trans. Sukanta Chaudhari, in *Words without Borders: The World through the Eyes of Writers*, ed. Samantha Schnee, Alane Salierno Mason, and Dedi Felman (New York: Anchor Books, 2007), 66.

a Chinese traveler how he has stayed in India's political good graces ("I've just arranged for everyone in the state to have a happy time—they're all stoned"), in a compact reference to the effects of British imperialism on China.[27]

As well as parodying British imperialism by reversing the order of things on the level of content, Basu also deploys parodic form. The play is not only fragmented and made modern by its rapid changes of scene but also by the extracts from newspapers and periodicals that are interspersed throughout it. Some of these are based on real Anglo-Indian periodicals such as the *Statesman*. But the fictional versions, like the rest of the play, reflect a topsy-turvy world. An ad in one of them for ambergris powder, for instance, declares that "memsahibs need not feel frustrated anymore. This miraculous powder will remove the unfortunate pallor of their skins and give them the complexion of Bengali women." Basu also plays on the divided public of the Indian Anglosphere, for the paper's other ad seems to be aimed at Indians rather than their British subjects and satirizes the ads in Anglo-Indian newspapers for packaged British goods: "Don't ruin your health by eating English biscuits larded with fat. Try our Joy-laddus. They strengthen your teeth. Nothing but ground rice and molasses. Not touched by machine: made by Bengali women with their own hands."[28] In a few short pages, Basu's writing exposes both the fallacies of its parodic object, liberal imperialism, and elucidates how it operates and circulates through modern forms like the novel, the newspaper, and the ads that appeared in both, as well as through institutions like schools.

As "The Scripture Read Backward" demonstrates, parody is like mimicry in that it imitates and produces difference from that which it copies, thereby calling the authenticity of the original into question.[29] But, as Carolyn Williams has contended, parody also makes the original an object of the *past*, by *surpassing* it. In her work on Gilbert and Sullivan, Williams defines parody as "powerfully modernizing": "In taking up its models, parody implicitly leaves

---

27. Parashuram, "Scripture Read Backward," 77.
28. Parashuram, "Scripture Read Backward," 70–71.
29. Bhabha makes this point in regard to mimicry and Judith Butler makes it in regard to gender parody and performativity. For Butler, the repetitive acts that constitute gender identity also allow for its contestation: "If the rules governing signification not only restrict, but enable the assertion of alternative domains of cultural intelligibility . . . then it is only within the practices of repetitive signifying that a subversion of identity becomes possible." The repetition with a difference that gay identity constitutes in relation to straight identity, she argues, calls the authenticity of the original—and its naturalness—into question. Judith Butler, *Gender Trouble: Feminism and the Subversion of Identity* (New York: Routledge, 1990), 185.

them behind or, rather ... casts them back into the past, treating them as outmoded relics compared with itself."[30]

In the colonial context, parodies that targeted colonial governance were able to hold British claims about the backwardness of Indian culture, which often relied on comparisons to Britain's own feudal past, up for scrutiny. Parody instead cast *British rule* into the past, both through its form, which leaves behind that which it critiques, and via its content, which represented colonial government as autocratic, fearful, and reactionary—hence backward and passé. Basu's alternative parodic history makes British rationales for imperialism appear ludicrously, transparently false, and dependent on the power of propagation; once this so-called scripture is read, or analyzed, from a different vantage point, it becomes untenable, as well as antiquated (as the word "scripture" indicates). Basu's piece was published in 1927, long after the first Indian *Punch*es began to appear in the mid-nineteenth century. But its wicked irreverence built upon the years and years of Indian parodies of imperialist forms, discourse, and imagery that rendered colonial views of India increasingly impotent and unconvincing.

Through the mechanism of parody, the Indian critique of British governance, even in very moderate journals such as *Hindi Punch*, came to stand in for the modern, both because it displaced and surpassed the object of its critique, to use Williams's terms, and because, like British *Punch*, it provided an up-to-the-minute commentary on political developments. In a preface to its 1903 annual, it explicitly identified itself as a modernizing force by taking on colonial stereotypes about Indian torpor: "*Hindi Punch* has often pondered upon the awful thought and marveled that men in this country should cling to the notion that the old is for ever to be with them.... But hark! There's a gentle whisper in the air! The spirit of novelty, bearing near kinship to change, is at last abroad. The murmur grows in volume." However ironically the idea of Indian passivity is staged here (as an "awful thought"), *Hindi Punch* allows it to stand in order to position itself as an engine of progress, sweeping in not only novelty but unity. *Punch*'s gift, it proclaims, is a meal "from which Hindus, Parsis, Mussalmans, Christians, and others of every caste and creed in this caste-ridden-land, may joyously partake together in one *pangat*, or company, without the least fear of Excommunication."[31] In this utopian image, imperial stereotypes of a divided, caste-ridden, and stagnant India are definitively surpassed.

---

30. Williams, *Gilbert and Sullivan*, 9.
31. *Hindi Punch*, "Preface to the Fourth Edition" (December 1902), in *Cartoons from the Hindi Punch*, edited by Barjorji Naoroji (Bombay: Hindi Punch Office, 1903–6).

The nature of parody, I am arguing, allowed writers and periodicals to contest and reshape the nature of the public sphere which they addressed and the ways it was defined by the criminalization of disaffection. In imitating British *Punch*, *Hindi Punch* performed both affection—the filial "taking after" its model that the government sanctioned—and disaffection, a rejection of the model that took the form of ridicule and critique. The Janus-faced nature of parody allowed the rhetoric of affection and disaffection and the space of public and counterpublic to exist simultaneously, while strategically making it hard to tell one from the other.

Punch Proliferates: British *Punch*, Indian *Punches*, and *Hindi Punch*

Hindi Punch was only one of many versions of *Punch* that circulated in India during the years of direct British rule.[32] Alongside other forms of comic journalism, there may have been as many as seventy Indian versions of *Punch*, according to one estimate.[33] While the greatest number of unofficial *Punch*es were produced in India, *Punch* takeoffs proliferated in other parts of the world as well, including Istanbul, Hong Kong, Tokyo, and Melbourne.[34] Though, as Ritu Khanduri demonstrates, both Indian cartoonists and *Punch* itself generally considered British *Punch* the original indigenous parent of all these copies, it was in fact itself derivative of the French satirical magazine *Le Charivari* (hence its subtitle, "The London Charivari") and the figure of Punch himself drew from Punch and Judy puppet shows influenced by the Italian Punchinello satiric puppet tradition—a tradition with roots as deep as the ancient world and with multiple global iterations, both ancient and modern.[35] Even though the Indian *Punch*es were accused of being upstart imitators of the British version, then, in the hall of mirrors that was the world of *Punch*es in the colonial period, there was no original.[36]

---

32. See Hans Harder and Barbara Mittler, eds., *Asian Punches: A Transcultural Affair* (New York: Springer, 2013). Other important work on *Punch*es in India include Mushirul Hasan's *The Avadh Punch: Wit and Humour in Colonial North India* (New Delhi: Niyogi Books, 2007) and *Wit and Wisdom: Pickings from the Parsee Punch* (New Delhi: Niyogi Books, 2012).
33. Harder, "Prologue," 2n3.
34. Harder, "Prologue," 1; and Mitter, "*Punch* and Indian Cartoons," 48; both in Harder and Mittler, *Asian Punches*.
35. Harder, "Prologue," 5.
36. The *Lytton Gazette* (what Khanduri calls "an example of the loyal faction of the press in India") complained that the *Punch*es abused the government. Ritu Gairola Khanduri, *Caricaturing*

The British version, *Punch; or the London Charivari*, did have an impressively broad reach, however, as the abundance of indigenous *Punch*es suggests. An illustrated satirical magazine founded in London by the journalist and social reformer Henry Mayhew, *Punch* was famous for the political caricatures and satirical drawings about contemporary events that filled its pages, many by influential artists such as John Tenniel. As well as popularizing the use of cartoons as a mode of political critique, it is credited with first giving the word "cartoon" its modern connotations (i.e., comic drawing, or caricature) by using it this way in 1843. By midcentury, it was widely read in literary and political circles and over the course of the century published significant Victorian writers such as William Thackeray, George du Maurier, and Douglas Jerrold and, later on, equally renowned twentieth-century ones such as P. G. Wodehouse, Sylvia Plath, and Penelope Fitzgerald (it survived, with varying degrees of success, into this century, finally folding in 2002).

By the middle of the nineteenth century, *Punch* was commercially successful, selling fifty to sixty thousand copies a week.[37] At this point, it had established itself as the magazine of respectable satire, staffed by members of the professional classes and with content that shied away from the politically malicious or sexually outré caricatures associated with other illustrated magazines. Yet it nonetheless "saw no contradiction between avoiding personality and caricature for elite politicians and subjecting minorities or marginal groups such as the Irish, Catholics, Jews, and colonial native peoples to unpleasant and cruel treatment."[38] *Punch* was produced by woodblock printing, which made the production of illustrated periodicals in particular faster and less work-intensive. The technique that allowed *Punch* to enhance its profitability and cultural influence by readily reproducing back issues and collected volumes was called stereotyping and the magazine's influence and reach also contributed to the etymological and phenomenological emergence of the other kind of stereotype—that associated with portable and recognizable racial and ethnic caricature.

Both *Punch*'s popularity, and its corollary ability to generate stereotypes, had much to do with its engagement with colonial events—in particular the 1857 Rebellion, which led to a surge in circulation. "Iconographic elements in *Punch* . . . emerged in

---

Culture in India: Cartoons and History in the Modern World (Cambridge: Cambridge University Press, 2014), 59.

37. Henry J. Miller, "John Leech and the Shaping of the Victorian Cartoon: The Context of Respectability," *Victorian Periodicals Review* 42, no. 3 (Fall 2009): 267–91, 267.

38. Miller, "John Leech," 282.

relation to the market in colonial India," Khanduri notes, because colonial administrators and military personnel were an important part of its readership.[39] Tenniel's famous cartoon about the Rebellion, "The British Lion's Vengeance on the Bengal Tiger," helped make empire a subject to which its visual style seemed well-suited, for cartoons could produce an immediate affective response more powerful than verbal accounts of political events; "cartoons evoked sense and sentiment: terror, horror, and fear constitute the vocabulary for translating a visual form."[40]

Punch's proprietors were aware not only of the importance of empire as subject matter but also as a source of potential markets and developed ambitions to produce multiple versions of their satirical magazine for different colonial regions; "*Punch* proclaimed its exalted status by noting its influence and its role as a model for political satire in the colonies and elsewhere."[41]

Figure 2.5 depicts Punch jumping through a hoop that is also a map of the world, held up by two figures of ambiguous ethnicity, but clearly meant to be indigenous. Punch himself wields a bow and arrow, another signifier of indigeneity, perhaps suggestive of his ability to beat indigenous *Punch*es at their own game. This goal was never achieved, however, for British *Punch* failed to expand significantly in India, perhaps because of the growing popularity and abundance of vernacular *Punch*es that rapidly entered the colonial public sphere from the mid-nineteenth century onward, muddying the commercial waters.[42]

Because of their appearance in the second half of the nineteenth century and decline after World War II, the existence of so many *Punch* variants has been read by critics as an effect of British global hegemony in the period and the flexibility of *Punch*'s form as a response thereto; the indirect and comic nature of this particular form of satire served as a mask for serious dissent.[43] Since both satire and parody had a long history in Britain, flourishing in periodical culture from the eighteenth century onward, it may have been more acceptable as a form of criticism than other, more direct modes.[44] In India in particular, the law

---

39. Khanduri, "Vernacular *Punch*es, 462–63.
40. Khanduri, *Caricaturing Culture*, 6.
41. Khanduri, "Vernacular *Punch*es," 462–63.
42. Partha Mitter contests this argument, however, claiming that there is little evidence that British *Punch* failed in India. "*Punch* and Indian Cartoons," 48n4.
43. Harder, "Prologue," 6–7.
44. On the eighteenth-century history of satire, see Dustin Griffin, *Satire: A Critical Reintroduction* (Lexington: University Press of Kentucky, 1994); and A. Marshall, *The Practice of Satire in England, 1658–1770* (Baltimore: Johns Hopkins University Press, 2013).

FIGURE 2.4 / "The British Lion's Vengeance on the Bengal Tiger" by Sir John Tenniel, *Punch* vols. 32–33, August 22, 1857, 76–77. Courtesy of NYU Special Collections.

against disaffection no doubt made *Punch* an attractive model, for its humor gave a light-hearted flavor to political critique and the Indian *Punch*es could appear to be eager students of British publishing norms. Indeed, as noted earlier, British *Punch* acknowledged *Hindi Punch* as colonial kin, referring to it as "family" and as its "Indian cousin."[45] But as Khanduri points out, the familial alibi performed by Indian journals was a recognizably cagey one: "Both officials of the colonial state and newspaper proprietors were cognizant that using the British *Punch* as a template for humor aesthetics offered a particularly effective challenge to British claims of liberal governance."[46]

The colonial state thus kept a close eye on the vernacular *Punch*es, just as it did on other potentially subversive publications; "For the colonial government, the profusion and popularity of the comic newspapers, particularly in the vernacular, transformed satire into something dangerous and therefore worthy of surveillance."[47] Notices that appeared in *Hindi Punch* from other newspapers

---

45. Harder, "Prologue," 4.
46. Khanduri, *Caricaturing Culture*, 54.
47. Khanduri, *Caricaturing Culture*, 58.

FIGURE 2.5 / Frontispiece to *Punch*, 1857. Courtesy of NYU Special Collections.

(including British ones such as the *Manchester Guardian* and the *Graphic*, as well as similar publications such as *Melbourne Punch*) suggested that the government had good reason to worry about its effects outside India as well as within. Applauding it for its illustrations and astute political sensibility, the *Manchester*

Guardian stated that *Hindi Punch* might well change British public support for empire by altering "the popular estimate of the Hindu as simply a 'native.' If these cartoons appeal to the average Hindu, he must be credited with a sense of humour and quite average intelligence."[48]

If the format of *Punch* was appealing to Indian journalists because it potentially helped mask the force of political critique, it may also have been popular because it fit well with existing Indian satirical and comic modes, such as the Kalighat caricatures (see chapter 1). Historians of the Indian *Punch*es have also noted that the character of Punch recalled the clown tradition of Sanskrit drama, while simultaneously evoking the word *panc*, which has connotations of local and collective wisdom (*panc* refers to the number five, and village councils, made up of that number, were known as *panchayats*, and the head of council as the *sarpanch*, or leader of five).[49] Furthermore, Mr. Punch as a narrator figure evoked the "figure of the kathak, a speaker or narrator of scriptural or mythological stories."[50] The fact that *Punch* was both a visual and verbal form also helps explain its appeal as a vehicle for political commentary, as it could be appropriated by a range of Indian languages ("Mr. Punch appeared in his various incarnations speaking Hindi, Urdu, Punjabi, Gujarati and English in colonial comic papers," Khanduri notes) and could potentially appeal to the nonliterate—a point that Trivedi, the contemporary satirist mentioned at the start of this chapter makes when he describes his desire to reach a mass audience through his cartoon website.[51] Produced more quickly and easily than many other forms of art, cartoons could also serve as a portable visual vocabulary for the burgeoning nationalist movement through the portrayal of iconic figures such as the Bengal tiger and the stalwart elephant (which came increasingly to represent the nationalist movement), as well as figures like Mother India. For all these reasons, the *Punch*es, and other publications that employed cartoons, were popular media forms during the colonial period which circulated as widely as regular nonillustrated newspapers.[52]

---

48. Cited in "Opinions of the Press," *Cartoons from the Hindi Punch* (1904 Annual), n.p.

49. Khanduri notes that "the Punch character was a fusion of the vidusaka traditions of the Sanskrit drama and also a play on the title of the judiciary head of the Indian village called (sar) panch." "Vernacular *Punch*es," 470. I am grateful to Sukanya Banerjee for further clarification of the etymological relation between *panc* and *panch*.

50. Chaiti Basu, "The Punch Tradition in Late Nineteenth Century Bengal: From Pulcinella to Basantak and Pācu," in Harder and Mittler," *Asian Punches*, 111.

51. Khanduri, *Caricaturing Culture*, 52. She also notes that "the cartoons' visual aspect rendered them available for interpretation even to those who could not read the newspaper" (26).

52. Khanduri, "Vernacular *Punch*es," 474.

The importance of cartoons to the nationalist movement is underscored by Gandhi's efforts to create a politicized, critically astute, and broad newspaper readership through his periodical *Indian Opinion*, published in South Africa in English, Hindi, Gujarati, and Tamil from 1903 to 1915.[53] Khanduri notes that "the term 'cartoon' made an early appearance in the political vocabulary that Gandhi formulated with the help of his readers," and that he emphasized the ways "the making and reading of the cartoon was a political act, deserving of their attention."[54] To emphasize their significance to political discourse, he reprinted cartoons from *Hindi Punch* and analyzed them in detail; "His exegesis of the cartoons signaled his recognition of the lack of cultural capital, thus political capital, among the expatriate Indian readers of *Indian Opinion*" and his efforts to remediate this lack.[55]

The Indian *Punch*es, particularly those that closely imitated the style of British *Punch*, did similar critical work by highlighting the verbal-visual semiotics of colonial discourse through their ongoing response to cartoons and caricatures in the British and Anglo-Indian press. If British *Punch* was parodic because of its irreverent imitation of the appearance, rituals, and rhetoric of British politics and public life, *Hindi Punch* was doubly so, for its imitative form satirized the visual-verbal forms of British *Punch* and the politics of racist representation and caricature. Of the many vernacular Indian *Punch*es that existed in the period, I focus on this publication because it was an influential example of the comic journal tradition, with a relatively long print run and robust sales compared to most of the other publications.[56] More importantly for this book, though, it was clearly in conversation with British and Anglo-Indian publications, not only because of its dual-language format and its close adherence to the form of British *Punch*, but also because it reached audiences in Britain. While *Hindi Punch* did not have a distribution office there, it sent copies to various British periodicals for commentary, and was frequently extracted in W. T. Stead's *Review of Reviews*. An ad for Stead's publication also appeared in its own pages, suggesting their synergistic relationship (Khanduri points out that cartoons were appealing to Stead because of their accessibility, a quality essential to his publishing philosophy, as

---

53. For more on how *Indian Opinion* worked formally to politicize its readership, see Isabel Hofmeyr, *Gandhi's Printing Press: Experiments in Slow Reading* (Cambridge, MA: Harvard University Press, 2013).
54. Khanduri, *Caricaturing Culture*, 76–77.
55. Khanduri, *Caricaturing Culture*, 85.
56. Khanduri, "Vernacular *Punch*es," 470.

discussed in the next chapter).[57] The fact that British *Punch* claimed kinship to *Hindi Punch* also suggests that it recognized the Indian publication's influence in the imperial public sphere more broadly—a space that the British publication was itself trying to impact.

Despite its name, *Hindi Punch* was published in English and Gujarati, not Hindi, and was originally named *Parsee Punch* (the word "Hindi" in the period was rarely a reference to the language, as it is today, but more often used to denote "India" in a nationalist tenor). One of the earliest Indian *Punch*es, it was founded in 1854, not long after British *Punch*, which launched in 1841.[58] *Parsee Punch* was initially designed to appeal to, and consolidate, the small but influential merchant class of Parsis in Bombay, but also to provoke a national conversation about reform; for this latter reason, it eventually changed its name to *Hindi Punch* to broaden its appeal.[59]

Unlike its British predecessor, which used wood engraving for its illustrations, *Hindi Punch* used lithography as its printing method, like many other Indian periodicals of the time. Graham Shaw traces the first example of lithography in printing in India to 1822, after which it was widely used (in Britain, by contrast, letter-press remained the chief means of print production). In India, Shaw argues, lithography was preferable to letter-press printing during this period of a burgeoning print culture for a number of reasons: "It was far simpler and quicker to master than typography; it was less cumbersome and more portable involving less equipment; and it was cheaper, appealing therefore to the amateur or small-scale operator in particular."[60]

The particular appeal of lithography to Indians is evidenced by the fact that it was not widely used by missionaries for Bible production, who may have found it more impermanent-feeling in comparison to the letter-press they were used to, and thus "totally inappropriate for a message of eternal truth." For Indian publishers, however, the reverse was true: "It was the letter-press printing page which lacked visual authority, being totally alien to traditional Indian book production. It was still the manuscript which was vested with visual and

---

57. Khanduri, *Caricaturing Culture*, 57.
58. On British *Punch* and the history of visual caricature in Britain specifically, see Brian Maidment, "The Presence of *Punch* in the Nineteenth Century," in Harder and Mittler, *Asian Punches*, 15–44, and *Comedy, Caricature and the Social Order, 1820–50* (Manchester: Manchester University Press, 2013).
59. For an extensive analysis of *Parsee Punch*, see Hasan, *Wit and Wisdom*.
60. Graham Shaw, "Lithography v. Letter-Press in India," *South Asian Library Notes and Queries* 29, no. 1 (1994): 988–98, 991.

cultural authority and this was the key to lithography's rapid acceptance and lasting appeal."[61] Lithography would have been particularly appealing to periodicals that used cartoons, and that were published in different languages—like *Hindi Punch*—because it allowed for different scripts and a greater range of visual effects, as well as the integration of text and image (whereas in letterpress printing, wood-engraved images are inserted independently of the letter blocks). Printing method was thus another difference between British *Punch* and the Indian *Punch*es that might have added to the satiric effect of the Indian caricatures; they looked (and were) hand-drawn and quickly produced, and thus more spontaneous and scrappy.

Hindi Punch announced its reformist agenda in its first editorial, stating that "A comic journal plays a good part in the development of the political and social reform of a country and it shall be always our aim and desire to advance that end."[62] But it also positioned itself as moderate and sent one of its issues to the India Office for approval. According to Partha Mitter, the journal did receive the government's "guarded approval" but "with the comment that the paper was necessarily one-sided."[63] After Congress was established in 1885, however, it became more explicitly political, especially in its commentary on freedom of the press and the animosity of Anglo-Indian newspapers toward reform and Indian culture in general.[64]

Punch, Counterpunch

In the turn-of-the century period I focus on here, *Hindi Punch* was run by Barjorji Naoroji, a supporter of moderate elements in Congress and a vociferous critic of the more revolutionary forms of nationalism that emerged over the course of his magazine's publication. Anarchism, for example, was just as often a target of satire as the colonial government. In fact, in its imitation of a British periodical and its use of English alongside Gujarati in its captions and articles, *Hindi Punch* could easily be read as a "loyal" publication: an explicit goal of editors who wished to evade censorship (because, according to Section 124a,

---

61. Shaw, "Lithography v. Letter-Press in India," 993.
62. Cited in Hasan, *Wit and Wisdom*, 12.
63. Mitter, *Art and Nationalism in Colonial India*, 156. Mitter's work on *Punch* versions in India and other "occidental orientations" is extensive. See also his essay in Harder and Mittler, *Asian Punches*, "*Punch* and Indian Cartoons: The Reception of a Transnational Phenomenon," 47–64; and "Cartoons of the Raj," *History Today* 47, no. 9 (September 1997): 16–22.
64. Hasan, *Wit and Wisdom*, 114.

critique of the government was acceptable as long as a publication demonstrated loyalty as well). The first title page of the journal thus announced that it was published "Under the Patronage of H. E. Lord Curzon of Kedleston, Viceroy and Governor-General of India" and many images and headings celebrated British rule and royalty in the manner of British *Punch*. Figure 2.6, for instance, was published to celebrate the succession of Edward VII as emperor of India after Victoria, and depicts a somber Panchoba (*Hindi Punch*'s Punchinello narrator figure) singing alongside equally devout-looking women.

But the magazine was increasingly ambivalent in its loyalties over time: seven years later, on the occasion of the Delhi Durbar held to commemorate the coronation of George V, an image of a different flavor appeared on the cover (Figure 2.7). Here, Panchoba is more comically rendered and the British flag is repurposed as an elephant diaper so that the publication's performances of loyalty read as insincere and its parodic elements as the "travesty of high genres and lofty models embodied in national myth" that Bakhtin associates with classical iterations of the genre. As in classical parody, the "high" culture of royal pageantry is "contemporized and brought low, into the everyday."[65] The image also echoes one that appeared on the cover of British *Punch* in 1858, after the quashing of the 1857 Rebellion and the Queen's Proclamation declaring that she had taken over governance of India from the East India Company (Figure 2.8).

In this illustration, the elephant kneels awkwardly, signifying its obeisance, and is dominated by Mr. Punch, who is disproportionately large and dances on the elephant's head, contributing to its discomfited appearance. The Indian version, however, reverses the elephant's stance, making it giddily, actively upright; rather than being danced *upon*, it dances beside Panchoba, who encourages its revelry.

Alongside its deployment of cartoons and caricature, *Hindi Punch*'s use of two languages helped it navigate the treacheries of a racialized public sphere. Most English-language periodicals were monolingual but nonetheless spoke to different audiences—those in Britain, the British in India, and formally educated Indians who could read English (though the Indian audience would have extended beyond this as individuals might have translated out loud for nonliterate or non-English-speaking listeners). *Hindi Punch*'s innovative dual-language format, on the other hand, made visible the different audiences

---

65. Bakhtin, *Dialogic Imagination*, 157.

FIGURE 2.6 / "Hind on the Delhi Durbar" from *Hindi Punch*, 1903-6, 4. Asia Pacific and Africa Holdings, British Library. Shelfmark SW 576, © British Library Board.

addressed by the English-language press and the role of perspective and language in the interpretation of events and their representation. Cartoons were often captioned in both languages: while translations of the Gujarati captions correspond closely to the English ones, the visual effect of the different scripts side by

PARODY / 95

FIGURE 2.7 / Elephant and Mr. Punch from the cover of *Hindi Punch*, 1910. Courtesy of New York Public Library.

side literalize the double-coding strategies of Indian Anglophone journals and suggest possible differences in interpretation of the images that might result from linguistic variations, or from the more distanced viewpoint provided by the lens of an Indian language. Some pages of the journal, meanwhile, were exclusively

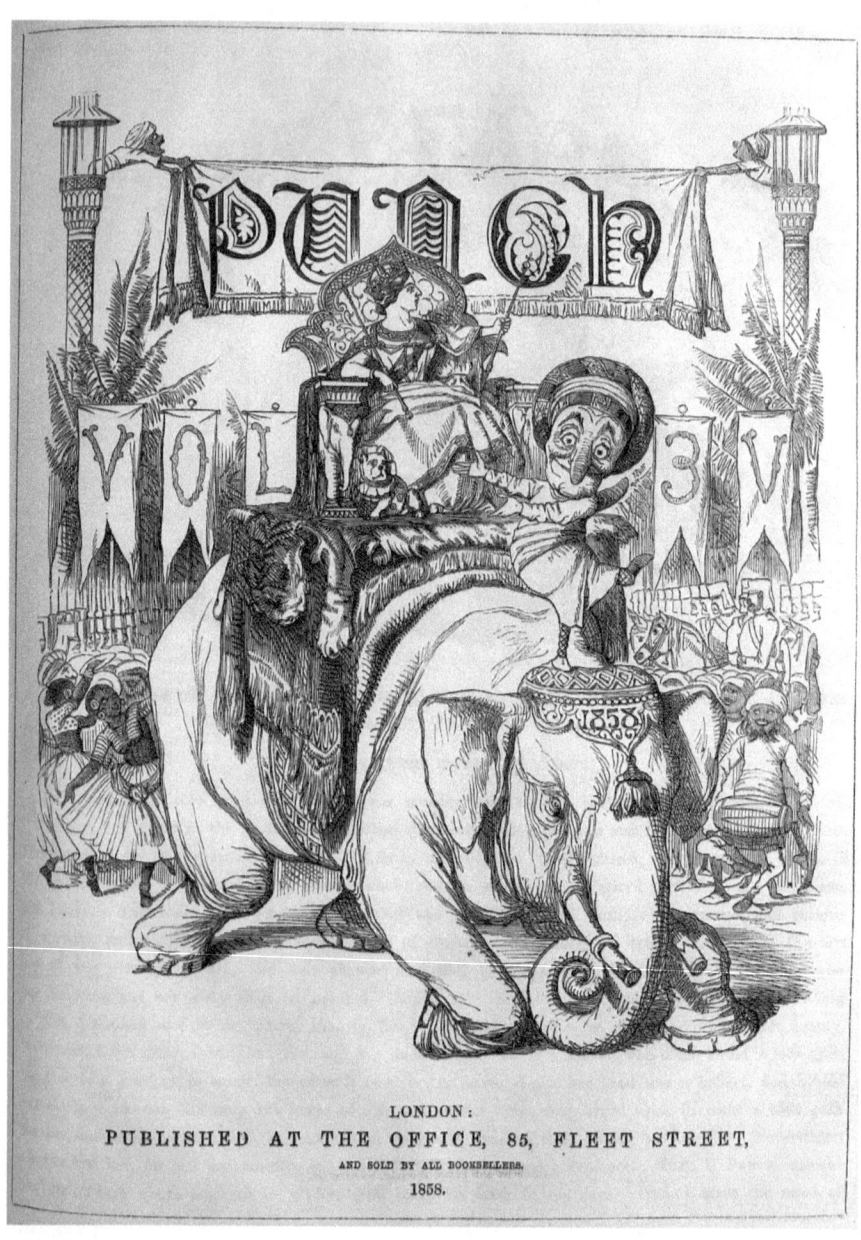

FIGURE 2.8 / Frontispiece to *Punch*, 1858. Courtesy of NYU Special Collections.

printed in Gujarati and addressed the Parsi and Indian communities directly with poems and articles, such as "A Parsi Manifesto," a short polemic urging the Parsi community to unite and strive for political power.[66]

But it is the journal's parodic criticisms of imperial rule, of press censorship, and of Anglo-Indian racism that seem most carefully designed to reshape the Indian Anglosphere into one in which the Indian, rather than Anglo-Indian, press, played a vital, truth-telling role as the voice of reason and moderation. *Hindi Punch*'s parodic cartoons about press censorship, in particular, drew out the race-baiting representations of the Anglo-Indian press and reframed them as the product of irrationality and hysteria.

The *Indian Charivari* was one of the Anglo-Indian periodicals to which *Hindi Punch* seemed to be directly responding. If the early Indian *Punch*es were a response to British *Punch* (and then to each other, as they proliferated), the *Indian Charivari* was probably itself a response to *them*, for it appeared in 1872, almost two decades after *Hindi Punch* was launched. Owned by Colonel Percy Wyndham, the *Indian Charivari* stated in its "Prospectus" that its goal was to direct "the sharp, pungent sting of wit and humour against the foibles of those around us." In practice, this usually meant the Indian press, in particular the Bengali *bhadralok*. The parrot-monkey image mentioned earlier was only one of many that degraded the babu to the position of ape to emphasize his imitative and atavistic qualities.

Figure 2.9, for instance, "The British Lion and the Bengalee Ape" (1873), takes aim at the criticism of the British in the Indian press (as did the doggerel in the parrot-monkey cartoon); the caption of this image specifically cites the *Hindoo Patriot*, a nationalist periodical, and pokes fun at the Raj's self-representation: "Therein the Lion has painted himself." But the lion's violence quickly changes the monkey's expression from smugness to pain, so that the cartoon's satire of the Indian press is also a tacit threat of violent reprisal. Ironically, since it takes issue with imitation via the baboo-monkey, the cartoon was itself a citation, based on an 1848 caricature in British *Punch*, "The British Lion and the Irish Monkey," that satirized the Irish nationalist and political journalist, John Mitchel (Figure 2.10).

Here, racism as well as the cartoon itself is derivative; a mode of defanging political critique borrowed from an earlier colonial context and imported to Calcutta to contend with a new form of nationalism.[67]

---

66. *Hindi Punch*, June 16, 1907, 11.
67. Stephen Morton notes that a cartoon in *Hindi Punch* that satirized terrorist activities in India seems to reference one in British *Punch* that depicted Gladstone fighting Irish problems in 1870

FIGURE 2.9 / "The British Lion and the Bengalee Ape" from *Indian Charivari*, January 24, 1873, 66. Asia Pacific and Africa Holdings, British Library. Shelfmark SW 238, © British Library Board.

Another cartoon from the same period, "The Baboo's Progress, or What We Are Coming To" (1873), similarly lampoons Indian presumptuousness; in this case it targets ideals of equality and self-rule that were increasingly circulating in the Indian press at the time. A parody of "The Origin of Species," meanwhile, combines the zoomorphic racism of the parrot-monkey and its critique of the press with the specific concerns about a burgeoning discourse of nationalism by lampooning the idea of Indian "progress" (Figures 2.11 and 2.12).

In response, *Hindu Punch* parodied the Anglo-Indian parody of the Indian press. Cartoons that did this explicitly were especially prevalent in the magazine after the 1905 Partition of Bengal—an act which separated the predominantly Muslim areas into East Bengal and the predominantly Hindu ones into West

---

(61)—the Ireland/India comparison was thus put to both colonial and anticolonial uses, as well as radical and conservative ones in each context (see also chapter 2 on coverage of Indian disaffection in the Irish press). "Terrorism, Sedition and Literature," in *Terrorism and the Postcolonial*, ed. Elleke Boehmer and Stephen Morton, 202–25. Chichester, West Sussex: Wiley Blackwell, 2010.

FIGURE 2.10 / "The British Lion and the Irish Monkey" by John Leech, *Punch*, vols. 14–15, April 8, 1848. Courtesy of NYU Special Collections.

Bengal. India's viceroy, Lord Curzon, who initiated the partition, cited administrative reasons for this drastic action, but it was seen by many Indians as a divide-and-conquer strategy deployed to weaken Bengali anticolonial activity. Instead, the act served as a turning point in the nationalist movement, inspiring political protests ranging from Swadeshi boycotts to terrorist bombings; this led, in turn, to repressive government actions, such as the imprisonment and exile of nationalist leaders, and the arrest of editors, printers, and publishers of nationalist articles. By 1911, however, alarmed by the amount of resistance the partition had inspired, the government reversed its decision and Bengal was reunited.

Hindi Punch remained relatively moderate during this galvanizing period, attacking radical leaders such as Tilak for the repression they had brought down upon moderates and revolutionaries alike and notably steering clear of the Swadeshi and Bande Mataram slogans that characterized the period. But it reacted to this moment through a series of cartoons that criticized both the government and Anglo-Indian newspapers by representing their response to nationalist agitation as overwrought, reactionary, and censorious: in figure

FIGURE 2.11 / "The Coming K——— (The Baboo's Progress, or What We Are Coming To)" from *Indian Charivari*, March 7, 1873, 110. As Asia Pacific and Africa Holdings, British Library. Shelfmark SW 238, © British Library Board.

FIGURE 2.12 / "Origin of Species" from *Indian Charivari*, January 9, 1874, 8. Asia Pacific and Africa Holdings, British Library. Shelfmark SW 576, © British Library Board.

2.13, for example, a doleful Panchoba looks on skeptically while a grotesquely enormous British policeman wields a barbaric torture instrument—the titular cat-o'-nine-tails, consisting of various repressive measures.

In its parodic criticisms of the Anglo-Indian press and the government, *Hindi Punch* drew upon many of the stereotypes about Indians that had by this time circulated widely in the press and colonial literature but recontextualized them as colonial fantasy. Thus, an image representing the repressive censorship that followed the Partition of Bengal, in its disturbing portrayal of two women bound and gagged, turns liberal British sentiment about the oppression of Indian women on its head by associating the violence of the image with censorious acts of government.

The women, identified by their dress as Muslim and Hindu, are drawn as twin images of Mother India, by now a familiar and iconic figure in the Indian press but, here, bound in a way that suggests sexual vulnerability. Their sisterly appearance and defiantly upturned heads counter British notions of Indian female modesty as well as the idea (notoriously used as a rationale for the partition) of India as internally divided by religion (Figure 2.14).

A cartoon that uses gender similarly, "Liberty in Fetters!" draws together elements of the two others, representing censorship through an image suggestive of sexual violence and the slave trade and thereby contrasting the repressed history of empire to its self-representation, embodied by the smug and dapper British administrator.

The slave cage in which Liberty (identified by her cap with the French Revolution) is of the type used for prisoners taken to the Andaman Islands, the destination for those punished by the state with "transportation for life" under Section 124a. As in figure 2.13, there are two female figures, both allegorical: the uncaged one, Mother India, looks on in "alarm and indignation" at the treatment of Liberty. Significantly, the text underneath this cartoon, which uses these affective terms, stresses the way British policy itself creates the disaffection it seeks to curb. During and after the 1857 uprising, the specter of sexual violence against British women played a crucial role in representations of reprisal and in justifications for various modes of illiberalism such as censorship. In both of these images, however, the bound and gagged women suggest metaphorically that empire acts as a form of violence against Indian integrity; on a more literal level, the intimations of sexual exploitation turn Mutiny-inspired lore about Indian men raping British women on its head by suggesting that Indian women are the ones vulnerable to the predations of British men. These images, then, prefigure the Trevedi cartoon mentioned at the beginning of this chapter (figure 2.1) and, like that one, exploit sexual violence as a bracing metaphor in their political commentary, leaving the lived reality of rape and its connection to political power dynamics to languish at the level of the literal.

FIGURE 2.13 / "A Terrible Cat!" from *Hindi Punch*, June 7, 1908, 16. Asia Pacific and Africa Holdings, British Library. Shelfmark SW238, © British Library Board.

FIGURE 2.14 / "Gagged!" from *Hindi Punch*, May 23, 1907, 17. Asia Pacific and Africa Holdings, British Library. Shelfmark SW238, © British Library Board.

FIGURE 2.15 / "Liberty in Fetters!" from *Hindi Punch*, April 1906, 39. Asia Pacific and Africa Holdings, British Library. Shelfmark SW238, © British Library Board.

Another cartoon from 1907, "The Lyre-(?Liar)-Bird" reverses the accusation of mimicry and irrationality so frequently leveled at the Indian press. The caption, "The Lyrebird is remarkable for its power of imitating the cries and songs of other birds," along with the words that appear as part of the bird's plumage,

FIGURE 2.16 / "The Lyre-(?Liar)-Bird" from *Hindi Punch*, June 30, 1907, 14. Asia Pacific and Africa Holdings, British Library. Shelfmark SW238, © British Library Board.

suggests that the British press and colonial public opinion, rather than Indians, are characterized by mindless imitation, hysteria, and dishonesty ("The Lyre-(?Liar)-Bird," reads the cartoon's title, spelling out the pun to emphasize its blunt accusation and the disparate resonances of such symbols across the Indian Anglosphere).

A similar critique is launched in an image of a witch doctor stirring a cauldron. In figure 2.17, small sticks representing "sedition," "strikes," "riots," and "dissent" are used to produce an enormous conflagration composed, like the plumage of the lyrebird, of "misrepresentation(s) of the truth" and hysterical affects: fear, panic, and above all, a sense of enmity (the rendering of the witch appears to draw on racial caricatures of colonial subjects—both African and Indian—but here the demonic and primitivized witch-doctor figure is identified with the British, in another instance of parody by reversal).

The caption refers to a speech by John Morley, secretary of state to India, to the British House of Parliament in which he says he must speak with reserve because what he says will be heard by "enemies" "thousands of miles away." Who are these enemies, Mr. Punch asks? His answer is that "the Scare Manufacturing Company in India and England" (i.e., the Anglo-Indian and English press explicitly named on the cauldron) "has succeeded in its object of creating a hue and cry in England against the political workers in this country and has poisoned the mind of the English public." This cartoon, then, is significant in its refiguration of disaffection in the public sphere as British rather than Indian.[68]

The cartoons reprinted in this chapter from three different versions of *Punch*—British, Anglo-Indian, and Indian—are only a tiny window onto the infinitely rich world of *Punch*es and of cartoons and caricature in India during the colonial period. But they give a sense of how closely the British, Anglo-Indian, and Indian presses were in conversation in the Indian Anglosphere, and the degree to which the Indian press actively and consciously engaged with the paradoxes of imperial rule and the parameters of the public constructed therein.

Mimicry and parody are both vital concepts for understanding this engagement. Not only are they closely related in terms of how they functioned structurally but also in terms of how they work together in a journal like *Hindi Punch*, which uses parody as a self-conscious form of mimicry. Taking the mimic man and mimicry as its object by commenting on representations of the Indian press, *Hindi Punch*'s parody captures the nuances of the mimetic problem, imitating in order to critique colonial assumptions about imitation. If parody provides valuable information about the style of the original text parodied, as Chatman argues, *Hindi Punch* provides insight not only into the visual-verbal style of *Punch* but into racism-as-style—a series of signifiers that can be imitated, imported from one context to another, and widely circulated in print culture.

---

68. "The Lyre-(?Liar)-Bird," *Hindi Punch*, June 30, 1907, 14; and "Our Enemies," *Hindi Punch*, June 16, 1907, 10.

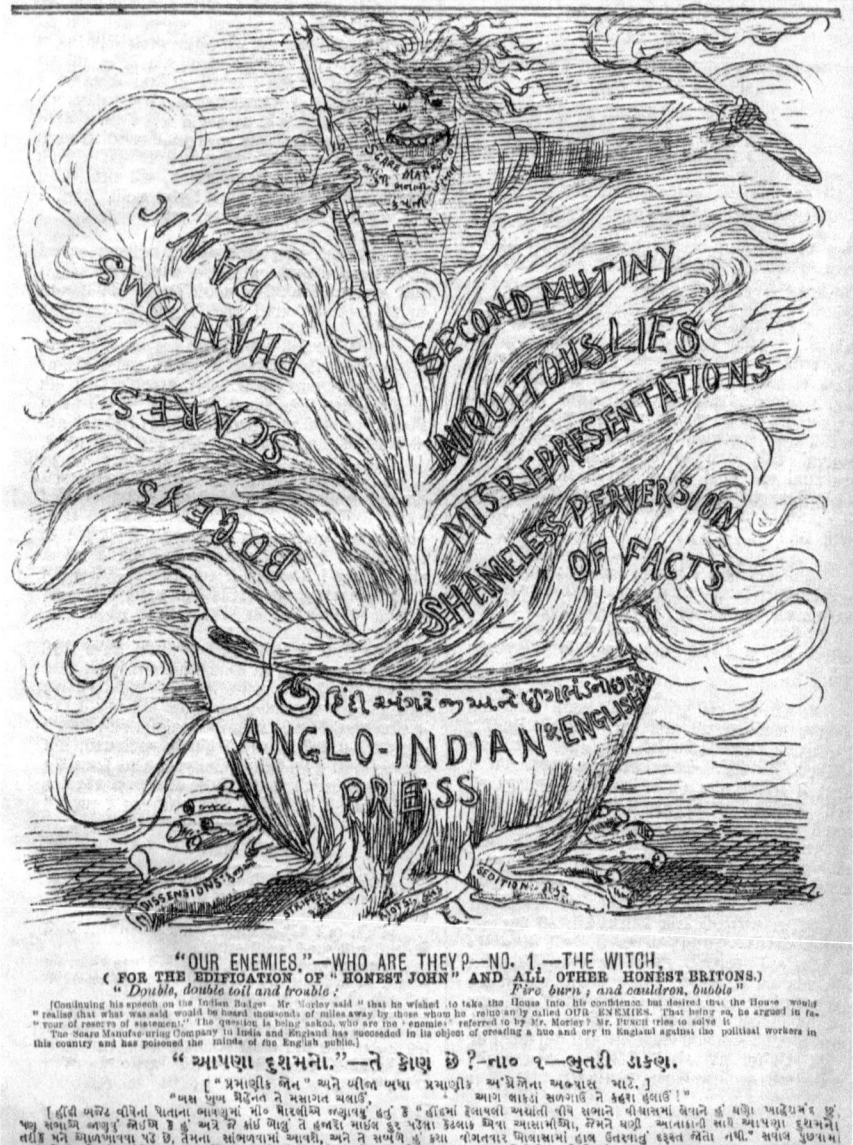

FIGURE 2.17 / "Our Enemies, Who Are They?" from *Hindi Punch*, April 1906, 39. Asia Pacific and Africa Holdings, British Library. Shelfmark SW238, © British Library Board.

Imitating *Punch* also allowed *Hindi Punch* to bypass local colonial hierarchies and address the metropole directly by invoking one of its most recognizable periodicals and thereby to contest the way India was represented, both governmentally and discursively, by the colonial administration. While the legislation against disaffection outlined in Section 124a was ostensibly designed to purge the public sphere of its excesses, the cartoons in *Hindi Punch*, by redrawing that sphere as a space of negative affect and bitter colonial contest, suggest it had the opposite effect. In parodying the forms and stereotypes of colonial discourse, *Hindi Punch* both exposed its logic and positioned it as antidemocratic *and* backward-looking. The critical, parodic distance of the Indian *Punch*, the periodical suggests through its tactical use of images and text, helps make sense of British representations of India, while self-representation within the imperial public sphere reveals itself, knowingly, as always already compromised.

Through the caricature of politicians, national iconography, and racial stereotypes, *Hindi Punch* made visible both the psychic and physical violence of imperialism and racism, so that disaffection became the text rather than subtext of public political discourse. In accounting for the disappearance of the journal in 1930 after its long and relatively successful run, Mitter speculates that it fell too far out of step with the more uncompromising forms of anticolonial nationalism that came to define the 1930s.[69] But looked at through the lens of the modernizing force of parody, the demise of *Hindi Punch* at the moment of nationalism's ascendance can be seen not so much as a failure of its ongoing relevance as the success of its built-in obsolescence.

---

69. Mitter, "*Punch* and Indian Cartoons," 63.

3

REVIEW / Worlding White Supremacy and Indian Nationalism

The law against disaffection was used to stymie and bar anticolonial critique in the Indian press, while racist and emasculating caricatures of the "scribbling classes" were designed to delegitimize and demoralize them. Another effect of this attempt to divide the imperial public sphere along racial lines was the emergence of new mass media forms that made this racial agenda explicit, affecting how audiences were addressed and how information was amassed and presented. This chapter examines how the transformation of white supremacy into a global project at the turn of the century influenced the emergence of two "reviews of reviews" that presented a range of periodicals in digest form in order to turn different forms of imagined community into lived realities.

Benedict Anderson's famous analysis of the novel and the newspaper as forms essential to the imagination of the nation, because they framed a readership brought together in the "homogeneous empty time" of national belonging, proceeds from the assumption that periodicals dwell in the space of the nation that they repeatedly conjure into being. But what about newspapers that traversed national borders by traveling along imperial circuits, addressing and imagining an international community not yet in evidence? As the literary review periodical was remade for what Antoinette Burton and Isabel Hofmeyr call "the imperial commons," its use of "scissors-and-paste" techniques, summary, and assemblage allowed for new and antithetical ideas of community, both imperialist and nationalist, to take shape.[1] In *Ten Books That Shaped the British Empire*, Burton and Hofmeyr argue that nineteenth-century print forms were often "the consequence of a variety of imperial trajectories: upcyclings from pamphlet material or recyclings from scissors-and-paste newspaper clippings—fragments remixed, in turn, through the 'geographically disaggregated networks' that

---

1. On the way periodicals and other publications borrowed from each other using what Hofmeyr, in *Gandhi's Printing Press*, calls "cut and paste" techniques, see Burton and Hofmeyr, *Ten Books*.

constituted the British Empire in its modernizing forms."[2] The imperial commons, as they imagine it, was composed of "forms of reading [that] depended on comparison and circulation, with readers juxtaposing different colonies or different imperial systems via a form which announced that it had come from a periodical elsewhere and was more than likely destined for another. This periodical format and its mode of reading constituted a widespread and homemade global idiom."[3] "Scissors-and-paste" periodicals, alongside books, pamphlets, and other forms of publishing, were thus instrumental in producing imperial publics and counterpublics.[4]

In 1890 W. T. Stead's audacious *Review of Reviews* took the encyclopedic comparativism of the Victorian periodical to its logical conclusion by publishing extracts from a vast array of literary reviews, including European, American, and colonial ones, for a mass audience. The imperialist motivations of Stead's ambitious project were bluntly laid out in his first editorial: by creating a global union of newspaper readers educated in the affairs of the world, the *Review of Reviews* would help "save the English Empire." The fact that this editorial was addressed to "English-speaking folk" was significant, for he used this term as a synonym for white Anglo-Americans, as he made clear in a special issue of the journal ("The Americanization of the World," discussed later in this chapter).

But the *Review* also generated an unofficial, anti-imperial spin-off. In 1905 its synthesizing format was borrowed by a Calcutta publication entitled the *Indian World*. This journal was explicitly and cannily derivative of Stead's, and subverted the global purview of his journal to the ends of Indian independence. Rather than surveying reviews from around the world, it collected articles about India from a series of British and European reviews and also reviewed the contents of noteworthy English-language Indian periodicals in order to create a holistic picture of Anglophone Indian nationalism. By emulating Stead and gaining his approval (Stead wrote a notice to the *Indian World*'s editor saying "I should esteem it a privilege to assist in the success of your admirable undertaking"), it simultaneously gained entrée for itself into the global forum of journalistic discourse that Stead sought to reshape.

While the *Indian World* was partly inspired by Stead's journal, it had an uncanny effect on it. By imitating Stead and inviting his letter of commendation,

---

2. Burton and Hofmeyr, "Introduction: The Spine of Empire?"
3. Burton and Hofmeyr, "Introduction: The Spine of Empire?," 5.
4. Burton and Hofmeyr, "Introduction: The Spine of Empire?," 9.

the journal drew itself into his orbit and became one of the informants on developments in India he cited most often. But it also used the *Review*'s form and its claims to worldliness as a way to mask its anticolonial disaffection as print culture cosmopolitanism, and to contest imperialist and white supremacist visions on the global platform that Stead's journal helped create. Stepping onto this platform through its address to Stead (and thus its subsequent appearance in extracted form in his journal), the *Indian World* was able to reach a larger public, disrupting the whiteness of the international reading public that Stead was trying to materialize. Furthermore, by becoming part of Stead's world, the *Indian World* eventually influenced his views of India and press censorship, unsettling his complacency about the progressive potential of liberal imperialism and making manifest the fissures in his influential vision of a global public sphere.

The Review Journal in the Imperial Commons

In his indispensable analysis of the emergence of eighteenth-century reading audiences, Jon Klancher argues that periodicals were central to the making of publics because they constructed "a knowable community of discourse that united its members and distinguished their social language from that of other audiences."[5] They helped shape "readers' interpretive frameworks and . . . their ideological awareness" and were "always supremely conscious of the audiences their writers imagine, assert, or entice."[6] The nineteenth-century review journal addressed itself to a range of different audiences depending on its political and class affiliations, but because it provided a rich survey of literary and political culture, this audience was most often imagined as a worldly one, educated and widely read enough to seek out a critical overview of significant current thought. Thus, James Basker describes "the highest aims of the learned journals" as "objectivity of treatment through abstract and summary, elevation of tone, selectivity of material, and above all the international cosmopolitanism that transcends national boundaries and defines enlightenment."[7] The Victorian

---

5. Jon Klancher, *The Making of English Reading Audiences, 1790–1832* (Madison: University of Wisconsin Press, 1987), 20.
6. Klancher, *Making of English Reading Audiences*, 4.
7. James Basker, "Criticism and the Rise of Periodical Literature," in *The Cambridge History of Literary Criticism*, vol. 4, *The Eighteenth Century*, edited by H. B. Nisbet and Claude Rawson (Cambridge: Cambridge University Press, 2005), 320.

literary review, an agglomeration of articles on cultural and political issues, book reviews, notices about current events, and advertising, inherited this cluster of cosmopolitan critical norms from Enlightenment print culture, a set of ideals I refer to as "print culture cosmopolitanism."[8]

In British publishing, a publication with "review" in its title was usually a monthly or quarterly journal that provided a forum for important contemporary ideas and political commentary. The *Fortnightly Review*, the *Edinburgh Review*, the *Contemporary Review*, and the *Westminster Review* generated and circulated some of the most influential writing of the period (as did others that followed a similar format without naming themselves reviews, such as *Fraser's Magazine*). Within these publications were numerous individual book reviews that were spun out into full-length essays, often formidable works in their own right: notable examples include William Gladstone's religious critique of *Robert Elsmere*, "The Battle of Belief," published in the *Nineteenth Century* in 1888 and Walter Pater's review of William Morris's *The Earthly Paradise* in the *Westminster Review* in 1868, the last section of which was later published as the famous "Conclusion" to *The Renaissance*.[9]

To review, then—to practice the work of the editor who assembles texts and critics in a way that aims to be representative of a cultural moment, or to provide an assessment of a text in the kind of lofty publications that tend to call themselves reviews—is both to exercise judgment and discernment and to display authority and cultural capital. In his materialist critique of judgment and taste, Pierre Bourdieu names this kind of authority "the authorized speech of status-generated competence, a powerful speech which helps to create what it says."[10] In this light, it seems apt that the verb form of "review" in the *OED* is associated with intellectual exertion (status-generated competence) while the

---

8. Elizabeth Eisenstein's *The Printing Press as an Agent of Change: Communications and Cultural Transformations in Early Modern Europe* (Cambridge: Cambridge University Press, 1979) provides a historical argument for the cosmopolitanism—in terms of circulation and ethos—of Enlightenment print culture in Europe.

9. Laurel Brake's essay, "Literary Criticism and the Victorian Periodical," *Yearbook of English Studies* 16 (1986): 92–116, provides a useful overview of how literary criticism and the periodical form were mutually influential in the Victorian period and how critical styles varied across and within journals.

10. Pierre Bourdieu, *Distinction: A Social Critique of the Judgement of Taste*, trans. Richard Nice (Cambridge, MA: Harvard University Press, 1984), 413.

noun form is associated with a military exercise (the power that accompanies that which can help create what it says):

> review, *n.*
> I. The action or an act of looking over or inspecting. 1. a. An inspection of military or naval forces; *esp.* a ceremonial display and formal inspection of troops or the fleet by a monarch, commander-in-chief, or high-ranking visitor.
> review, *v.*
> 2. a. The action of looking (again) over something, as a book, text, etc., with a view to its correction or improvement; revision.[11]

In reference to the review journal, at once a survey of contemporary thought and a collection of critical judgments, both these denotations have resonance.

In the Indian Anglosphere, the review journal was initially a British cultural import, adapted to the task of assimilating colonial knowledge while paternalistically modeling a civic culture and asserting British values. *Asiatic Researches*, one of the first and most influential British journals in India, was a publication of William Jones's Asiatic Society of Bengal. Its first issue in 1789 interpellated its readers into its project of building an imperial archive: "You will investigate whatever is rare in the stupendous fabric of nature; will correct the geography of Asia by new observations ... will trace the annals ... of these nations ... and bring to light their various forms of government, with their institutions civil and religious."[12] By the nineteenth century, however, English language journals addressed Indian audiences as well. Henry Schwarz's work on aesthetic imperialism highlights the way that literary criticism, as part of a larger project of aesthetic education, was one of the ways that writers sought to "influence the colonial government in the creation of a bourgeois, capitalist, Christian civil society, using the vast publishing industry already in place and mobilizing the alleged Indian disposition for aesthetic literature, in accordance with pseudo-Kantian principles."[13]

Ironically, the secular public sphere that initially emerged alongside Anglo-Indian governance was formed largely by Christian evangelicals and took shape around demands for a policy of religious neutrality on the part of the East India Company, who had initially sought to influence the region through the patronage

---

11. "review, n.," *OED Online*, accessed June 28, 2017, http://www.oed.com/view/Entry/164850?rskey=5bYCRL&result=1&isAdvanced=false.
12. Klancher, *Making of English Reading Audiences*, 25.
13. Schwarz, "Aesthetic Imperialism," 573.

of Hindu institutions. The aim of these evangelicals was "not to be hindered by the state in their efforts to convert people in the free market of opinion and [ideally] to have that aim supported by the state."[14] The *Calcutta Review* is a good example of this endeavor. Founded in 1844 by a British military historian and colonial administrator, Sir John Kaye, and a missionary, Rev. Alexander Duff, the *Calcutta Review* changed editorial hands several times before finding a permanent home at the University of Calcutta in 1921, where it is still being published.[15] Along with similar Anglo-Indian publications, the *Calcutta Review*, whose editorial boards "were largely staffed with clergymen," served as a supposedly neutral space in which to engage the educated Indian bourgeoisie in a rational debate about the relative merits of the Hindu and Christian faiths— a debate within which Hinduism and Christianity were typically identified respectively with fiction and fact, poetry and prose, irrationality and rationality, tradition and modernity, and autocracy and democracy.[16]

For example, when reviewing an English translation of a Sanskrit poem published in the *Calcutta Review*, the writer remarks of Hindu religious texts that "all is dreamy and visionary.... The relation between cause and effect is utterly overlooked."[17] Quoting the translator, the reviewer concurs with him that indulgence in poetic ingenuities has "diverted [Hindu] minds from that correct and dignified style of *prose* composition in which the Greek and Latin writers (and *we* add, those of all other western nations) so much excel them; and which, to a nation, is of far greater importance than all the embellishments of poetry."[18] Another review article, entitled "Transition States of the Hindu Mind," noted that Hindu sages are "possessed of a poetic and contemplative imagination in common with all Asiatic philosophers—ignorant of that inductive and analytic process of reasoning which is the glory of modern science, and little disposed to test out their aphorisms by laborious experiments."[19] Pieces such as these drew attention to the ways the review periodical, with its emphasis on nonfiction, rational discourse, and the cross-cultural comparison of ideas, served as a useful vehicle

---

14. van der Veer, *Imperial Encounters*, 22.
15. The University of Calcutta maintains a useful website documenting the periodical's history (http://www.caluniv.ac.in/academic/arts_english.htm#research).
16. See Schwarz, "Aesthetic Imperialism."
17. "Art I. The Nalodaya or History of King Nala, a Sanskrit Poem by Kálidàsa. Accompanied with a Metrical Translation, an Essay on Alliteration, an Account of Other Similar Works, and a Grammatical Analysis. By W. Yates," *Calcutta Review* 3, no. 5 (January 1845): 1–36, 13.
18. "Art I. The Nalodaya or History of King Nala," 33 (original emphasis).
19. "Transition States of the Hindu Mind," *Calcutta Review* 3, no. 5 (January 1845): 102–47, 105.

for Anglicization. The cosmopolitanism of British print culture was demonstrated pedagogically through its juxtaposition with Hindu obscurantism.

By progressively including more and more Indian writers in its issues over the course of the nineteenth century, however, the *Calcutta Review* and other Anglophone reviews strove to become the face of gradualist, liberal change—change that was understood to proceed from a transnational dialogue moderated by the British press. Increasingly, however, reviews that published both Indian and British authors became forums in which Indians could lay claim to the rights of citizens in a global public sphere by performing the roles of critics. By the end of the century, as well as writing for extant publications such as the *Calcutta Review*, Indian critics could also publish in a range of Indian-owned English-language reviews, such as the *Modern Review* and *East and West* (see chapter 4). While modeled on the British review periodical, these Anglophone Indian periodicals were designed to reject British paternalism by modeling self-determination and bringing into view a vibrant modern Indian culture that negated the depictions of Indian backwardness in the Anglo-Indian press.

For example, in an 1879 article on "British Rule in India," Syed Mahmood (the first Muslim to serve as a high court judge under the Raj) points to racial inequities across the imperial community when he complains of references to "our Indian subjects" in the British press: "We do not remember ever hearing Englishmen employ the expression 'our subjects' towards the people of Canada or Australia," he notes.[20] A book-length article serialized in the *Calcutta Review* in 1890, "An Introduction to the Study of Hinduism" by Guru Prosad Sen, also targeted the fallacy of print culture cosmopolitanism. Sen took issue with the characterization of Hinduism in earlier versions of the journal, when it was dominated by Anglo-Indian writers. Parodying the evolutionary language that situated the glories of Indian civilization irretrievably in the past, he states that "it is interesting to observe the various phrases through which the minds of educated Indians have passed [in relation to this idea].... The earliest stage was to take the result of European thought, even though not strictly scientific, on trust." Disdainful of the quietism produced by this trust, Sen names it "a kind of cosmopolitanism which ... is no better than cynicism."[21]

---

20. As Sukanya Banerjee has shown, the Queen's Proclamation of 1858, which spoke of extending to India "the same obligation of duty which binds us to all our other subjects," was seized upon as a text that seemed to promise Indians the same right to governmental representation that pertained in the white settler colonies. Sukanya Banerjee, *Becoming Imperial Citizens*, 22.

21. Guru Prosad Sen, "An Introduction to the Study of Hinduism," *Calcutta Review* 91, no. 182 (October 1890): 226.

Efforts to expose the ways in which liberal universalist ideals masked the racist paternalism of the imperial public sphere happened on the level of form as well as content, as we have seen in the case of *Hindi Punch*. W. T. Stead's *Review of Reviews* and the *Indian World*, because they surveyed reviews, which themselves surveyed literary culture, were also significant interventions in the Indian Anglosphere, and classic examples of the kind of "scissors and paste" journalism that thrived in the messy, multitudinous space of the imperial commons.

Worlding White Supremacy

Launched in 1890, the *Review of Reviews* addressed—and helped create—a certain vision of the imperial public sphere by attempting to provide a comprehensive redaction of journalistic writing from around the world. Experimental in its metaform, it set out to review, extract, index, and synthesize all major English monthly periodicals (such as the *Fortnightly Review* and the *Westminster Review*), as well as some American and European ones. The *Review*'s globalizing mission was evident in all aspects of its endeavor. It was a monthly, and focused on reviewing other monthlies, because Stead believed this to be a necessary interval for global circulation; he also chose its price of sixpence in order to promote its "universal accessibility." Like other publications that made up the imperial commons, it "routinely depended on extant copy, which was selected, fragmented, re-phrased, listed and re-circulated."[22] Before it foundered under his financial mismanagement, it was considered a commercial success, selling a robust 220,000 copies a month by 1897.[23]

In Victorian studies, Stead is best known for helping to invent muckraking journalism through a series of articles about child prostitution and white slavery collectively entitled "The Maiden Tribute of Modern Babylon." In order to publicize his exposé, Stead arranged to "purchase" a thirteen-year-old girl, Eliza Armstrong, from a chimney sweep in order to show how easy it was. The stunt was a success: his paper, the *Pall Mall Gazette*, sold out and his articles have been credited with helping to pass the Criminal Law Amendment Act of 1885 which raised the

---

22. Laurel Brake, "Stead Alone: Journalist, Proprietor, and Publisher 1890–1903," in Brake et al., *W. T. Stead*, 84.
23. J. O. Baylen, "Review of Reviews Office," in *Dictionary of Literary Biography*, vol. 112, *British Literary Publishing Houses 1881–1965*, ed. Jonathan Rose and Patricia J. Anderson (Detroit, MI: Gale Research, 1994), 266. For another useful overview of Stead's work on the *Review* by Baylen, see "W. T. Stead as Publisher and Editor of the 'Review of Reviews,'" *Victorian Periodicals Review* 12, no. 2 (Summer 1979): 70–84.

age of consent from thirteen to sixteen—but which also produced new legislation criminalizing prostitution and homosexuality (see chapter 1). Stead was eventually charged with abduction for his "purchase"; the girl's father's permission had not been sought and her mother claimed she was misinformed about the nature of the sale, so Stead ended up serving three months in prison. The way Stead became the victim of the very disciplinary system he was attempting to strengthen in the "Maiden Tribute" scandal prefigures the unintended consequences the *Review of Review*'s engagement with Indian journalism would have for him; as we will see, his imperialist venture, designed to bolster and extend Britain's role in the colonies and the world, would also land him on the wrong side of the law.

Though feminist scholarship of the 1990s drew ample attention to the Maiden Tribute scandal as a pivotal moment in the history of gender and sexuality, another scandal is visible in plain sight: the fact that the *Review of Reviews* was an attempt to create a white supremacist empire in print. Stead started the *Review of Reviews* in 1890 with George Newnes, proprietor of *Tit-Bits*, another publication that extracted information from a wide range of books and periodicals and presented it in condensed form for mass consumption. Stead was already renowned in the world of British publishing for his work as editor of the *Northern Echo* and the *Pall Mall Gazette*, as well as for the "Maiden Tribute" scandal. His work was influentially dubbed the "New Journalism" by Matthew Arnold, who accused Stead's muckraking form of reportage of being "featherbrained." By favoring dramatic storytelling over the truth, Arnold argued, Stead was miseducating the increasingly literate working classes:

> We have had opportunities of observing a new journalism which a clever and energetic man has lately invented. It has much to recommend it; it is full of ability, novelty, variety, sensation, sympathy, generous instincts; its one great fault is that it is feather-brained. It throws out assertions at a venture because it wishes them true; does not correct either them or itself, if they are false; and to get at the state of things as they truly are seems to feel no concern whatever. Well, the democracy, with abundance of life, movement, sympathy, good instincts, is disposed to be, like this journalism, feather-brained; just as the upper class is disposed to be selfish in its politics, and the middle class narrow.[24]

Stead was undaunted by Arnold's disdain, however, for he began the first issue of the *Review of Reviews* by evoking Arnold's famous definition of culture ("the

---

24. Matthew Arnold, "Up to Easter," *Nineteenth Century* 73 (May 1887): 629–43.

best that is known and thought in the world") in his claim that his periodical would "make the best thoughts of the best writers in our periodicals universally accessible."[25] By glossing Arnold, the *Review* was also echoing Newnes's introduction to *Tit-Bits* in 1881, which promised that the journal would amass "the best things that have ever been said and written."[26] As Richard Menke has suggested, Newnes adapted this idea of culture from Arnold's. But rather than focusing on that which has "timeless literary value" as Arnold sought to, *Tit-Bits* strove for a broad audience by offering "light diversion rather than important news, intellectual edification, or cultured leisure." Despite the difference between Newnes's and Arnold's ideas of what kind of text should reach the "new mass education market of the 1880s," Menke argues, they both depended on excerpting to address that market, for Arnold's "The Study of Poetry" used fragments of poems, or "touchstones," to give a sense of what counted as excellence in poetry.[27]

In Stead's case, excerpting was a means to bring different parts of the world's knowledge into proximity so as to make his publication as synthetic an image of global thought as possible. While the "best things" were inevitably British, Arnold's writing on criticism also evoked Enlightenment values of comparative critique when he argued that "the English critic of literature ... must dwell much on foreign thought."[28] The *Review* followed Arnold's lead in this view of cultured reading as well, for it published extracts from a wide array of literary reviews. Stead profiled German, French, Italian, Russian, and American as well as British reviews and also devoted space to coverage of the Indian press and colonial affairs more broadly.

Stead's deployment of Arnold's definition of culture was just one of many universalizing discourses he used in the *Review*, which was at once international, imperialist, and populist. However, unlike Arnold's Enlightenment-derived cosmopolitanism, which imagined culture as an exchange within a world republic of letters, Stead's internationalism was more geopolitical in outlook and instrumentalist in execution, motivated in part by his prescient fear of large-scale war in the coming century. He promoted his version of cosmopolitanism ardently, both through the form of his periodical and other venues: he became involved

---

25. Matthew Arnold, "The Function of Criticism at the Present Time," in *Poetry and Criticism of Matthew Arnold*, ed. A. Dwight Culler (Boston, MA: Houghton, 1961): 237–59, 246.
26. Richard Menke, "Touchstones to Tit-Bits: Extracting Culture in the 1880s," *Victorian Periodicals Review* 47, no. 4 (Winter 2014): 559–76.
27. Menke, "Touchstones to Tit-Bits," 568.
28. M. Arnold, "Function of Criticism," 246, 256.

with the Hague Peace Conference of 1899, championed pacifist organizations, and wrote frequently in support of Esperanto (the international language invented as a contribution to world harmony). He also experimented with a short-lived journal called *War against War: A Chronicle of the International Crusade for Peace*. The *Review of Reviews*, then, was at once a repository of British thought, and an attempt to give shape to a global network of political and cultural activity.

The globe that appeared on its cover makes these aspirations clear, along with the scope of the articles highlighted in the list above the title. As Laurel Brake points out, "Stead's commitment to the global character of journalism" was reflected in the use of the globe not only on the cover but also "as the principle graphic image for the firm, the journal and the monthly and annual indexes that followed."[29] Stead's monthly column "The Progress of the World" provided a narrative summary of the global overview the journal aspired to, while a page listing highlights from a range of literary journals both local and foreign gave a composite picture of elite periodical culture. While these aspects of the journal provided condensed snapshots of a world republic of letters, Stead used the journal to encourage looser networks of connection as well. One proposed project, for instance, sought to link lonely people up to each other through the journal's correspondence section, and another encouraged readers to trade different monthly issues with each other if they could not afford to buy more than one (both projects drew on the idea behind the *Link*, a periodical he cofounded with Annie Besant in 1888 in an effort to link social activists across local communities).

In its attempts to make itself a vital repository of Anglocentric knowledge and a web of connections that spanned the globe—to provide a literary corollary to the political and cultural project of empire in other words—the *Review* took a redactive approach to content, focusing on lists and summaries of articles rather than full-length pieces. This also furthered its goal of educating the busy worker by encouraging skimming rather than analysis, and information gathering rather than immersion—reviewing in the style of militaristic inspection (*OED* noun) rather than critical practice (*OED* verb).

On the surface, with its reference to a more global range of subjects and its sampling of diverse editorial visions extracted from different reviews, the *Review of Reviews* seemed to be a more multivocal reflection of British cultural discourses

---

29. Brake, "Stead Alone," 78.

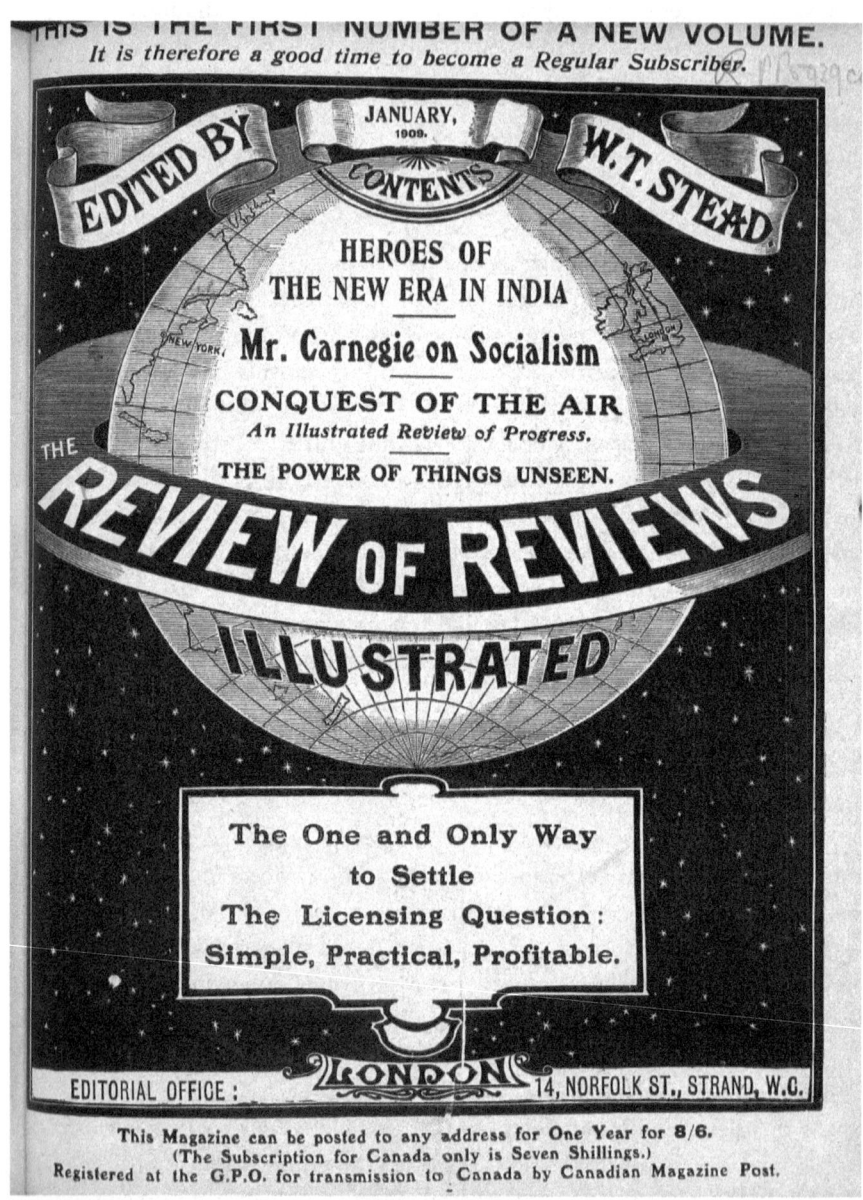

FIGURE 3.1 / Cover of *Review of Reviews*, vol. 29, January 1909, 585. General Reference Collection, British Library. Shelfmark P.P.6365.d., © British Library Board.

than that found in the average monthly. Yet Stead's editorial voice permeated the paper, much of which he wrote himself, and proffered his own interpretations of the issues covered.[30] Readers were thus discouraged from active critical engagement with the articles in the review which, as isolated fragments of long-form and ongoing conversations in other journals, were already decontextualized. On the one hand, his attempt to offer working people a window onto a larger world reflected Stead's populist outlook; on the other, it functioned as a mini-empire unto itself, with Stead at the helm. Aspiring in his editorial role to the overview of an omniscient narrator, Stead declared "The ideal of the journalist should be . . . to know every one and to hear everything." In attaining this ideal, he argued, the successful editor will have such "far-extended influence and world-shaping power" that he will "influence the destinies of the human race" and ultimately be the "most permanently influential Englishman in the Empire."[31] The centrality of the word "influence" to his vision of journalism speaks to the grandiosity of his vision; Stead literally wanted to change the world and believed he could do this by generating what he dubbed a "civic faith" in politics through the assimilation and circulation of print culture.[32] He imagined his journal read across the world "as men used to read their Bibles . . . to discover the will of God and their duty to man."[33]

Stead's influential essays "The Future of Journalism" and "Government by Journalism" (both published in the *Contemporary Review* in 1886) also made it clear that he saw his journalism as a crucial mediator between the government and the public and thus essential to the progress of democracy:[34] "The telegraph and the printing-press have converted Great Britain into one vast agora, or assembly of the whole community, in which the discussion of the affairs of State is carried on from day to day in the hearing of the whole people."[35] It is telling that the "agora," in this modern iteration, is one in which the public is comparatively

---

30. Baylen notes that Stead's business manager estimated that "Stead personally wrote and dictated over 80,000 letters during the period 1890–1912, in addition to personally writing the monthly 'Progress of the World' and 'Character Sketches,' generally the 'Book of the Month,' and numerous articles for the periodical and daily press." Brake, "Stead Alone," 76.
31. W. T. Stead, "The Future of Journalism," *Contemporary Review* 50 (November 1886): 663–70.
32. W. T. Stead, "To All English-Speaking Folk," *Review of Reviews* 1, no. 1 (January 1890): 15.
33. Stead, "To All English-Speaking Folk," 20.
34. For further discussion of these essays and their role in Stead's vision of the public sphere, see Graham Law and Matthew Sterenberg, "Old vs. New Journalism and the Public Sphere; or, Habermas Encounters Dallas and Stead," *19: Interdisciplinary Studies in the Long Nineteenth Century* 16 (2013), http://doi.org/10.16995/ntn.657.
35. W. T. Stead, "Government by Journalism," *Contemporary Review* 49 (May 1888): 653–74, 653.

passive since, for Stead, democracy functioned as a tool in the service of the Anglo-American world domination his journal hoped to promote. Global leadership, he argued, required a more robustly educated populace, now that colonized people were increasingly agitating for self-determination. Championing the kind of gradualist reform advocated by liberal supporters of empire, Stead noted darkly that imperial subjects "if not enfranchised and brought within the pale by being allowed a voice in deciding the policy of the Government of the Empire . . . will inevitably seek enfranchisement in another direction."[36]

Part of his *Review*'s function, then, was to prepare all English-speaking peoples to lead a future Anglo federation based on a simultaneously expanding and liberalizing empire—a structure that would preserve British hegemony through a strategic alliance with America. This plan, he believed, was necessary to "the salvation of the world" because "the English-speaking race is one of the chief of God's chosen agents for executing coming improvements in the lot of mankind."[37] Gauri Viswanathan's work has demonstrated how English culture and literature became the secular tools of choice in the conversion of Indians to English subjects by the mid-nineteenth century.[38] In Stead's version of the imperial educative project, however, it was not colonized subjects but English ones that were most desperately in need of conversion—from being a slum-dwelling drain on the nation to a lucrative member of the colonial ruling class—through a sense of their own formidable destiny and heritage:[39] "That red-haired hobbledehoy, smoking his short pipe at the corner of Seven Dials, may two years hence be the red-coated representative of the might and majesty of Britain in the midst of a myriad of Africans or Asiatics."[40]

This destiny was, for Stead, explicitly racialized because his internationalism was both complemented and compromised by his dedication to an exclusively white, Anglocentric version of imperialism. His promotion of Esperanto, for example, was eclipsed by the importance he placed on English in his publication, not just as a world language but as the basis for the new form of global empire

---

36. Stead, "To All English-Speaking Folk," 13.
37. Stead, "To All English-Speaking Folk," 17. Stead understood "salvation of the world" in both secular and religious terms, as indicated by his use of the phrase in his publication *The Americanization of the World* (London: Review of Reviews Office, 1902), and his idea that it was the duty of the English-speaking race to "secure the peace of the world."
38. Viswanathan, *Masks of Conquest*.
39. On how this sense of destiny operated in settler colonial contexts, see Jason Rudy, *Imagined Homelands: British Poetry in the Colonies* (Baltimore: Johns Hopkins University Press, 2017).
40. Stead, "To All English-Speaking Folk," 16.

he envisioned. Hence the article addressed "To All English-Speaking Folk" in the first issue of the *Review* made it clear that the journal's mission was to help create a global union of the white readers it addressed, and to educate them in the affairs of the world so that they might "save the English-speaking race": a bizarre term linking language and race to name white Anglo-America and the settler colonies that would later be taken up by Winston Churchill in the service of his own vision of Anglophone world domination (delineated in his four-volume tome, *A History of the English-Speaking Peoples*).[41]

Like Churchill, Stead imagined "a great federation of English-speaking commonwealths" that would include America as well as the settler colonies; in this vision, he was heavily influenced by the "Greater Britain" imaginary that effloresced at the end of the century, when the "Scramble for Africa" and other forms of imperial competition on the Continent brought the persistence of British global hegemony into question. Proponents of a Greater Britain believed that Britain and its settler colonies would function best as "a single transcontinental political community, [or] even ... a global federal state."[42] Stead's ideas for imperial federation went even further. In the *Review of Reviews* annual of 1902 entitled *The Americanization of the World, or the Trend of the Twentieth Century*, he laid out in detail his ideas for how to preserve the empire through a strategic Western alliance. The only way to preempt the eclipse of British by American power and avoid the competition, or full-scale war, that might ensue would be to pursue "the great ideal of Race Union" and unite both powers.[43] *The Americanization of the World* was a comprehensive geopolitical survey of the world at the turn of the century and a series of predictions based on this analysis that lent support and urgency to his argument. The idea of imperial federation was not an intellectual dalliance for Stead, then, but the motivation for much of his work; "When it came to imperial federation, Stead expounded the same views consistently and over a period of decades," Simon Potter notes.[44]

In both his address "To all English-Speaking Folk" in the *Review* and in the special annual on Americanization, Stead made it clear that "English-speaking" was a racialized geopolitical term: "The real kernel and nucleus of both States is to be found in their white citizens. The mutual influence of Britain on America

---

41. Stead, "To All English-Speaking Folk," 19.
42. See Duncan Bell, *The Idea of Greater Britain: Empire and the Future of World Order, 1860–1900* (Princeton, NJ: Princeton University Press, 2007), 1.
43. Stead, *Americanization of the World*, 5.
44. Simon J. Potter, "W. T. Stead, Imperial Federation and the South African War," in Brake et al., *W. T. Stead*, 117.

and of America on England depends upon the number and the intelligence of their citizens and the intensity of their cohesion. That cohesion is not necessarily geographical. It is in its essence moral, emotional, and intellectual."[45] Comparing British and American populations, he subtracts people of African descent from the American population and counts only white British people across the empire as subjects, arguing that "if anyone objects that we have not included the myriads of India among British subjects, the answer is easy.... The right of leadership does not depend upon how many millions ... of colored people we have compelled to pay us taxes. It depends upon the power, the skill, the wealth, the numbers of ... white citizens of the self-governing State."[46] His support for Irish Home Rule and critique of the Boer War derived from the fact that he saw these colonial entrenchments as "the Achilles heel of the Empire."[47] Citing America's history as a self-liberated colony as the reason for its advancement, he argued throughout *Americanization* for self-governance as a key principle of progress, but only in reference to white colonies (at least for the foreseeable future). An article reprinted in the *Review* entitled "What Is My Duty to the People of India?," first written for the Indian periodical *East and West*, suggests some sympathy for Indian nationalism but also cites political "superiority" and the benevolent effects of British paternalism as the reason why Indians must remain under colonial rule indefinitely.[48]

A map that appeared in the annual entitled "The Possessions of the English-Speaking Race" demonstrates in stark visual terms that "English-speaking" does not include those "compelled to pay us taxes" but settler colonials, Americans, and British subjects, those who are, at least nominally, "self-governing" rather than fully colonized.

Ample facts, figures, and charts bolster Stead's racial geopolitics, as he lays out the facts of colonial appropriation in language that both emphasizes its brutality and presents it as the incontestable logic of white supremacy: "The English-speaking States, with a population of 121,000,000 self-governing white citizens govern 353,000,000 of Asiatics and Africans. Under their allied flags

---

45. Stead, *Americanization of the World*, 19.
46. Stead, *Americanization of the World*, 5.
47. In his declamation that just "as a father endeavors to make his son an independent man, so English dominion in India ought to have as its ultimate aim the establishment of the principle of self-government," Stead suggests that independence is still a long way off. Stead, *Americanization of the World*, 21.
48. W. T. Stead, "What Is My Duty to the People of India," *Review of Reviews* (December 1901): 616.

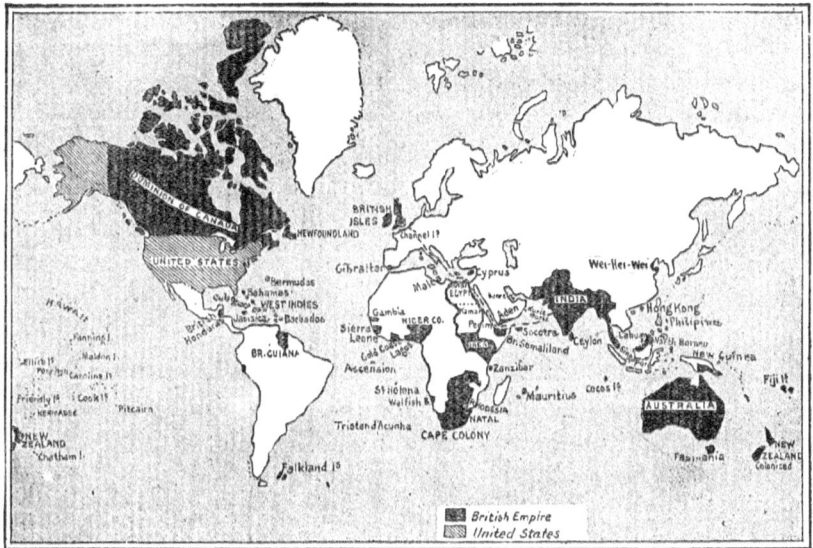

THE POSSESSIONS OF THE ENGLISH-SPEAKING RACE. "Here sit the people of one language."—SIR GEO. GREY.

FIGURE 3.2 / "The Possessions of the English Speaking Race" from W. T Stead, *The Americanization of the World* (New York: H. Markley, 1902), Internet Archive, https://archive.org/details/americanizationo01stea.

labour one-third of the human race. . . . Of the dry land, they have occupied and are ruling all the richest territories in three continents. With the exception of Siberia they have seized all the best gold-mines of the world. There is hardly a region where white men can breed and live and thrive that they have not appropriated. They have picked out the eyes of every continent."[49] At the end of one section of this narrative and statistical account of Anglo-American global dominance, Stead concludes: "The lion's share of the world is ours, not only in bulk but in tit-bits also."[50]

The fact that "tit-bits," the name of Newnes's journal, is repurposed as a geopolitical reference here is significant. "Tit-bits," and their amassing into a "bulk" that represented a "lion's share" of knowledge in the service of imperial power and white supremacy was how Stead, with Newnes at his side, imagined the work of his journal and how he believed it would lubricate and shape the future of

49. Stead, *Americanization of the World*, 9.
50. Stead, *Americanization of the World*, 10.

empire. If the English language and the Arnoldian cultural values that Stead attached to it were to spread across the world, becoming severed from place and cultural specificity in the process, the journal's encyclopedic form would serve as a repository of Englishness, distilling and assembling the best of British culture. Two non-British spin-offs of the *Review*, the *American Review of Reviews* and the *Australasian Review of Reviews*, would help preserve cultural specificity in those regions while generating more connections across the so-called English-speaking world. In this way, Stead's newspaper empire might support not only the Greater Britain project but also the white supremacist ideology that underwrote it.

As Andrew Griffiths has argued, the sensationalism of the New Journalism and the jingoism and scientized racism of the New Imperialism were closely linked in Stead's work (and were more broadly linked together "in a mutually supportive cycle" by the 1880s).[51] Stories from imperial campaigns and battles helped provide sensational news stories, while these in turn helped stir up imperialist sentiment among a burgeoning readership. The new media forms created by enterprising journalists like Stead, with their savvy appeal to a mass audience, were also crucial to the shape of the New Imperialism. In her work on imperial publics, Karin Barber describes the relationship between address and genre as follows: "New forms of address are the key to new genres. New genres take shape as writers/composers of texts convoke new audiences (or old audiences in new ways)."[52] Stead's *Review of Reviews* helped usher in a new form of global journalism—simultaneously fragmented and totalizing—that is now most often identified with the internet and internationally influential sites such as Reuters or CNN.

To say that Stead's global vision both imaginatively and materially anticipated the world wide web—and its contribution to contemporary neoimperialism and white supremacy—would not be a stretch. The fact that he exclusively addressed "English-speaking folks," or white Anglo-Americans, in his contribution to this new genre identified it squarely with the audience to which much Anglophone writing is still tacitly addressed. In both address and form, then, Stead's journal created an image of the world governed by an Anglo-American political alliance whose values would be upheld by Anglo-American liberal culture. Amalgamating a month's worth of news and commentary from a stunningly wide range of

---

51. Andrew Griffiths, *The New Journalism, the New Imperialism and the Fiction of Empire, 1870–1900* (Houndsmills, Basingstoke: Palgrave, 2015), 12.

52. Karin Barber, *The Anthropology of Texts, Persons, and Publics* (Cambridge: Cambridge University Press, 2007), 138.

sources into a single issue, the *Review* compressed space and arrested time in a way which made that image tangible and its racism enduringly potent.

Worlding Indian Nationalism

Only a few years after its first appearance, the redactive format of Stead's periodical was borrowed by a publication entitled the *Indian World*. Edited by Prithwis Chandra Ray, the journal was published in Calcutta from 1905 to 1912. Like Stead's journal, the *Indian World* was a monthly that devoted the majority of its content to reviewing other reviews, summarizing their content, and reprinting choice selections. It also mirrored Stead's *Review* by having a section entitled "Notable Articles of the Month" as well as a "Progress of the World" column similar to his, with a diary for each month surveying major political events.

Just as the early issues of the *Review of Reviews* were filled with "autographs"—blurbs written by famous figures greeting its arrival and commending Stead on his project—the *Indian World* presented a range of complimentary "opinions" on its opening page, including the one from Stead cited earlier ("I should esteem it a privilege to assist in the success of your admirable undertaking. I sincerely wish you all success"). Stead also profiled the *Indian World* in his journal, calling it, paternalistically, "a plucky attempt to create the *Review of Reviews* for the Indian World."[53]

Other publications cited in the "Notices" section of the *Indian World* highlighted the resemblance to the *Review* as well. The British periodical the *Statesman* described Ray's review as "a new and ambitious publication which, in spite of the modesty of its advertisement, aspires to fulfill in India the function which Mr. Stead and the *Review of Reviews* perform with reference to the Empire at large." The *Englishman* also noted the *Indian World*'s resemblance to the *Review*, along with its "modesty" and "judicious and detached tone." As evidence of this modesty, it cited the placing of the editorial notes at the back of the paper, when the common practice of most journals, "and [of] Mr. Stead not least," it added archly, was to allot them "the first and foremost place." The *Indian World*'s "modest" self-presentation and balanced tone may have been an attempt to present itself as a model of English influence and liberal, rational values—a successful incarnation of empire's educative mission. But this so-called modesty, along with

---

53. W. T. Stead, "The Reviews Reviewed: *The Indian World*," *Review of Reviews* 32, no. 187 (July 1905): 83.

the mantle of Stead's approval, would also have helped it fly under the radar of British censorship. In a self-advertisement published in one of its issues, the *Indian World* compares itself to Stead's journal as a way to emphasize its respectability, as well as its influence: "[The *Indian World*] is now the recognized *Review of Reviews* of India and has many features in common with Mr. Stead's world-renowned organ."

Imitating Stead may have seemed merely like a legitimizing move (to censors, for example) but it served the paper's nationalist purposes well: the reviewing reviews format, as Stead's deployment of it illustrated, was useful to the work of cultural consolidation. Rather than surveying reviews from around the world, however, the *Indian World* collected articles about India from a series of British and European reviews and also redacted the contents of noteworthy Anglophone Indian periodicals.

Ray's focus on India as the subject matter that unified the different kinds of reviews he extracted, as opposed to a universalist understanding of culture, had two interrelated effects. First, many of the selections from articles on India extracted from British, European, and American reviews were sympathetic to Indian nationalism (if often in attenuated or compromised ways) and helped create an image of India as a modern dynamic subject of contemporary critical discourse, in direct contrast to the antiquated and stagnant version of India found in Orientalist and missionary writing in Anglo-Indian publications. Second, if the Indian nation was called into being by its existence as the subject of criticism, the *Indian World* also represented India as a critical subject. Through its practice of reviewing prominent English-language Indian monthlies that regularly published nationalist critiques of British rule, the journal also highlighted, and helped consolidate, a forceful discourse of dissent.

The *Indian World* thus reversed the formal effects of Stead's journal. As opposed to an image of a world of "English-speaking folk" with the British nation at its center, it hypothesized an Indian nation situated within a world republic of letters. By assimilating and reviewing contemporary discourses on India, the journal's format contributed to a sense of India as a modern subject—unitary but self-reflective—that was crucial to the performance of national identity on the world stage (the lasting effect of this kind of move is visible in what critics describe as the English-dominated and "deracinated cosmopolitan" nature of the present "globalized South Asian literary scene").[54]

---

54. Sarah Brouillette uses these terms to summarize the ways Aijaz Ahmad and others critique Indian literature in English. But she also shows how they romanticize local vernacular literature,

Despite its riff on Stead's imperial project, then, the *Indian World* was a looking-glass version of it, with an anti-imperial, nationalist agenda that reversed and opposed the goals of Stead's paper. Its first issue stated that "the *Indian World* shall not concern itself with any subject that does not bear upon India—directly or indirectly." In his efforts to make his journal embody India on every level—materially, as well as in content and form—Ray at one point printed an apology that read: "We are sorry that, in spite of our best efforts to obtain countrymade antique paper for this review, we have failed to procure any.... We have therefore been obliged to print this number of *The Indian World* on foreign paper." In this way, the journal identified itself explicitly with the emergent Swadeshi movement, which saw economic self-sufficiency as essential to national self-determination (see ad for "Gupta's Teas," figure. 3.3).

Several different review functions were performed by Ray's journal. Its survey-like review of India in the world press elevated the spectral image of a modern Indian nation that was constantly belittled by the Anglo-Indian press. A complementary focus on Indian periodicals, meanwhile, helped outline a counterpublic within the Indian Anglosphere. Furthermore, the process of editorial selection, compression, and summary that the "review of reviews" format demanded allowed Ray to reproduce the most explicitly nationalist articles and the most rhetorically powerful parts of them. In his way, his journal takes on a potent critical tone that emphasizes the corrective function of the "reviewing" process—for, while most of the English-language Indian reviews it surveyed were literary in outlook, the commonest targets of their critiques were aspects of British rule and British attitudes toward Indian culture.

The review of reviews format thus enabled Ray to create a much more focused and homogenized overview of nationalist and anticolonial critique than that found in its contemporaries. Even more significantly, the title of his periodical proposed that this conversation represented the "Indian World" as a whole. Just as Stead's review format was useful to Ray's project, so was the world-encompassing outlook that underwrote it. The "world" of Ray's title functioned as a synecdoche for nation, a word he could not yet use, and simultaneously put India center stage in a picture of global periodical circulation diametrically opposed to Stead's, drawing attention to India as a cosmopolitan culture in its own right.

---

obscuring the way it is itself subject to the market logic of globalization. See Sarah Brouillette, "South Asian Literature and Global Publishing," *Wasafari* 22, no. 3 (2007): 34–38, 35.

FIGURE 3.3 / Advertisement for Gupta's Tea in the *Indian World*. General Reference Collection, British Library. Shelfmark P.P.3779.hfb., © British Library Board.

One of the reasons cosmopolitanism played an important role in the formation of Indian nationalism was that it undermined the British argument that India's internal divisions of caste and religion necessitated imperial supervision. Many nationalists, therefore, increasingly used Indian diversity as an argument in favor of the country's unique modernity: India, unlike Western Europe, the argument went, had already learned to live with difference. The journal also stressed its cosmopolitan version of nationalism through a series of articles on the nationalist leader Sister Nivedita. Nivedita (originally Margaret Noble) was a Scots-Irish woman whose tactics for promoting Indian nationalism drew upon those of the Irish literary revival; she consequently saw the arts as central to the project of nationalist consolidation. Writing on what she labeled "cosmo-nationalism," she called for a "great literature which can not 'only utter India to the world but also . . . voice India to herself." Though the journal was not necessarily the kind of literature she had in mind, it performed exactly this task—accumulating and reifying a critical Indian voice and situating this voice within a global discursive field.

The *Indian World*'s role as a survey of other periodicals in the Indian Anglosphere also made it well-positioned to comment on India's representation in the English and Anglo-Indian press, which both fostered, and was a focal point of, anti-colonial discourse. In this way, it resembled *Hindi Punch*, whose satirical format offered similar opportunities for metacommentary. In 1907 an editorial column in the paper contained a full-blown critique of the way India was portrayed in the British press. The column argued that most English reporting on India relied on misleading or false reports produced by correspondents who visited India without acquiring any "reliable and accurate first-hand knowledge." Instead, their view of the colony was shaped exclusively by Anglo-Indians—men who "bear an unconquerable hatred against the educated Indians . . . inspired by their passions and prejudices." Their writing has an inordinate influence on public opinion in Britain, according to the editorial, affecting the colonial government by causing it to "pour out all its venom against the educated Indians," and thus generating still more dissent and distrust—a vicious cycle that was rendering the colonial relationship increasingly untenable. A case in point, the article argued, was British anxieties about Indian unrest in the wake of the 1905 Partition of Bengal, an act which provoked both widespread critique of the government and a wave of bombings (see chapter 2). Despite these protests, the British press was sensationalizing and exaggerating the gravity of the moment, the editorial contended, fallaciously making "the English people believe that the sedition-cobra has raised its hood in India against the English."

Two cartoons accompanying this article depict "'The Indian Unrest' as viewed by the English Press" and "The Indian Unrest—as Viewed by the Indian People." One is a hand-copied reproduction of a cartoon from British *Punch* that depicts John Morley, then secretary of state in India, as a secretary bird with its feet crushing "sedition" in the form of a snake (see Figure 3.4 for the original *Punch* version). Since secretary birds are known for killing snakes in this way but are native to sub-Saharan Africa, not India, this is a telling and possibly deliberate conflation of colonial contexts, given that Gandhi was publishing on satyagraha in *Indian Opinion* in South Africa at this time. The image was designed to celebrate the wave of arrests for seditious writings and gatherings that Morley oversaw during this period. "Emergency" government actions in 1907 included an ordinance that suspended public meetings; the deportation of political leaders without trial; repressive actions against certain "seditious" newspapers (included the banning of the radical journal, the *Indian Sociologist*); and a Prevention of Seditious Meetings Act.

The second *Indian World* riff on the *Punch* cartoon, drawn in the same style, serves as a rebuttal to the first and includes the words "apologies to Mr. Punch" in the caption to accentuate its parodic aims (the first one simply says "from Punch" even though it was a replication rather than a print of the original). In the *Indian World*'s satirical version, the secretary bird is not fiercely heroic but instead "duped" into turning against liberal values—an about-face of which Morley was frequently accused when he supported the suppression of disaffection in India after having championed freedom of the press in Britain as an MP, as well as a range of democratic and anti-imperialist positions (he was against the Boer War and in favor of Irish Home Rule, for example). The subtitle of the caption, "Mr. Morley Throttles Peace, Progress and Liberty in India," curtly summarizes the image's attempt to allegorize the hypocrisies of liberal imperialism. Its abandoned ideals are represented by two smaller birds (Peace and Progress) and a doll (Liberty) that the secretary bird is strangling with its claws; the bird's vacant stare, meanwhile, suggests it is unaware that the snake it is killing is a toy being manipulated from a distance by a monkey. Sitting on a whole box of provoking toy snakes, the monkey's head is turned to look knowingly at the viewer. The monkey is an obvious stand-in for the babu figure who was frequently caricatured as a species of primate, as chapter 2 demonstrates. By evoking this trope, the image suggests that babu journalists have created the *impression* of sedition via anticolonial writing, thus duping Morley and his government whose repression of the press, political gatherings, and books (all of which were criminalized in this period) is an overreaction that exposes the hypocrisies of liberal empire.

FIGURE 3.4 / First illustration of "The Indian Secretary Bird" accompanying an article entitled "Reflections of Men and Things" from the *Indian World*, vol. 28, July 1907. General Reference Collection, British Library. Shelfmark P.P.3779.hfb., © British Library Board.

FIGURE 3.5 / Second illustration of "The Indian Secretary Bird" accompanying an article entitled "Reflections of Men and Things" from the *Indian World*, vol. 28, July 1907. General Reference Collection, British Library. Shelfmark P.P.3779.hfb., © British Library Board.

Most obviously, this editorial, and the cartoons that accompanied it, offered a counternarrative to India's depiction in the British and Anglo-Indian press. But, significantly, it did so by employing the very journalistic norms most influentially articulated in the period by Stead, the *Indian World*'s implied mentor. As mentioned earlier in this chapter, Stead's two major essays on journalism— "Government by Journalism" and "The Future of Journalism"—spoke of the sanctity of public opinion, and an accurate analysis of it, to democratic governance; of the value of sensationalism as a way to generate reform; and, significantly for this *Indian World* article, of the importance of gleaning information from local informants—those best positioned to understand public opinion on the ground. The *Indian World*, however, suggests that the British press is falling short on all these counts and that its sensationalism produces the opposite effect from the one desired by Stead, generating hysteria and antidemocratic legislation rather than progressive reform.

FIGURE 3.6 / "The Indian Secretary Bird: Mr. Morley Puts His Foot on Sedition in India," from *Punch*, June 5, 1907, 407. Courtesy of NYU Special Collections.

Whether or not Stead felt the sting of this rebuke (and whether or not it was specifically addressed to him), the *Indian World* and the perspective reflected in the 1907 editorial—along with the other English-language Indian newspapers he published and their increasingly vocal critique of British repression—had an impact on Stead's journal and its imperial project by contributing to his growing sense of the adverse effects of colonial law on freedom of speech more broadly. But because the *Indian World*, like his own journal, offered a synthetic view of contemporary perspectives (and perhaps seduced by the fact that it had explicitly sought his patronage), Stead reprinted its articles in his section on Indian affairs more often than the other Indian journals he cited, such as *East and West*, the *Hindustan Review*, and the *Calcutta Review*. In 1908, a year after the editorial critiquing the way India was portrayed in the British press, he published large sections of an *Indian World* article on "The Arrival of the Bomb in India."

LEADING ARTICLES IN THE REVIEWS. 37

THE ARRIVAL OF THE BOMB IN INDIA.
WHAT IT MEANS AND WHAT SHOULD BE DONE.

THE *Indian World* for May publishes two notable articles upon the recent outburst of revolutionary violence in India.

WHAT ARE THE FACTS?

The facts so far as they can be determined would seem to be as follows: A handful of young men formed a secret society with no very settled objects in view, shortly after the partition of Bengal. Some thought that by that organisation they should ultimately succeed in upsetting British rule, while others more sanely thought that they would strike terror among "the oppressors of their race" and teach the people to dare and die. Their first efforts seem to have been devoted to physical training of young men and to preaching independence, and the destructive propaganda, if contemplated, would not seem to have been materially furthered. It was and appreciate. But this is not all. The character of most of the young men who are undergoing their trial at Alipore reveals not only a striking amount of boldness and determination, but also a certain degree of heroism which constitutes the real essence of patriotism.

Why these young men face death so willingly is thus explained:—

The failure of all our attempts in recent years to make the present administration more sympathetic and just, to purge it of its evils, and to make it acceptable to the people, probably stands out as the most potent cause of the present unrest and discontent in India. Your rule may be good, but that is not enough, nor the whole of it. You must make us feel that it is good—that constitutes the essence of all loyalty. Measures that have been badly wanted have been continually put off; reforms that have been loudly demanded have been quietly ignored; bills that have been strongly opposed have been rushed through the Legislature. Public opinion has been flouted in almost all questions that have come to the front in the lifetime of this generation; and a thousand and one things have been done just in the way in which the people would not have them done. No doubt, much wild writing and wild speaking have fanned the flame of Indian unrest; but it remains a fact that the flame thus fanned has been kindled by British insolence, British contumely, and British disregard for Indian public opinion.

"A FEW OUT OF A HUNDRED GRIEVANCES."

The editor, condescending upon particulars, mentions—

The quiet shelving of the principal recommendations of the Public Service Commission, the imposition of a countervailing excise duty on Indian cotton manufactures, the closing of the mints to the free coinage of silver, the amendment of the sedition section in the Indian Penal Code, the officialisation of the Indian Universities, the Partition of Bengal, the prohibition and the breaking-up of public meetings by a *posse* of constables armed with bludgeons, the irritating prosecution of irresponsible journalists and stump orators, the penalising of swadeshi activity, the whipping of young political offenders, the vexatious shadowing of innocent public men, the expeditious removal of

Hindi Punch.]   [Bombay.
The Anarchist Octopus.

FIGURE 3.7 / "The Arrival of the Bomb in India" from *Hindi Punch*, reprinted in the *Review of Reviews*, vol. 38, July 1908, 37. General Reference Collection, British Library. Shelfmark P.P.5939.ca., © British Library Board.

While his framing of the article attempts to reign in its relatively sympathetic view of the bomb-throwing revolutionaries, the bulk of the article is reproduced in the *Indian World*'s own words, many of which echo the critique of the 1907 editorial and blame the outbreak of violence on British disregard for Indian public opinion: "Public opinion has been flouted in almost all questions that have come to the front in the lifetime of this generation. No doubt, much wild writing and wild speaking have fanned the flame of Indian unrest; but it remains a fact that the flame thus fanned has been kindled by British insolence, British contumely, and British disregard for Indian public opinion."[55] Here, the *Indian World* takes up the idea of disaffection as a form of danger propagated by the ("wild") Indian press but also positions it as a reaction to Britain's bad affects—"insolence" and "contumely."

Stead finally arrived at a similar position. The coverage of "the arrival of the bomb in India" in Stead's *Review* was the first of a series of articles published between 1908 and 1909 on Indian disaffection, including one published under the title "The Real Secret of Indian Unrest" in which the *Review* summarizes an article as follows: "The Indians have been goaded into disaffection by the brutality with which they have been treated by the British." Another article in 1908 begins with a quote about the inevitability of Indian nationhood and also reprints nationalist articles from various Indian reviews; in 1909 a section of the periodical entitled "Character Sketches" was devoted to "Heroes of the New Era in India" and included a long biographical essay by the nationalist writer Saint Nihal Singh that focused on the more radical activists in the movement, such as Tilak and Lajpat Rai. It was these men and their ilk, Stead notes, whose voices were being repressed by sedition charges and thus most urgently needed a hearing.

From this point onward, the use of sedition legislation as a way to criminalize the Indian press seemed increasingly to irk Stead. In 1909 an article by the nationalist leader Chandra Pal, entitled "The Aetiology of the Bomb in India," was published in London in the journal *Swaraj*, and then suppressed in India for being "calculated to incite disaffection." In response, Stead published a virulent attack on the colonial government in the form of an editorial entitled "Freedom of the Press in India: A Typical Instance of Repression." Arguing that the *Swaraj* article was merely pointing out the causes of disaffection in order to alleviate it, and disgusted by what he saw as an "unwarrantable outrage upon the most elementary principles of a free Press," he reprinted "the strongest passages from the

---

55. Cited in *Review of Reviews* 38, no. 233 (July 1908): 37.

incriminating article . . . for the purpose of exciting discontent with [Morley's] administration of the Press Law in order to obtain either a reform in the law or an improvement in its administration."[56]

Stead's article is interestingly similar in its diagnosis of India's problems to the *Indian World*'s, for it blames violence and political unrest on Britain's inability to properly assess and respect Indian public opinion. "Had not the bureaucracy, in a fit of fear, magnified this 'toy revolution' into a huge political conspiracy in this way, the situation in India . . . would have been less complex and tense today," Stead writes, using the journalistic trope—common in the Indian press and depicted in the *Indian World* cobra cartoon mentioned earlier—of characterizing recent political violence as toylike and trivial rather than threatening. His citation of other periodicals as a way to air unorthodox views (in this case, anticolonial ones) while evading direct responsibility for them also borrows from, or mirrors, the editorial strategy of the *Indian World*.

A few months later, Stead wrote a follow-up article, dramatically entitled "A Plea for a Censorship on the English Press Circulating in India: An Open Letter to Lord Morley." Morley is the target of Stead's rant not only because of his position as secretary of state but because of the hypocrisy of his policies in India in light of his liberalism in Britain. As Stead notes, Morley was the editor of the *Pall Mall Gazette* when Stead was building his journalistic career there, and once wrote radical articles on "the Aetiology of Crime in Ireland" that blamed anticolonial violence on British repression. "If such an article be seditious under English law," Stead says of the Indian bomb article, "then the *Pall Mall Gazette*, under Mr. Morley's editorship, was full of sedition from first to last."[57]

Stead's plea for censorship reflects the outcome of his republication of "The Aetiology of the Bomb." While the *Review of Reviews* was not censored by the colonial government, as Stead had dared it to be, the periodical was turned over to the colonial police by the Indian newsagents who had been criminalized for selling *Swaraj*, the journal that had initially published the article. This event drove Stead to articulate in print the contradiction at the heart of the liberal imperialism that he sought to champion through his periodical—its will to repress those it claimed to be leading to freedom, threatening British freedoms in the process. Specifically, for Stead, this meant the freedom to circulate his periodical as

---

56. W. T. Stead, "Freedom of the Press in India: A Typical Instance of Repression," *Review of Reviews* 40, no. 238 (October 1909): 348.

57. W. T. Stead, "A Plea for a Censorship on the English Press Circulating in India: An Open Letter to Lord Morley," *Review of Reviews* 40, no. 240 (December 1909): 542.

widely as possible in order to further its imperialist aims for, as he put it, "there is not an English newspaper or review which circulates in India that can henceforth publish any independent comment on Indian affairs without rendering its newsagents liable to be sent to jail."[58] The irony of this turn of events was not lost on Stead, who wrote "It is somewhat galling, I admit, that the *Review of Reviews*, which for 20 years has been recognized as a loyal and intrepid defender of the free and sane Imperialism on which alone the Throne can rest should be practically suppressed in India by a Bombay police magistrate without being afforded any opportunity of being heard in its own defence. At the same time it is perhaps as well that I should experience in my own property if not in my own person, the extent to which the great traditions of English liberty are being trampled underfoot in India."[59] In response to this topsy-turvy scenario, and playing on his new sense that liberalism in the colonies was an oxymoron, Stead called for censorship as a solution to censorship. Requesting, in earnest, the establishment of an agency in London to vet periodicals being sent to India, he argues that the "official imprimatur of the Censor" would reassure Indian newsagents that they would not be criminalized for selling them and would thus save British editors the fear and expense of being cut off from circulation in the colonies.

If the logic of imperialism meant that the liberal ideals which served as its rationale were always being dynamically compromised by the imperial project on the ground, the logic of Stead's imperialist print project meant that his ideals, too, could be undermined by the dynamics of the imperial public sphere. Stead was committed to covering the colonial press because of his own ambition to build an Anglo-empire in print form that would undergird, over time, a geopolitical reality. But the form he created to do this was adapted by Ray to the *Indian World*'s postcolonial vision, which turned redactive form to its own ends. Stead used Ray's periodical because it seemed to be doing the work of his own journal, synthesizing and packaging information into a miniature colonial world, but the *Indian World*—entering Stead's orbit in the guise of mimic—attained the global circulation that its cosmopolitan rhetoric aspired to through its reproduction in the *Review of Reviews*.

Ray and Stead were engaged in a tacit yet high-stakes journalistic contest, in which Ray's journal subverted Stead's imperialist goals by reversing the outward-looking stance of his review and consolidating a national rather than international community, influencing other Anglophone Indian journals along the way

---

58. Stead, "Plea for a Censorship," 542.
59. Stead, "Plea for a Censorship," 542.

(such as the *Indian Review of Reviews*, a 1920s periodical subtitled "A Monthly Journal of Indian Nationalism"). Journals such as the *Indian World*, meanwhile, were part of the reason for the *Review of Reviews*'s existence; even as Stead's journal predated Ray's, his anxiety about the status of Anglo-American culture and its present and future geopolitical hegemony was fueled by his heightened sense of how global print culture, and the English language itself, was being transformed by the literary endeavors of colonial subjects such as Ray.

Stead's and Ray's mutual citation shaped both their political projects. If Ray used print mimicry to cite Stead and borrow his legitimacy in the context of censorship, Stead used a similar strategy, citing the *Indian World* in order to air the views of Indian nationalists without necessarily valorizing them, demonstrating his investment in open-minded dialogue in the process. In a 1901 article entitled "What Is My Duty to the People of India?"—published in the first issue of *East and West* and redacted in his *Review*—Stead stated that as a journalist he "endeavored to minimise . . . the inevitable evils of such a position as that which we occupy in India, and have endeavored also to promote . . . the feeling of mutual self-respect, sympathy, and fraternity between my own countrymen and my fellow-subjects in India."[60] While invested in British hegemony, Stead also believed in the democratizing effects of journalistic exchange and, judging by the extracts he published, seemed increasingly sympathetic to the critiques of British rule he encountered in his efforts to survey, and reproduce in condensed form, the Anglophone Indian press.

By incorporating the *Indian World* into his own editorial vision, and performing a kind of brownface in the process, Stead made his journal newly vulnerable to criminalization: a turn of events which compelled him to confront the fact that taking in the world meant being irrevocably changed by it. As in the case of the "Maiden Tribute" incident that landed him in jail, his engagement with Indian journalism made him a potential victim of the very system whose reach he was attempting to expand (criminal law in the first case, imperialism in the second).

As well as setting up print networks like the *Review of Reviews*, Stead also pursued global connectivity via the occult world, which lent itself in a still loftier way to his ambitions to connect people across space and time. By networking the spirit world, Stead believed he would reach beyond his own present and assure (or at least be assured of) his own immortality. He thus promoted the activities of

---

60. Cited in Stead, "What Is My Duty to the People of India," *East and West* 1 (November 1901): 70.

the influential Society for Psychical Research in his *Review*, and in 1893 founded a whole periodical devoted to occultism, *Borderland*, that was similar in form to the *Review*.[61] An occasional participant in séances, he was known to ventriloquize spirit voices, translating them into "Steadese" to make them comprehensible—just as many of the redacted articles in his *Review* were reframed in his own voice. On the relationship between Stead and the networks he created, Laurel Brake and James Mussell note that "Stead's prolific activity among the living was only possible because of the network of men and women with whom he worked.... Stead's colleagues, in effect, had to learn to channel Stead, dispersing his presence; however, when he came to channel the voices of others, he had difficulty with the required passivity.... It was commonly accepted that medium and spirit control could affect communications from the other side but, as Stead himself noted, 'my spook writes Steadese.'"[62] Yet, as stories of the supernatural warn us, letting the spirit world in is fraught with risk. Inhabited by voices from the "other side" of empire, Stead, in his encounter with the *Indian World*, became estranged from his own enterprise, transformed into the other of the imperial public sphere he had helped create.

---

61. On Stead's interest in psychical research, see Justin Sausman, "The Democratisation of the Spook: W. T. Stead and the Invention of Public Occultism," in Brake et al., *W. T. Stead*, 149–65.

62. Laurel Brake and James Mussell, introduction to *19: Interdisciplinary Studies in the Long Nineteenth Century* 16 (2013), http://doi.org/10.16995/ntn.669.

4

SYNCRETISM / From East and West to the Darker Nations

> Passage to India!
> Lo, soul, seest thou not God's purpose from the first?
> The earth to be spann'd, connected by network,
> The races, neighbors, to marry and be given in marriage,
> The oceans to be cross'd, the distant brought near,
> The lands to be welded together.
>
> —"Passage to India," Walt Whitman (1871)

In a laudatory review of Rabindranath Tagore's *Gitanjali* published in the little magazine the *Blue Review* in 1913, a few months before Tagore received his Nobel Prize for Literature, the British poet Lascelles Abercrombie connects the import of Tagore's work to its ability to fuse East and West—the kind of world-unifying alchemy that Whitman associates with network technology in the extract from *Leaves of Grass* above. By performing this synthesis, Abercrombie contends, Tagore's collection contributes to "world politics as well as to poetry":

> As I read his own exquisite prose translation of his songs, I seem to have jumped right over that formidable clash which is, or ought to be, at the back of everybody's mind—the coming clash of East and West; I seem to have landed magically in its serene and triumphant conclusion. All the great original civilizations of the world . . . have resulted from the East fusing somehow with the West. And always it has been the East that supplied impulse—Dionysus, the West that supplied form—Apollo. Now this seems to me exactly what has happened afresh in "Gitanjali." The book is not only noble poetry, it is a new civilization.[1]

---

1. Lascelles Abercrombie, "Poetry," *Blue Review* 1, no. 2 (June 1913): 117.

On the one hand, he warns ominously of an epic "coming clash"—a popular notion related to the rise of anticolonial movements across the French and British empires and the perception of Japan as a newly formidable global power in the wake of the 1905 Russo-Japanese War. On the other, he imagines a triumphant union of East and West based on complementary aesthetic elements ("impulse" and "form") that allow for a "magical" transcendence of conflict and give rise to "a new civilization."

This version of the East-West binary, wherein Eastern spirituality was seen as a redemptive and renovating counter to Western materialism, had much currency at the time. Protap Chunder Mozoomdar, a representative of the Brahmo Samaj at the World's Parliament of Religion in 1893, described the reformed Hinduism practiced by the Samaj as a "commonwealth of affection"; in his speech at the Parliament and elsewhere, Eastern spiritualism serves as the affective glue of world unity.[2] Similar syncretic ideals circulated between Britain and India in the works of theosophists like Annie Besant; literary figures such as W. B. Yeats, Sarojini Naidu, and E. M. Forster; spiritual leaders such as Sri Aurobindo, Swami Vivekananda, and Sister Nivedita; and, of course, the writings and lectures of Tagore himself. For these thinkers, as for Abercrombie, East-West syncretism in the cultural sphere was imagined as a potential remedy for conflict in the political sphere.

The purchase of this idea extended to organizations such as theater groups and presses. A group called the Indian Art and Dramatic Society of London renamed itself the Union of the East and the West in 1914 and put on Indian plays (many by Tagore) for the British public as a way to promote cross-cultural understanding; John Murray's publishing house, meanwhile, launched a series called "The Wisdom of the East" which ran from 1905 until the 1960s and published 122 translations of classical and modern Middle Eastern and Asian literary and religious texts. An editorial note on the series used idealistic language that recurs repeatedly in descriptions of East-West syncretism in the early twentieth century:

> The object of the Editors of this Series is a very definite one. They desire above all things that, in their humble way, these books shall be the ambassadors of good-will and understanding between East and West, the

---

2. J. Barton Scott, "A Commonwealth of Affection: Modern Hinduism and the Cultural History of Religion," in *Constructing Nineteenth-Century Religion*, ed. Joshua King and Winter Jade Werner (Columbus: Ohio State University Press, 2019), 57–61.

old world of Thought and the new of Action. In this endeavour, and in their own sphere, they are but followers of the highest example in the land. They are confident that a deeper knowledge of the great ideals and lofty philosophy of Oriental thought may help to a revival of that true spirit of Charity which neither despises nor fears the nations of another creed and colour.[3]

But despite its utopian articulations, East-West syncretism was an ideologically fraught project. Michael Adas notes that because Indian versions of modernist syncretism often involved the adoption of Western-inflected views of India and Asia, "pre–World War I challenges to assumptions of Western superiority . . . were highly essentialist, mainly reactive rather than proactive, and framed by Western gauges of human achievement and worth."[4] In the works of modern Indian writers like Tagore, syncretism functioned as a cosmopolitan ideal that united spiritual and scientific worldviews, but it was also used by spiritual leaders as a way to harness cosmopolitanism's normative power to the ends of Indian nationalism by asserting the world-historical import of Indian religions and literatures—most often Hinduism.

As many have argued, the ways in which an ahistorical view of Hinduism as the locus of authentic Indian identity became central to the nationalist movement in the early twentieth century would have disastrous consequences for the postcolony that can be traced up to the rise of the extreme right and attendant communal violence in contemporary India.[5] Ironically, syncretism—despite its constitutive openness to multiple faiths—would contribute to this development more than mitigate it. In "Beyond Orientalism," Gauri Viswanathan explores broader meanings of "syncretism," tracing its uses to the rise of Protestantism in the seventeenth century when Christian theology sought a more democratic basis for faith located in "the people" as opposed to the clerisy. Rooted in this

---

3. Description of the aims of the Wisdom of the East series found in *The Classics of Confucius: Book of Odes (Shih-King)*, by L. Cranmer-Byng (London: John Murray, 1906), Editorial Note, 5. I am grateful to Alexander Bubb for drawing my attention to this series.

4. Michael Adas, "Contested Hegemony: The Great War and the Afro-Asian Assault on the Civilizing Mission Ideology," *Journal of World History* 15, no. 1 (March 2004): 31–63, 86.

5. See, for instance, Gauri Viswanathan, "Beyond Orientalism: Syncretism and the Politics of Knowledge," *Stanford Humanities Review* 5, no. 1 (1995), https://web.stanford.edu/group/SHR/5-1/text/viswanathan.html; Srinivas Aravamudan, *Guru English: South Asian Religion in a Cosmopolitan Language* (Princeton, NJ: Princeton University Press, 2006); and Lise McKean, *Divine Enterprise: Gurus and the Hindu Nationalist Movement* (Chicago: University of Chicago Press, 1996).

history, syncretism is best described as "an embodiment of disinterestedness [that] creates conditions for a form of governance where class differences, allegiances and interests vanish." But, Viswanathan argues, it must also be seen as "a specific position from which certain interests are advanced, presumably in the name of a larger comity of universal brotherhood."[6] Used both to assimilate Indians to British rule via Christianity and to ground Indian nationalism in broad religious movements such as the Brahmo Samaj, syncretism was at once a form of "nostalgia for an undivided community that preceded the state" and "constitutive of the will to nationhood."[7]

By examining the way syncretic ideals circulated between Britain and India in speeches, journalism, and the form of periodicals themselves, I show how what Viswanathan calls "syncretism-as-strategy" operated on either side of the colonial divide and helped shape political and literary debates in the first two decades of the twentieth century. I am using syncretism in a narrower sense than Viswanathan, however, to name a type of modernist cosmopolitanism that was visible in the imperial public sphere in both Indian and British publications.[8]

In the face of large-scale war (the Russo-Japanese War and then World War I), modernist syncretism imagined East-West exchange, or a synthesis of East-West ideas, or both, as the basis of world progress and peace. But in practice, as Abercrombie's word "magical" suggests, syncretism in European writing tended to build on essentialist ideas of East and West, as well as the racist and "sometimes eugenicist" ideas about civilizational clash that circulated in this period in the work of many influential European writers, such as Oswald Spengler and Henri Massis.[9] Even as the modern version of the East-West binary was informed

---

6. Viswanathan, "Beyond Orientalism," 4, 7.

7. Viswanathan, "Beyond Orientalism," 5, 8.

8. On the varied uses of cosmopolitanism in this period, see my earlier work, *Urban Realism and the Cosmopolitan Imagination in the Nineteenth Century: Visible City, Invisible World* (Cambridge: Cambridge University Press, 2011). On earlier forms of Indian cosmopolitanism and syncretism in the periodical press and popular culture, see Daniel E. White, *From Little London to Little Bengal: Religion, Print, and Modernity in Early British India, 1793–1835* (Baltimore: Johns Hopkins University Press, 2013).

9. Andrzej Gasiorek, "War, 'Primitivism,' and the Future of 'the West': Reflections on D. H. Lawrence and Wyndham Lewis," in *Modernism and Colonialism: British and Irish Literature, 1899–1939*, ed. Richard Begam and Michael Valdez Moses (Durham, NC: Duke University Press, 2007), 94. Gasiorek describes how anxieties about the "fate of Europe" affected the emergence of East and West as Manichaean categories. Also see Christopher GoGwilt, *The Invention of the West* (Palo Alto, CA: Stanford University Press, 1995). GoGwilt discusses both the implications of the idea of the "West" in this period and the "double-mapping" of Europe and empire wherein Europe becomes divided between East and West at the same time that the paradigm is applied to a broader globalized landscape.

by fears of the West's decline and Asia's ascendancy, the meanings of East and West continued to be figured, in the words of Antonio Gramsci, "from the point of view of the European cultured classes who, as a result of their world-wide hegemony, have caused them to be accepted everywhere."[10] East and West are nominally symmetrical in the opposition but "the East is marked—stereotyped, labeled, named—while the West is not."[11]

Building on the work of Edward Said, with whom this view of the West's unmarkedness in the development of Orientalism is most often associated, Saree Makdisi argues for a more nuanced view of the East-West binary. In his account, Occidentalism emerged alongside Orientalism in the eighteenth century as a way to mark the Other within—the British and Irish working classes, as well as the decadent aristocracy. Orientalism was not just outward- but inward-facing, designed to differentiate the civilized bourgeoisie, uniquely associated with the West, from those both within and outside the nation.[12] But if civilizational ideas of the West took shape in this earlier moment, the term "the West" itself—and the ways we use it today—developed later, in the turn-of-the-century period covered in this book. As Christopher GoGwilt notes in his analysis of Conrad and the "invention of the West," "It is only relatively recently—between the 1880s and the 1920s—that formulations of "the West" came to mean a relation between a structure of international political power, and imagined cultural identity and a discrete historical development within world history."[13] Both East and West, then, were being freshly rearticulated in relation to each other in the imperial public sphere during this period, in both cultural and geopolitical terms.

The first two decades of the twentieth century produced various forms of transnational antiracism and anticolonialism still inadequately attended to. Manu Goswami points out that "we know a good deal more about the afterlife of colonial internationalism ... than its crisis-borne appearance between WWI and WWII" despite the fact that "from the standpoint of anti-imperial intellectuals and activists, the interwar moment marked a crisis not just within but of an extant geopolitical order."[14] If, as GoGwilt argues, now-dominant ideas about

---

10. Antonio Gramsci, "Some Problems in the Study of the Philosophy of Praxis," in *Selections from the Prison Notebooks*, ed. and trans. Quinton Hoare and Geoffrey Nowell Smith (New York: International, 1985), 447. Cited in GoGwilt, *Invention of the West*, 15.
11. GoGwilt, *Invention of the West*, 22.
12. Saree Makdisi, *Making England Western* (Chicago: University of Chicago Press, 2013).
13. GoGwilt, *Invention of the West*, 15.
14. Manu Goswami, "Imaginary Futures and Colonial Internationalisms," *American Historical Review* 117, no. 5 (2012): 1461–85, 1485, 1463.

"the West" (and thus implicitly of the East) were "constructed *after* and *in reaction to* the process of decolonization," what was happening to those ideas in the colony as the process of decolonization began to take shape?[15] How did they, for better and for worse, shape the process of decolonization itself, and the discourse of anticolonialism across the imperial Anglosphere?

In our contemporary moment, when the geographic terms that prevail in colonial and postcolonial studies have shifted axis from East and West to North and South—at least in part to escape the stereotypes and ideologies that overdetermine the older binary—it is worth revisiting the specific uses of "East and West" at the historical juncture that foreshadowed the concept's loss of power. In what follows, I look in detail at two specific and significant uses of the East-West binary in the imperial public sphere, the first focused on its geopolitical usages (at the Universal Races Congress of 1911), the second on its cultural ones (in the modernist Indian journal *East and West*). Whereas the preceding chapters have paired British and Indian events and texts to demonstrate their overlapping and mutually influential print cultures, this chapter's doubled structure focuses on the way the metropole/colony dialogue was made explicit and staged as such in two venues—an international conference that took place in London, and a journal published in Bombay that contained texts written by both Indian and British authors.

In both cases, notions of affection and disaffection had a key role to play for, like the colonizer-colonized relationship, the East-West one was frequently figured as a friendship or romance. As we have seen in the other case studies examined in this book, Indians who sought to intervene in the imperial public sphere had to do so strategically because of the law against disaffection. The wide range of texts that use tropes of cross-cultural friendship and romance in the colonial context thus had much to do with the coercive conditions that underlay the affection allegory, for they offered a way for writers and politicians to engage elliptically yet pointedly with the political dimensions of the colonial encounter.

My aim in this chapter, however, is not only to show how syncretism functioned as a form of cosmopolitanism and a tactic for navigating press censorship, but also how modernism—both Indian modernism and "high" European modernism—was shaped in part by ideas about East and West that were being debated in cultural and political forums by key players on each side of the colonial divide: indeed, nothing demonstrates the interdependence of British and

---

15. GoGwilt, *Invention of the West*, 9.

Indian literary publics upon which this book is focused more fully than the transnational circuit and global imaginary of modernist syncretism. Though scholarship on Indian modernism focuses on art, literature, and artsy literature (such as "little magazines") produced later, from the 1930s through the 1960s and beyond, the discourse I trace here, and the existence of a periodical such as *East and West* that was thoroughly modern in both form and content, demonstrates that the syncretic ideals and geopolitical realignments crucial to our understanding of transnational modernism were very much in play at the beginning of the century.[16] The colonies may have served as a colorful backdrop for individual self-making and unmaking in the works of European writers such as Joseph Conrad, Virginia Woolf, and George Orwell, but the forms of criticism and comparison practiced by colonial subjects in the same period were part of the impetus for existential crisis in the West.[17] In short, this chapter encourages us to see modernism as a dialogue structured by colonial relations and, as such, one ineluctably shaped by colonial censorship.

Not Yet, Not Here: The Failures of Friendship

The uses of friendship in literary and political discourse analyzed here offer a contrasting view to scholarship of the last two decades that has taken up the trope of friendship as a way of understanding and celebrating various forms of anticolonial resistance otherwise invisible to view. In *Affective Communities*, for instance, Leela Gandhi looks at "minor narratives of crosscultural collaboration between oppressors and oppressed" and charts a history of anticolonialism located in the metropolitan center, where imperatives of empire were refused via alliances forged across the East-West binary.[18] Seth Koven's *The Match Girl and the Heiress* reconstructs the unlikely friendship between two women of starkly

---

16. Examples of works on Indian modernism focusing specifically on periodical writing include Anjali Nerlekar, *Bombay Modern: Arun Kolatkar and Bilingual Literary Culture* (Chicago: Northwestern University Press, 2016); Supriya Chauduri, "Modernist Literary Communities in 1930s Calcutta: The Politics of *Parichay*," in *Modernist Communities across Culture and Media*, ed. Caroline Pollentier and Sarah Wilson (Gainesville: University Press of Florida, 2019), 177–96; and Laetitia Zecchini, *Arun Kolatkar and Literary Modernism in India: Moving Lines* (London: Bloomsbury), 2016.

17. On questions of empire and the novelistic form of development/underdevelopment, see Joseph Slaughter, *Human Rights, Inc.: The World Novel, Narrative Form, and International Law* (New York: Fordham University Press, 2007); and Jed Esty, *Unseasonable Youth: Modernism, Colonialism, and the Fiction of Development* (New York: Oxford University Press, 2011).

18. L. Gandhi, *Affective Communities*, 6.

different class backgrounds and the way they deployed it to enable and energize their anticolonialism, grassroots activism, and utopian community building.[19] Elleke Boehmer's essay on Robert Baden-Powell's *Scouting for Boys*, meanwhile, suggests that the scouts' emphasis on friendship as a mode that might cut across "cultural, racial, or social divides" was taken up by nationalists like Rabindranath Tagore to promote a different vision of "transnational and intercultural attachment."[20]

The intricate histories uncovered by these approaches contribute in salutary ways to our understanding of empire. But it is hard to see friendship as a category that might operate outside the space of normative politics if we consider the legal and rhetorical history of affection as an imperial trope: can friendship be a space of freedom if it is also a coercive requirement of intercultural contact? Part of the reason relationships understood in affective terms have been appealing to critics of empire and theorists of affect alike is that they can be seen as forms of voluntary filiation unmediated by the ineluctable identities of nation, class, or culture. But because affection was a mandate of loyal imperial subjecthood, it was always being performatively produced or refused in print circulation and was thus as highly mediated as any other category of sociability.

Two of the most well-known examples of friendship being used to surmount the fraught politics of British-Indian relations in Anglophone modernist literature are Rudyard Kipling's *Kim* (1901) and E. M. Forster's *Passage to India* (1924). Famously, the friendship between the eponymous character and the lama in *Kim* serves both as a spiritual and moral counter to, and cover for, the cynical machinations of the Great Game. A lesser-known and later work of Kipling's, *The Eyes of Asia*, puts the rhetoric of imperial friendship to work in similar ways, but rather than merely representing war games, like *Kim*, it was actively engaged in them and is thus an even better example of the dubious ways in which friendship and affection were deployed in the period surrounding World War I.

After the start of the war, the British government, concerned about the radicalization of Indian immigrants in the United States by the revolutionary Ghadar movement and about potential discontent among Indian soldiers fighting in France, recruited a number of famous authors to write propagandistic articles that would sell the war to the American and British publics while convincing them of the ongoing value of empire. Thus, in 1917, at the instigation of a British

---

19. Seth Koven, *The Matchgirl and the Heiress* (Princeton, NJ: Princeton University Press, 2015).
20. Elleke Boehmer, "The Text in the World, the World through the Text: Robert Baden-Powell's *Scouting for Boys*," in Burton and Hofmeyr, *Ten Books*, 131–53, 133, 149.

intelligence officer, Kipling published four stories in British and American newspapers that read as letters from Indian soldiers deployed in France to their families on the subcontinent.

Though he did not like to think of his writing as propaganda, much of Kipling's literary output during the war functioned this way in practice: for instance, he was allegedly responsible for the widely used term "Huns" to describe Germans.[21] But he also participated actively in official propaganda campaigns, and in 1916 stated in a letter to a friend that, while retaining copyright, he had allowed his writing to be used "as articles in newspapers or as pamphlets in propaganda work in all countries."[22] His propagandistic output, Anurag Jain notes, included poems, speeches, and articles aimed at British and imperial audiences, alongside letters and verse addressed specifically to Americans that cajoled them to "face up to their duty to help the Allies in the war."[23]

Kipling's four fictional letters by Indian soldiers were serialized in the American *Saturday Evening Post* and the British *Morning Post* in 1917 and later published together in book form under the title *The Eyes of Asia*. The letters borrowed liberally from actual soldiers' letters secretly forwarded to him by a British intelligence officer; they are thus reminiscent of some Indian accounts of the war, but minus the reports of war fatigue, criticisms of leadership and of European moral barbarism, and warnings to others to avoid enlistment at all cost that could be found in actual sepoy letters, as well as other Indian war narratives such as Mulk Raj Anand's novel *Across the Black Waters*. The title of Anand's book alludes to one of the worst punishments for disaffection under Section 124a—transportation for life. Those punished in this form were sent to the Andaman Islands, a locale chosen specifically—and sadistically—because it was across the "Black Waters" of the Indian Ocean and therefore proscribed by the Dharma Sutra, which identified travel to foreign countries with the loss of *varna* (caste status). Of his chapter on punishments in the Indian Penal Code, Thomas Babington Macaulay stated that "the consideration which has chiefly determined us to retain that mode of punishment is our persuasion that it is regarded by the natives of India, particularly those who live at a distance from the sea, with particular fear. The pain

---

21. David Gilmour, *The Long Recessional: The Imperial Life of Rudyard Kipling* (New York: Farrar, Straus and Giroux, 2002), 206.

22. Kipling to Sir Douglas Brownrigg, April 24, 1916, *The Letters of Rudyard Kipling*, vol. 4, *1911–19*, ed. Thomas Pinney (Iowa City: University of Iowa Press, 1999), 363.

23. Anurag Jain, "The Relationship between Ford, Kipling, Conan Doyle, Wells and British Propaganda of the First World War" (unpublished doctoral thesis, University of London, 2009), 105.

which is caused by punishment is unmixed evil."²⁴ By associating serving in the war with the proscription against crossing the ocean, the title of Anand's novel equates loyalty to the empire with literal bad faith.

Thus, while Kipling strove to represent a range of Indian experiences in his fictional letters, including the voices of Sikhs, Muslims, and Hindus, his version of the sepoy was many degrees removed from the actual experience of Indian soldiers. But these were highly mediated in multiple ways. To begin with, there was the retrospection of the writing process, the polite conventions of the letter form, and the role of scribes (used by many soldiers who dictated their communiqués with friends and family). Once finished, the letters were subject to translation and two rounds of inspection. Finally, they were submitted for possible censorship at different levels of army administration before being released for travel to their intended audiences. Gujendra Singh describes the censorship operations at the government level as follows: "A special Chief Censor of Indian Mails was appointed whose purpose, with the help of his staff, was to read, analyse, translate and record every letter sent by and to a sipahi in the field. At first this was just for sipahis serving in the operational theatre of France, but, by WWI, this more stringent censorship covered sipahis wherever they served—from N Africa, Italy and the Mediterranean to Burma, Malaya and the Far East."²⁵ The goal of these censors was to suppress any content that betrayed covert information, discouraged enlistment, sapped morale, or was explicitly critical of the empire and its allies.

By 1915 sepoys had become aware of the censorship to which their letters were being subjected and—like many journalists and authors in India—changed their writing accordingly, using conventional British phrases and stock characterizations of warfare to appear adequately loyal, as well as cryptic references, allegories, and poems to convey negative sentiments that might otherwise provoke redaction.²⁶ These tactics confounded British censors even when they were alert to them. One censor complained, for example, that it is "almost impossible . . . for any censorship of Oriental correspondence to be effective as a barrier. Orientals excel in the art of conveying information without saying anything definite."²⁷

---

24. Cited in Gajendra Singh, *The Testimonies of Indian Soldiers and the Two World Wars: Between Self and Sepoy* (London: Bloomsbury Academic, 2014), 57.
25. Singh, *Testimonies of Indian Soldiers*, 63.
26. Santanu Das, *India, Empire and First World War Culture: Writing, Images, and Songs* (Cambridge: Cambridge University Press, 2018), 207.
27. Singh, *Testimonies of Indian Soldiers*, 66.

In keeping with the doppelgänger effect produced by colonial censorship in other texts examined in this book, Kipling's sepoy letters mimicked Indian soldiers performing the role of mimic man, professing and enacting loyal subjecthood by avoiding critique and voicing affection for their rulers (or in this case, the Allied troops and their commanders). Of the many British writers enlisted to produce war propaganda, Kipling would have been especially comfortable with this role because he had helped invent the mimic man a decade and a half earlier through his character Hurree Chunder Mookerjee in *Kim* (see chapter 1). Predictably, the sepoy letters are written in a Hurree-esque voice, complete with linguistic error, comical malapropisms, and wide-eyed naivete. In the punningly titled fiction "A Private Account," for example, a mother whose son is reading to her from a letter is impressed by the fact that the French could apparently leave expensive clothing hanging in unsecured spaces because of their honesty: "That is the country for me! Dresses worth 200 rupees hanging on nails! Princesses all they must be."

But Kipling's soldier-mimic had to be more serious than comic, so as to encourage his readers to believe in the authenticity of the war experiences recounted, and the pro-Allies and anti-German sentiment professed. Thus, one of the "letters" that appeared under the heading "A Retired Gentleman," written in the voice of an elderly sepoy convalescing at an English hospital, represents the Germans as follows: "The nature of the enemy is to commit shame upon women and children and to defile the shrines of his own faith with his own dung. It is done by him as a drill. . . . We did not know they were outcaste. Now it is established by the evidence of our senses. They attack on all fours running like apes." The reference to the caste system and empirical evidence augment the authentic ring of the letter, which is focused on dehumanizing the Germans while emphasizing the modesty of the British: "Their greatness is to make themselves very small," the retired gentleman writes, concluding that "we are not even children beside them."[28] Another of the letters based its extensive arguments for why more Indians should enlist on the superiority of French culture. "No man molests any woman here," the soldier writes; touting the war as a form of cultural tourism, he insists his compatriots should come to the front as fast as possible to learn the French ways of life because "such opportunities will not occur again."[29]

---

28. Rudyard Kipling, *The Eyes of Asia* (New York: Doubleday, Page, 1918), 16. In *The Long Recessional*, Gilmour notes that Kipling instructed newspaper editors not to capitalize "Hun" and refer to him as "it" (117).

29. Gilmour, *Long Recessional*, 99.

Because they were based on actual letters, Kipling's letters are charged with affection for their addressees, the beloved family back home. But he also saturates his letters with a rival affection for the colonizer so that they might counter affect pointed toward India, and the possibility of seditious disaffection, with a sense of imperial belonging. Thus, the Retired Gentleman writes that he has no desire to return home to India after his convalescence because of the loving care of the nurses in Britain and his many "friends among the English." Another letter, "The Fumes of the Heart," devotes several lines to the kindness of a French woman who treated its writer like a son and wept for him accordingly: "I had never believed such women existed in this Black Age," the imaginary soldier writes in awe.[30]

At a point where censorship in India could no longer contain anticolonial writings as they spread around the world, from Ghadar newspapers in America to letters written in the trenches of France, Kipling was forced to invent the loyal Indian wholesale and to become his own mimic subject. For if the soldiers Kipling created in his letters resemble his babu character Hurree, Kipling himself, performing in brownface by producing "authentic" accounts from the front, resembles the shape-shifting Kim, who passes as an Indian while performing espionage for the British.

The title of the collection given to the four fictional letters, *The Eyes of Asia*, is reminiscent of travelogues of the period, such as Behramji Malabari's 1893 autobiographical work *An Indian Eye on English Life*, that sought to reverse the anthropological colonial gaze and decenter Western culture by subjecting it to the detached scrutiny of the colonial outsider. The focus on the eye in these titles suggests the disembodied perspective of an eye in the sky, a phrase once evocative of a watchful god or an objective overview but now associated primarily with security cameras, satellites, and drones. Given these current-day militaristic connotations, it is fitting that Kipling's appropriative voice turns the disinterested gaze of the traveler into one of surveillance, trained on the very subjects it claims to represent in an effort to curb their dissent. The "eyes of Asia," Kipling's letters, are tools of the state and as such recall not so much participant observation as dismemberment: the body parts of soldiers drawn into a war that mobilized their labor and lives against their own interests.

Forster's representation of East-West exchange a few years later engaged explicitly with the discourse of friendship and affection as well, but in a mode that

---

30. Kipling, *Eyes of Asia*, 36.

simultaneously illuminated its radical potential and its fallacies. Like Kipling's, Forster's writing about India was influenced in part by the stereotypes that circulated in the Anglo-Indian press (some of these written by Kipling himself or published by him during his editorial stint at the *Pioneer*). Forster borrowed lightly from the babu figure in his representation of Aziz, for instance, and personified the kind of spiritual cosmopolitanism popularized by Tagore and Vivekananda in the comic-enigmatic figure of Godbole. But he tried hard to refuse the terms of both Anglo-Indian racism and liberal imperialism in his engagement with India, and used friendship as a central metaphor for this refusal.[31]

For example, his essay "Three Countries" stressed that his motivation to go to India was to see a friend rather than to "govern or make money or improve people,"[32] and in *Two Cheers for Democracy* he famously stated: "If I had to choose between betraying my country and betraying my friend, I hope I should have the guts to betray my country."[33] In *Passage to India*, these ideas are acted out in the friendships between Fielding and Aziz, and Aziz and Mrs. Moore, characters whose appeal is rooted in their determination to dodge the ideological imperatives of the colonial encounter through a focus on personal experience and interpersonal loyalty. After Aziz shows Fielding a picture of his wife, they become "friends, brothers. That part was settled. . . . They trusted each other, affection had triumphed for once in a way."[34]

But if friendship is the guiding ethos of the novel, with Aziz's meeting with Mrs. Moore serving as the first embodied encounter of East and West and Fielding's loyalty to him dominating the "Cave" section, the last section, "Temple," the novel's ending famously draws this ethos into question. When the homoerotic friendship of Fielding and Aziz ends with a missed kiss as Aziz rides off into the sunset in a burst of nationalist fervor, we learn that the characters may be able to transcend ideology in individual moments but cannot transcend the dialectics of history.

One of the canniest aspects of Forster's novel is the way it embeds this history in the novel's settings. The bridge party where the ill-fated trip to the caves is dreamed up is a satire of actual bridge parties held by the British in the early 1900s in an attempt to stave off disaffection through displays of friendly

---

31. See Lauren M. E. Goodlad, "Where Liberals Fear to Tread: E. M. Forster's Queer Internationalism and the Ethics of Care," *Novel: A Forum on Fiction* 39, no. 3 (2006): 307–36; and L. Gandhi, *Affective Communities*.
32. Cited in Wendy Moffat, *E. M. Forster: A New Life* (London: Bloomsbury, 2010), 109.
33. E. M. Forster, *Two Cheers for Democracy* (New York: Harcourt Brace, 1951), 68.
34. E. M. Forster, *Passage to India* (London: Harcourt Brace, 1985), 115.

East-West contact. The cave outing initiated at the party demonstrates the superficiality of this kind of endeavor by returning to the scene of colonial trauma and allegorizing the way an imagined drama of sexual violence (a phantasmatic reversal of conquest) generates disaffection by legitimizing racial hatred and accelerating the sedimentation of power, as it did in the case of the 1857 Rebellion.[35] This event leads to the trial scene, in which British legal reasoning proves unequal to the task of managing the effects of affect—as it would in the case of disaffection trials like Gandhi's which helped bolster rather than dispel an ethos of disaffection. Mid-trial, Adela breaks down and the Indian characters emerge from the scene of dissolution with a new sense of anticolonial resolve. At the end of the novel, this resolve is manifested not only in Aziz's hardheaded nationalism but in the ecosphere and built environment as well. The horses, earth, birds, and sky, as well as the temple, tank, jails, and palace all help generate the unbridgeable rift between Aziz and Fielding with their chorus of refusal: "no not yet . . . no not there."[36] Though affection and friendship are the ostensible ideals of the novel, the novel ultimately relies on moments of disaffection and repudiation to highlight the grandiose delusions of liberal humanism and its modernist analogue, East-West syncretism.

Significantly, *A Passage to India* was published at the end of the period of syncretism covered in this chapter, for it outlines both the naive but appealing idealism of friendship as a space outside politics and the inevitability of disaffection with colonial governance.[37] The Universal Races Congress (URC) and the journal *East and West* are less well-known examples of modernist syncretism than the writings of Kipling and Forster but they illuminate these better-known texts by demonstrating the degree to which they were engaging with constructs—East-West exchange, friendship, and affection—that were part of a much larger conversation within the imperial public sphere.

While the URC helped reify rather than successfully deconstruct race as a category of political analysis, it also marked a moment when proto-nations and minority subjects became openly critical of the West and increasingly turned to each other, rather than imperial interlocutors, in their imagination of the future. Race at the URC may have been biological for many commentators, but for many

---

35. On sexual violence in the imagination of empire, see Sharpe, *Allegories of Empire*.
36. Forster, *Passage to India*, 316.
37. For a useful analysis of how these issues intersect with Forster's ideas about secularism and religion, see Dustin Friedman, "E. M. Forster, the Clapham Sect, and the Secular Public Sphere," *Journal of Modern Literature* 39, no. 1 (2015): 19–37.

of the non-Western attendees it came to signify a shared embodied experience of oppression and manipulation that could serve as the basis of new alliances and solidarities. *East and West* demonstrates how this dynamic played out in the periods before and after World War I and how the journal's syncretic cosmopolitanism, as it began to reject the West as the model for modernity, opened both onto Hindu nationalism and emancipatory visions of grassroots transnational solidarity. The period of modernist syncretism, then, was one of divergent imaginative possibilities, the best promises of which remain unrealized.[38]

"So-Called White and So-Called Coloured Peoples": The Universal Races Congress and the Racialization of East and West

The Universal Races Congress of 1911 has yet to receive robust critical attention but was a pivotal event in the history and circulation of transnational racist and antiracist discourses.[39] At the turn of the century, global networks of white settler colonists, projects of Anglo-Saxon unity, and imperial agendas such as that of "Greater Britain"—each intertwined to different degrees with ideologies of white supremacy—were all gathering momentum and taking advantage of the faster circulation and wider reach of print culture (as we saw in the case of W. T. Stead's *Review of Reviews* in chapter 3).[40] Yet these ideas and movements were both driven by, and provoked responses from, anticolonial movements and antiracist thinkers in the global South, as well as some in the West.

The Hungarian sociologist Gustav Spiller, chief organizer of the URC, envisioned the conference as an intellectual, interrogative response to the rise of racial thinking. Making the subject of race the basis for an international

---

38. Gary Wilder's analysis of the moment of decolonization in the Francophone context demonstrates the fuller flourishing of this promise at midcentury in the works of Aimé Césaire, Léopold Senghor, and other anticolonial intellectuals. Developing the glimmerings of radical possibility visible at the URC and in *East and West*, these thinkers attempted to think through "an alternative global order that would promote civilizational reconciliation and human self-realization. At stake, for them, was the very future of the world." See Gary Wilder, *Freedom Time: Negritude, Decolonization, and the Future of the World* (Durham, NC: Duke University Press, 2015), 2.

39. This section owes much to the work of Ian Christophe Fletcher, Seth Koven, and Mia Bay, each of whom invited me to participate in projects on the topic; their insight and enthusiasm was invaluable, as was that of all the participants in the 2014–15 working group on the URC initiated by the Rutgers British Studies Center and coconvened by the Rutgers Center for Race and Ethnicity; a number of the ideas here were first developed and presented in that seminar.

40. Nico Slate, *Colored Cosmopolitanism: The Shared Struggle for Freedom in the United States and India* (Cambridge, MA: Harvard University Press, 2012), 8–9.

conference in this incendiary moment turned out to be a winning idea: Spiller generated considerable interest in his potentially quixotic venture and more than two thousand representatives from all over the world assembled at the University of London from July 26 to July 29, 1911. These included such notable and disparate figures as W. E. B. Du Bois, Annie Besant, Franz Boas, Sister Nivedita, Ferdinand Tönnies, and J. A. Hobson.[41]

As the first international conference organized specifically to investigate the category of race, the URC offers a window onto the way race was understood and instrumentalized across a range of disciplines and geographies in this moment, as well as the way these ideas were challenged by prominent intellectuals and politicians. In this regard, it should be seen as a crucial forerunner to more well-known anticolonial formations such as the Bandung conference of 1955 and the Non-Aligned Movement, as well as "the series of Pan-African Congresses that took place beginning in 1900 . . . the League against Imperialism meeting held in Brussels in 1927, and the two Pan-Asian People's Conferences held in Nagasaki (1926) and Shanghai (1927)."[42]

In this transitional period, when race was increasingly being used as a scientific paradigm to explain a wide variety of sociological and anthropological phenomena, it was also a way of reconceiving global space. The varieties of informal and scientific racisms that justified slavery and imperialism have a history that significantly predates the URC, of course. But in creating an international venue in which various forms of racial thought, validated by the academic credentials of those who professed it, came into contact with the antiracist critique being developed by formidable thinkers such as Du Bois, the URC created a vision of the globe in which people were divided not only by nation, region, or religion, but— more fundamentally and incontrovertibly—by race. For the URC systematically brought the civilizational opposition of East and West imported from Orientalist discourses together with the opposition of "white" to "colored" even as it called such racial categorizations into question. The purpose of the conference was described in its official records as follows: "To discuss, in the light of science and the modern conscience, the general relations subsisting between the peoples of the West and those of the East, between so-called white and so-called coloured peoples with a view to encouraging between them a fuller understanding, the

---

41. Robert John Holton, "Cosmopolitanism or Cosmopolitanisms? The Universal Races Congress of 1911," *Global Networks* 2, no. 2 (2002): 153–70.

42. Christopher J. Lee, ed., *Making a World after Empire: The Bandung Moment and Its Political Afterlives* (Athens: Ohio University Press, 2010), 9–10.

most friendly feelings, and a heartier co-operation."[43] Here, the division between East and West is reimagined as a color line even as race is de-essentialized with the word "so-called"—a tension in the conception of the conference that was evident across the event as a whole. For some attendees, race was a fiction, while for others it was a fundamental truth underlying global schisms.

The introduction to the URC's papers also highlights the slipperiness of race at the conference: "No impartial student of history can deny that in the case of nearly all recorded wars, whatever the ostensible reasons assigned, the underlying cause of conflict has been the existence of race antipathies—using the word race in its broad and popular acceptation."[44] The reference to "race in its broad and popular acceptation" acknowledges the complexity of the term in this period. Race could refer to a family or clan; a tribe, nation, or ethnic group; or it could refer to what the *OED* calls "any of the (putative) major groupings of mankind, usually defined in terms of distinct physical features or shared ethnicity, and sometimes (more controversially) considered to encompass common biological or genetic characteristics."[45] Though still used varyingly today, it is most often deployed in this latter way, with particular reference to skin color. While the "broad and popular acceptation" to which the URC materials refers presumably encompasses all these meanings, it draws attention to the fact that the conference, with its repeated references to East and West and its many papers on biological difference, was funneling the term toward its narrower contemporary resonances.

In their effort to demonstrate their investment in the cosmopolitan spirit of the conference, Spiller and the other organizers endeavored to establish a genuine dialogue between East and West by inviting a number of non-Western speakers; by permitting some "Oriental" languages alongside the European ones that dominated the conference; and by acknowledging that "in a Congress of this comprehensive character each people should speak for itself; and it is for this reason that every paper referring to an Oriental people will be found written by an eminent person belonging to it."[46] Yet, in practice, the conference tended to rehearse racist presumptions of Eastern backwardness in the face of anxieties about the rise of anticolonial nationalisms and industrialized economies in Asia. The introduction to the conference papers thus describes the emergence of Japan

---

43. Preface to Spiller, *Papers on Inter-Racial Problems* (1911), v.
44. Lord Weardale, introduction to Spiller, *Papers on Inter-Racial Problems* (1911), vii.
45. *OED Online*, s.v. "race (*n*.6)," accessed July 22, 2019.
46. Weardale, introduction, vii.

as a world power as an instance of "the most remarkable awakening of nations long regarded as sunk in ... depths of somnolence."[47] The day soon approaches, the writer ventures, "when the vast populations of the East will assert their claim to meet on terms of equality the nations of the West, when the free institutions and the organized forces of the one hemisphere will have their counterbalance in the other ... when, in short, the colour prejudice will have vanished."[48] As this statement suggests, the URC was at once a moment of utopian internationalism and an endeavor to neutralize anticolonial, anti-Western sentiment through the discourse of friendship and understanding. The confused causality in this quotation indicates the ambivalence about East-West equality that persisted throughout the conference: Is Western "colour prejudice," as a justification for imperialism, responsible for the fact that the East is not yet on terms of equality with the West? Or is it the color prejudice of those in the East that holds them back? Both? The anaphoric sentences of the introduction imply an ordered logic but leave the underlying premise unclear. The organizers' purportedly antiracist benevolence and idealism (the idea that the principle of equality will produce "free institutions" across the globe via the spread of Western liberalism) is interwoven with political cynicism, for the shifting balance of power (the "organized forces" on either side of the world) is just as explicitly at stake.

The logo of the conference in which two female figures representing East and West shake hands, gives visual form to the ambivalence legible in the introduction. An allegory of East-West parity and friendship, the image seemingly makes race irrelevant by rendering the figures as classical statues and hence without obvious racial markers, similar to the handshake logo that appeared after the list of conference attendees.

Yet Lady East is partially nude and her hand covers part of her face because of her awkward stance: a consequence of her holding up the banner "Concordia" to her right with her left hand so that she can use her right hand to shake that of Lady West, who stands firm and poised because the banner is conveniently to her left and thus requires no contortions. Given its emergence alongside so many other representations in this period that equated Western supremacy with liberal attitudes toward gender and Eastern backwardness with unevolved ones, this image asks us to read the physically weaker position of Lady East allegorically.

Ironically yet symptomatically, then, one of the most striking aspects of the URC from today's perspective is the way it epitomized the tenacity of ideas of

---

47. Weardale, introduction, v.
48. Weardale, introduction, v.

FIGURE 4.1 / URC logo from cover of *Papers on Inter-Racial Problems*, ed. Gustav Spiller, (London: P. S. King and Son, 1911), Hathi Trust, https://catalog.hathitrust.org/Record/001742063.

FIGURE 4.2 / Illustration of handshake from *Papers on Inter-Racial Problems*, ed. Gustav Spiller, (London: P. S. King and Son, 1911), Hathi Trust, https://catalog.hathitrust.org/Record/001742063.

racist essentialism even as many participants in the event claimed to be debunking them. Papers ranged from sociological and anthropological theories of race—such as Franz Boas's "Instability of Human Types"; "On the Permanence of Racial Mental Differences" by Charles Myer; and John Gray's "The Intellectual Standing of Different Races and Their Respective Opportunities for Culture"—to broad-strokes theoretical papers on gender, language, religion, and economics. In the spirit of critical inquiry, a number of these papers isolated one contemporary notion of racial difference to deconstruct only to erect another in its place. The Austrian anthropologist Felix von Luschan, for instance, wrote in favor of monogenesis and against the idea of "civilized" as opposed to "savage" races but also argued that "racial barriers will never cease to exist, and ... it will certainly be better to preserve than to obliterate them" because of what he saw as the overriding drive of the struggle for survival and its tendency to coalesce around nation and race.[49] Boas, one of the more progressive racial anthropologists by today's standards, spoke of the plasticity of race and the tendency of both cultural and physical racial characteristics to change quickly over time under the influence of

---

49. Felix von Luschan, "Anthropological View of Race," in Spiller, *Papers on Inter-Racial Problems* (1969), 23.

different environments. But in using this position to argue in favor of immigration and more porous borders by claiming that admitting "degenerate" Italians into the United States would accelerate their racial advancement, he also demonstrated the tenacity of specious ideas about race.[50] The British colonial administrator Harry Johnston, meanwhile, railed against aesthetic hierarchies based on racial difference while declaring himself in favor of polygenesis and the impossibility of a common ancestor.[51] The majority of the papers at the conference, then, ended up freshly legitimizing the idea of racial difference at the very moment it was supposedly being questioned, while also putting it front and center as the defining characteristic of social and political life and of the twentieth-century geopolitical imaginary.

Papers by non-Western delegates were fewer in number and for the most part segregated into a session entitled "Conditions of Progress (Special Problems)" that made manifest the presumption of Eastern belatedness that framed the conference. Rather than naming a theoretical argument, titles in this section named regions and religions, such as "China," "Japan," "Shintoism," "Egypt," "The Bahai Movement," and "East and West in India." But some of these delegates were nonetheless able to introduce a significant strain of anti-essentialism into the congress, using their speeches and comments to historicize race and subject it to materialist and rhetorical analysis. Du Bois, for example, gave a speech that focused on the way racism in the United States was being reformulated in response to increasing African American social mobility: "The Negro is rapidly developing a larger and larger class of intelligent property-holding men of Negro descent; notwithstanding this more and more race lines are being drawn which involve the treatment of civilised men in an uncivilised manner."[52] Challenging the notion that racist ideas were justified by black backwardness, he connected them instead to white social and class anxieties, while simultaneously decoupling the term "civilization" from its traditional usages in the East-West binary and affixing it to humane behavior (and also, less constructively, to "intelligent property-holding" men in particular).[53] Rev. M. D. Israel, a Tamil Christian and the only attending

50. Franz Boas, "Instability of Human Types," in Spiller, *Papers on Inter-Racial Problems* (1969), 99–104.
51. Harry H. Johnston, "The World-Position of the Negro and the Negroid," in Spiller, *Papers on Inter-Racial Problems* (1969), 328–36.
52. W. E. B. DuBois, "The Negro Race in the United States of America," in Spiller, *Papers on Inter-Racial Problems* (1969), 362.
53. I owe this insight to Janet Neary's work in Tanya Agathocleous and Janet Neary, "Before Bandung: Afro-Asian Cross-Referencing and Comparative Racialization," *Journal of Social History* 55, no. 2 (Winter 2021): 1–24.

member who identified himself with the lower castes of India, took particular issue with the rhetoric of anthropological rather than social racism, citing "the bad feeling [created] when Europeans use the [word] 'native' to represent any nation or race who are not 'white.'"[54] Antiracism and anti-imperialism, as the ongoing conflation of "race" and "nation" at the conference suggested, were often closely connected, if not conflated, in these speeches.

The URC was an ideal rhetorical moment to garner global support for decolonization by joining the growing transnational critique of imperialism to that of racism. A sizable number of international speakers assembled there and the speeches, which were precirculated and printed together in a volume that was distributed both in Britain and America, had the potential to reach an audience that extended beyond the metropole: G. K. Gokhale's speech (discussed later in this section) was reprinted in several Indian newspapers as well as in Gandhi's South African periodical *Indian Opinion*, for example. Indian politicians in particular were clearly aware that the URC presented a unique opportunity to pressure the British for political reform on an international platform by calling them to moral account: the list of the conference's "General Committee" names ninety delegates from India, the largest number from a non-Western nation (Brazil only sent three, for example, and Japan sent nine).[55]

The rhetoric of East-West affection and friendship that undergirded the conference, moreover, provided a way for Indian speakers to intervene in the coercive discourse of affection generated by Section 124a by changing its connotations, for in the global arena affect was more often associated with the language of diplomacy and accord than with colonialism and conquest. The use of the word "friendship" in treaty negotiations, alliances, and informal exchanges between leaders has ancient roots: "A *philia*, or treaty of friendship, was one of the most important of the treaties used by the Greeks.... In the case of Roman foreign relations, friendship was also considered to be a suitable concept to refer to relationships between states."[56] Scholars of its historical usages, such as Heather Devere, Simon Mark, and Jane Verbitsky, trace the concept of friendship from ancient Greece and Rome through the Middle Ages to the modern period, when the invocation of friendship became largely strategic rather than idealistic.

---

54. *Record of the Proceedings of the Universal Races Congress* (London: P. S. King and Son, 1911), 41.
55. This was the same strategy Gandhi would later use with such panache in his sedition trial of 1922 (see chapter 1).
56. Heather Devere, Simon Mark, and Jane Verbitsky, "A History of the Language of Friendship in International Treaties," *International Politics* 48, no. 5 (2010): 46–70.

Rarely based on equal partnership, so-called "friendship treaties" are frequently used as "a tool of public relations and spin, rather than diplomacy and peacebuilding."[57] However, they also qualify this statement to exclude full-scale imperialism: "The terminology of friendship was not used when treaties involved the surrendering of land or resources."[58] James Fitzjames Stephen (the architect of Section 124a), aligning himself with this understanding of the British presence in India and blithely throwing liberal rationales under the bus, stated in a letter to the *Times* that the British government in India was "an absolute government, founded not on consent but on conquest."[59]

Notwithstanding Stephen's brutal candor, many involved in British governance in the early twentieth century found the language of East-West amity strategically useful as a counter to the rise of nationalism. Carl Schmitt's notion of the friend-enemy distinction as fundamental to the formation of political community is relevant here. In his analysis, political community is called into being by the delineation of an enemy with which one might go to war. One is willing to die for their "friend"—a member of one's political community—and to kill one's political enemy. The fear that Indians were organizing a proto-nationalist political community and increasingly imagining Britain as the enemy was a good reason for those invested in empire to insist on friendship as the connective tissue between colonized and colonizer, so that they could be imagined as part of the same polity rather than as political antagonists.[60] Meanwhile, Indians engaging in the discourse of friendship in this period employed it to introduce a presumption of equality into the colonial dialogue and to create a vision of India as a modern liberal nation frustrated with its "ally," rather than a colony pleading for release from bondage or poised for a violent liberation struggle. The language of friendship as it was deployed in colonial contexts in the early twentieth century, then, helped fudge the line between alliance and conquest for the colonized as well as the colonizer who, for opposing reasons, could pretend their relationship was strategically advantageous and consensual rather than coercive.

Gokhale's speech at the URC is a case in point. Gopal Krishna Gokhale was a key figure in Indian nationalism, influential on Gandhi among other major figures of the movement. A Brahmin with an English education, he was part of the cosmopolitan elite class that made up the most internationally visible part

---

57. Devere, Mark, and Verbitsky, "History of the Language of Friendship," 1.
58. Devere, Mark, and Verbitsky, "History of the Language of Friendship," 64.
59. Thomas R. Metcalf, *Ideologies of the Raj* (Cambridge: Cambridge University Press, 1995), 210.
60. See Carl Schmitt, *The Concept of the Political* (Chicago: University of Chicago Press, 1995).

of the Indian nationalist movement and eventually became one of the leaders of the Indian National Congress. As a political moderate, he advocated gradual reformist progress toward self-rule and was considered by more revolutionary leaders, such as his political rival Tilak, to be pro-British. Before the URC, he had been to London a number of times; in 1898, for example, he visited in order to protest the exploitation of Indian revenues and resources by Britain before the Welby Commission, convened by Parliament. He thus had ample experience in trying to leverage the terms of the system to the ends of the reformist Congress Party.

At the URC, Gokhale's strategy was to inhabit the imperial language of friendship in order to expose its hypocrisies to the British on their own turf. He thus evoked the conference's desire to encourage "the most friendly feelings and the heartiest cooperation" as a way to critique British rule in India; point to the naïveté of the conference's ideals in the light of imperial exploitation and the racist ideas that enabled it; and directly address and challenge presumptions about the binary that structured the conference. His paper was bluntly titled "East and West in India" and notes early on that "with the commencement of the twentieth century the relations between the East and West may be regarded as having entered a new phase."[61] Arguing that "the traditional view ... of the changeless and unresisting East" had been historically used to justify Western expansion "in utter disregard of the rights or feelings of Eastern peoples," he used intimations of the rising power of the East, including "the victories of Japan over Russia," "the awakening of China," and "the spread of the national movement in India" as a backdrop for a thinly veiled call to national self-determination across the empire and to the idea of Asia as a newly formidable entity on the world stage.[62] He stressed, therefore, "a new pride in the special culture and civilization of the East" and "a new impatience of Western aggression and Western domination and a new faith in the destiny of Eastern peoples. India could not but be affected by these thought-currents with the rest of Asia."[63]

While the speech emphasized the rise of the East and the West's loss of stature, morally if not politically, a key part of Gokhale's argument relied on his inhabiting the ideology of Eastern backwardness for, strategically at least, it allowed him to chastise the British for not leading India toward democracy.[64] He states,

---

61. G. K. Gokhale, "East and West in India," in Spiller, *Papers on Inter-Racial Problems* (1969), 158.
62. Gokhale, "East and West in India," 158.
63. Gokhale, "East and West in India," 161.
64. On internalized Orientalism, see Adas, "Contested Hegemony," 76–77.

for example, that British conquest was facilitated by the fact that "India did not develop the national idea or the idea of political freedom as developed in the West" and that therefore the point of English rule was to help "the people of India ... to advance steadily to a position of equality ... so that they might in due course acquire the capacity to govern themselves in accordance with the higher standards of the West."[65]

But he uses this assumption to drive home the argument that the British have betrayed their initial promise to India—"English administrators were not in practice as ready to advance along lines of constitutional development as had been hoped, and ... the bulk of Englishmen in the country were *far from friendly*, even to the most reasonable aspirations of Indians in political matter" (my emphasis).[66] Here, the language of friendship underscores British political betrayal, but also highlights the racial condescension whereby Indians have been encouraged to learn about the West while the English have not correspondingly learned about "Indian culture and civilization."[67] Whereas Indian universities encouraged insight into Western culture that was "sympathetic and marked by deep and genuine appreciation," this openhearted affect had gone unreciprocated, Gokhale argued.[68] There were no grounds for good feeling between colonizer and colonized, in other words, because the former had betrayed all their promises, proving themselves unworthy of love and admiration.

One passage is particularly effective in delineating the relationship between colonial power, coercion, and affection:

> The soul of social friendship is mutual appreciation and respect, which ordinarily is not found to co-exist with a consciousness of inequality. This does not mean that where equality does not exist the relations are necessarily unfriendly. It is not an uncommon thing for a party which is in what may be called a state of subordinate dependence on another to be warmly attached to that other party. But such relations are possible only if the subordinate party—assuming, of course, that its sense of self-respect is properly developed—is enabled to feel that its dependent state is necessary to its own interest, and that the other party is taking no undue advantage of it for other ends.[69]

---

65. Gokhale, "East and West in India," 159.
66. Gokhale, "East and West in India," 160.
67. Gokhale, "East and West in India," 164.
68. Gokhale, "East and West in India," 164.
69. Gokhale, "East and West in India," 163.

The triple negative in the second sentence ("This does not mean that where equality does not exist the relations are necessarily unfriendly"), followed immediately by the double negative in the next sentence ("It is not an uncommon thing"), brings into view the frictive and unsustainable nature of the imperial relationship and the reluctance and ambivalence with which Gokhale buys into the romance allegory that accompanied it. The relationship between Britain and India is described in terms vaguely reminiscent of an S and M contract for good reason: Gokhale is working hard to disentangle coercion from consent and thus to make an intervention that cuts to the heart of the imperial imaginary. If the subordinate is not self-hating and can act in their own best interest; if the dominant party cares about the subordinate's well-being and is not being exploitative; if, in other words, the relationship is voluntary on both sides, it can sustain affection. While canny about the way the fiction of romance serves as a thin veneer for a sexualized threat of violence, this strange attempt to distribute agency across a relationship that even British administrators like Stephens admitted was founded "not on consent but on conquest" demonstrates how much currency the language of affection had in this moment, and how hard people worked rhetorically to bend it to their advantage.[70]

Gokhale's paper was reprinted in the Indian English-language journal the *Hindustan Review* and generated much commentary from Indians and English writers there, as well as in other publications. The missionary Rev. Edwin Greaves's response to Gokhale's piece reveals how unsettling Indian versions of the East-West binary were to Anglo-Indians. Citing a range of cosmopolitan lessons from the conference ("There are not many races but one; differences from, say, a Western standard do not necessarily involve inferiority," and "the onward march of humanity [is] towards the desired goal of unity in diversity"), Greaves nonetheless takes to task Gokhale's sidestepping of questions of religion. "Difficult though the problem may be," he states woefully, "we have to face the fact that the great dream of the brotherhood of humanity can never be realized until the reality be fully accepted that there is one God who is the common Father of us all."[71] This remark makes apparent the degree to which the norms of the imperial public sphere had shifted by the early twentieth century. As I noted in the introduction, the fiction of free and rational debate in colonial periodicals was initially governed by a Christian conversion imperative; by this point in the

---

70. Metcalf, *Ideologies of the Raj*, 210.
71. Edwin Greaves, "The Universal Races Congress," *Hindustan Review* (September 1911): 327, 329, 330.

new century, however, the Christian framework needed to be articulated as such because it was no longer hegemonic.

What we see in Gokhale's speech, then, are two versions of the East-West affect allegory, both influential in this moment. One version describes a soured romance between East and West that can only be rectified by the West being properly supportive of its dependent (by living up to its liberal ideas and promoting progress toward self-rule). The other version is of a kind of East-West death match—an agonistic struggle in which the East is swiftly gaining advantage in strength by rejecting Western materialism in favor of solidarities based on difference from, and moral superiority to, the West.

In the next section, the scene shifts from London to Bombay, home of the Indian modernist periodical *East and West*. The journal shared with the URC the utopian idea that the right platform for East-West exchange would lead to greater understanding and mutual respect, thereby undermining racial biases and political conflict. But if the URC serves as a still shot of the way amity and animus were intertwined in early twentieth-century conceptions of East vs. West, the editorial trajectory of the journal reflects a movement from one stance to the other, as the idea of East-West cultural exchange gave way to more openly anti-Western writing and the imagining of new solidarities inspired by pan-Asian and international labor movements. While the URC registered the ambivalence surrounding ideals of racial equality and international amity at the threshold of World War I, *East and West* reflects the way the war impacted views of the West and of empire, and fomented new political imaginaries. Writing of the effect of the war on Afro-Asian views of the civilizing mission, Adas states that "the crisis of the Great War gave credence to Gandhi's contention that the path for humanity cleared by the industrial West was neither morally or socially enabling nor ultimately sustainable."[72] Gandhi was perhaps the most famous proselytizer of this position but after the war it was visible everywhere, including in the genteel and relatively moderate editorial columns of *East and West*.

Never the Twain: Dialogue and Dialectic in *East and West*

In 1905 the *Malabar Quarterly Review* published an article on "The Prospects of an English Literature of Indian Growth." It spoke of Sarojini Naidu, the Indian

---

72. Adas, "Contested Hegemony," 63.

nationalist poet who wrote in English and was lauded by British writers such as Arthur Symons and Edmund Gosse, as the harbinger of a harmonious union of East and West, despite the ill omens which the author of the article associates with "Kipling and his ilk." "The growing exhaustion of the imaginative spirit," he writes, "has been a complaint whose doleful accents have been resounding through the dim corridors of the last century. That the aggressions of science are broadening the conquests of knowledge is a matter of everyday experience to us; that the fount of imaginative glow is ebbing out is equally evident.... May not the Oriental warmth of colour be inoculated into the Western hardness of outline?"[73] In this version of the East-West encounter, we see an Indian version of the Western modernist call to "make it new" through literary hybridization. Before the project of writers such as W. B. Yeats, T. S. Eliot, E. M. Forster, and Gertrude Stein to renovate Western culture through the incorporation of Asian and African elements became legible as such, Indian writers were calling for a similarly synthetic undertaking, in part because of the coercive conditions under which they contributed to the imperial public sphere. This version of the modernist idea, however, had Eastern literary output—the "Oriental warmth of colour"—forming the substance of artistic work, with the West providing only the vehicle of language (the "hardness of outline"). Here, Indian writing in English is figured not as mimicry but as the grounds for a new aesthetics.

An influential journal with a two-decade print run, *East and West* was invested in this form of syncretism both formally and ideologically; the hemispheric categories functioned as synecdoches for India and Britain respectively and the journal sought to create "a larger understanding" between the two cultures. The exchange of ideas that would lead to this understanding was showcased through its attempt to balance and alternate Eastern and Western perspectives in its pages.[74] *East and West* published articles by British writers about India and Indian writers about Britain, ones in favor of imperial policy and others critical of it (by both British and Indian writers), while literary debates between British and Indian writers, often with a pointed political subtext, raged in the correspondence column. In this way it sought to enact in the reader's experience of the periodical a sense of parity and exchange between perspectives that champions of this brand of syncretism believed would benefit both sides.

---

73. M. N. Rama Aiyar, "The Prospects of an English Literature of Indian Growth," *Malabar Quarterly Review* 5 (1906–7): 286.

74. From a recurring announcement to advertisers in *East and West*. For the full quote, see 22.

Yet the ways in which the vision of the journal changed between 1901, when it first came into print, and 1921, when it folded, reveal the malleable function of syncretic ideals in the colonial context and the pivotal role of World War I in changing the nature of these ideals. In *East and West*, syncretism functioned as a form of modernism that mediated between an Enlightenment-inflected public sphere cosmopolitanism and an anti-Western spiritual cosmopolitanism more amenable to pan-Asian and Afro-Asian solidarities. From a chronological perspective, the journal's investment in these different cosmopolitanisms gradually shifted over its print run from one affiliated with the West to one affiliated with the East. In performing this shift, the journal made explicit a crucial change in the public sphere more broadly. Even as the early years of *East and West* subscribe to a cosmopolitanism that upholds the public sphere ideals mandated by the British government, during and after the First World War the journal begins to flip the dynamic of the East-West binary in an attempt to defamiliarize and deconstruct Western supremacy. In doing so, it demonstrates a broader discursive shift within the Indian Anglosphere from Enlightenment public sphere norms, developed through imperial ideology and law to promote white supremacy and maintain imperial order, to an anti-Western vision both aesthetic and political. Although the utopian internationalism of this vision was to be upstaged by the various forms of nationalism that eventually dominated the Indian press, the journal, like the URC, represents a vital moment in the history of alternative forms of anticolonialist modernism.[75]

Published in Bombay from 1901 to 1921, *East and West* was an English-language monthly founded by Behramji Malabari, a poet, reformer, and journalist who enacted his interest in East-West syncretism through a variety of literary pursuits.[76] He wrote two books addressed to both Indian and British audiences: *The Indian Muse in English Garb* (1876), a collection of poetry written in English that attracted the notice of Alfred, Lord Tennyson and *The Indian Eye on English Life*, mentioned earlier—a flaneurian account of London that challenged and

---

75. Another periodical study that covers some of the same period as this one, of the Bengali journal *Kallol*, also focuses on the way it created an internationalist imaginary. See Kris Manjapra, "From Imperial to International Horizons: A Hermeneutic Study of Bengali Modernism," *Modern Intellectual History* 8, no. 2 (August 2011): 327–59.

76. As Isabel Hofmeyr points out in her work on *Gandhi's Printing Press*, many of those involved in what she calls "printing culture" were part of reform movements: "Among proprietors, printing acquired a strong aura of reform and progress, with the figure of the printer-editor-proprietor an almost stock character of reformist movements across the sub-continent" (36). Editors such as Malabari belonged to the world of the "educated amateur.... These editors had to be men of many parts: lawyers, journalists, editors, social workers, historians, and politicians" (43).

reversed stereotypes of Western travel literature.[77] He also helped disseminate the work of the Orientalist scholar Max Müller in India, who in turn garnered British publicity for Malabari's reform campaigns against child marriage and in favor of widow remarriage. An article commemorating Malabari's work as a reformer published in *East and West* in 1913 shortly after his death stressed not only his contribution to women's rights but also his importance as an "interpreter" between Britain and India and his willingness to bring about "peace and goodwill between the rulers and the ruled . . . by telling each how to meet the other halfway."[78]

Malabari was no radical, then, but by creating a structural tension between East and West, his journal brought into view the cultural biases that guided these public sphere norms and provided both a context and forum for their redefinition. If the relationship between East and West was often imagined as a romance in British and Indian writing of the early twentieth century—the aesthetically satisfying "fusion" of complementary elements that Abercrombie's review of *Gitanjali* describes—it was also depicted as a dialectical struggle for civilizational supremacy. These two versions of the relationship were often visible in *East and West* at the same time, but as anti-Westernism and nationalism gained traction after World War I, the more optimistic view of East-West interaction that defined the journal at its outset grew darker. Correspondingly, the journal's cosmopolitanism, initially invested in public sphere norms of transparency, objectivity, and liberal critique, became allied with pan-Asianism, spiritualism, and anticapitalist critique instead—a formation Peter van der Veer usefully terms "spiritual cosmopolitanism."[79]

Since the turn of our century, a number of critics have addressed the diverse ways in which various versions of spiritual cosmopolitanism emerged at the turn of the last one. Alongside van der Veer, Gauri Viswanathan, Srinivas Aravamudan, Leela Gandhi, Elleke Boehmer, Nico Slate, and others have illuminated the fascinating networks and exchanges whereby many revered religious leaders of the early nationalist movement, from Swami Vivekananda to Gandhi, developed their forms of Hindu universalism in direct and indirect conversation with westerners interested in Indian spiritualism, from W. B. Yeats and Madame Blavatsky

---

77. On Malabari's writing about Britain, see Burton, *At the Heart of the Empire*.

78. Rai Bahadur Lala Baij Nath, "Three Modern Indian Reformers," *East and West* 12, no. 137 (March 1913): 225.

79. Peter van der Veer, "Colonial Cosmopolitanism," in *Conceiving Cosmopolitanism: Theory, Context and Practice*, ed. Steven Vertovec and Robin Cohen (Oxford: Oxford University Press, 2002), 177.

to Max Müller and W. E. B. Du Bois.[80] Together, these different accounts provide a thick description of spiritual cosmopolitanism as a discourse derived from the colonial experience that had significant cultural and political effects, some salutary and some less so, from its originary moment to our own (in Aravamudan's account, its legacies range from the commercialized spirituality of yoga to the violent excesses of contemporary Hindu nationalism). Adding *East and West* to this picture, however, allows us to see the degree to which spiritual cosmopolitanism was shaped by modernism, the periodical genre, and the strictures of imperial censorship, which encouraged the rejection of Western public sphere norms. Spiritual cosmopolitanism took shape in both the content and form of *East and West* as a disaffected stance on the exclusions of Enlightenment cosmopolitanism and a strategy whereby to wrest from the British the vocabulary of moral superiority and aesthetic-philosophical vanguardism.

Published during a period when radical periodicals in Britain and experimental Indian publications such as the South Africa–based *Indian Opinion* sought to intervene in public discourse by changing the nature of print culture, *East and West* was both intriguingly innovative and profoundly mainstream. Elizabeth Miller and Isabel Hofmeyr explore the ways in which late nineteenth- and early twentieth-century figures who sought radical political change, such as William Morris and Gandhi, intervened in their respective commercial print worlds by eschewing advertising, running collaborative presses, and producing periodicals that contested mass industrialized culture both through their anticapitalist content and through their approach to periodical form.[81] Gandhi's *Indian Opinion*, for example, strove for a "slow reading" experience whereby readers would learn *swaraj* (self-rule) through "the process of learning to read in a patient, concrete, nonteleological way."[82] *East and West*, on the other hand, flagrantly played to bourgeois aspirations. It carried advertisements for gold watches, insurance, and

---

80. I refer respectively to Peter van der Veer, *Imperial Encounters: Religion and Modernity in India and Britain* (Princeton, NJ: Princeton University Press, 2001); Gauri Viswanathan, *Outside the Fold: Conversion, Modernity, and Belief* (Princeton, NJ: Princeton University Press, 1998); Srinivas Aravamudan, *Guru English: South Asian Religion in a Cosmopolitan Language* (Princeton, NJ: Princeton University Press, 2006); Leela Gandhi, *Affective Communities: Anticolonial Thought, Fin-de-Siècle Radicalism, and the Politics of Friendship* (Durham, NC: Duke University Press, 2006); Elleke Boehmer, *Empire, the National, and the Postcolonial, 1890–1920: Resistance in Interaction* (New York: Oxford University Press, 2002); and Nico Slate, *Colored Cosmopolitanism: The Shared Struggle for Freedom in the United States and India* (Cambridge, MA: Harvard University Press, 2012).

81. Elizabeth Carolyn Miller, *Slow Print* (Stanford, CA: Stanford University Press, 2013); Hofmeyr, *Gandhi's Printing Press*.

82. Hofmeyr, *Gandhi's Printing Press*, 150.

new inventions from London and Paris exhibitions and avoided articles with politically radical content, focusing instead on the type of thoughtful but politically benign essays on literature, history, and politics that characterized highbrow British periodicals such as the *Westminster Review*, the *Edinburgh Review*, and comparable Indian reviews, like those regularly redacted in the *Indian World* (the *Malabar Quarterly Review*, *Indian Review*, *Calcutta Review*, *Modern Review*, and *Madras Review*).

While all these English-language Indian reviews published British as well as Indian writers, *East and West* was innovative because of the way it built divisions between East and West into its structure. If *Indian Opinion*, as Hofmeyr argues, sought to intervene in contemporary debates by creating a new form of imagined community—namely, an Indian diaspora united around ideals of swaraj—*East and West* produced an impression of divided community by giving imaginative form to the colonial public sphere and (usually) invisible racial boundaries.

Yet the journal also had utopian aspirations throughout its run. Within its pages, East and West were not always associated respectively with materialism and progress, and spiritualism and tradition, per the essentialist categories that tended to characterize modernist syncretism. Though this binary was important to the journal's anticolonialism and its critical response to World War I, an Eastern mentality of antimaterialism was one designed to be embraced by those from the West as well, for East and West came to be figured as philosophies rather than racialized geographies. The 1917 masthead enacts this figuration by displaying Europe and India together on a globe over which the word "East" is superimposed, while the "West" is represented by North and South America. The illustration thus highlights the arbitrary nature of geographical perspective and the journal's willingness to debunk Orientalist versions of the East-West binary.

In an early issue, the journal's utopianism used the language of Enlightenment cosmopolitanism. A notice to advertisers read: "*East and West* has a mission, to bring about a larger understanding between men of all races and creeds. It treats life as a whole and aims at a symbiosis of all nations." The journal's publication strategy and the range of subjects it addressed accentuated its cosmopolitan ambitions. It was printed in London and Paris as well as Bombay and covered an eclectic range of international subjects including, Julie Codell notes, "Hungarian writers, feminism in New Zealand, Irish Home Rule, ancient Egypt and Greece, Japanese education . . . Booker T. Washington, and American universities."[83] It attracted notable British, Anglo-Indian, Indian, and even American contributors

---

83. Codell, "Getting the Twain to Meet," 215.

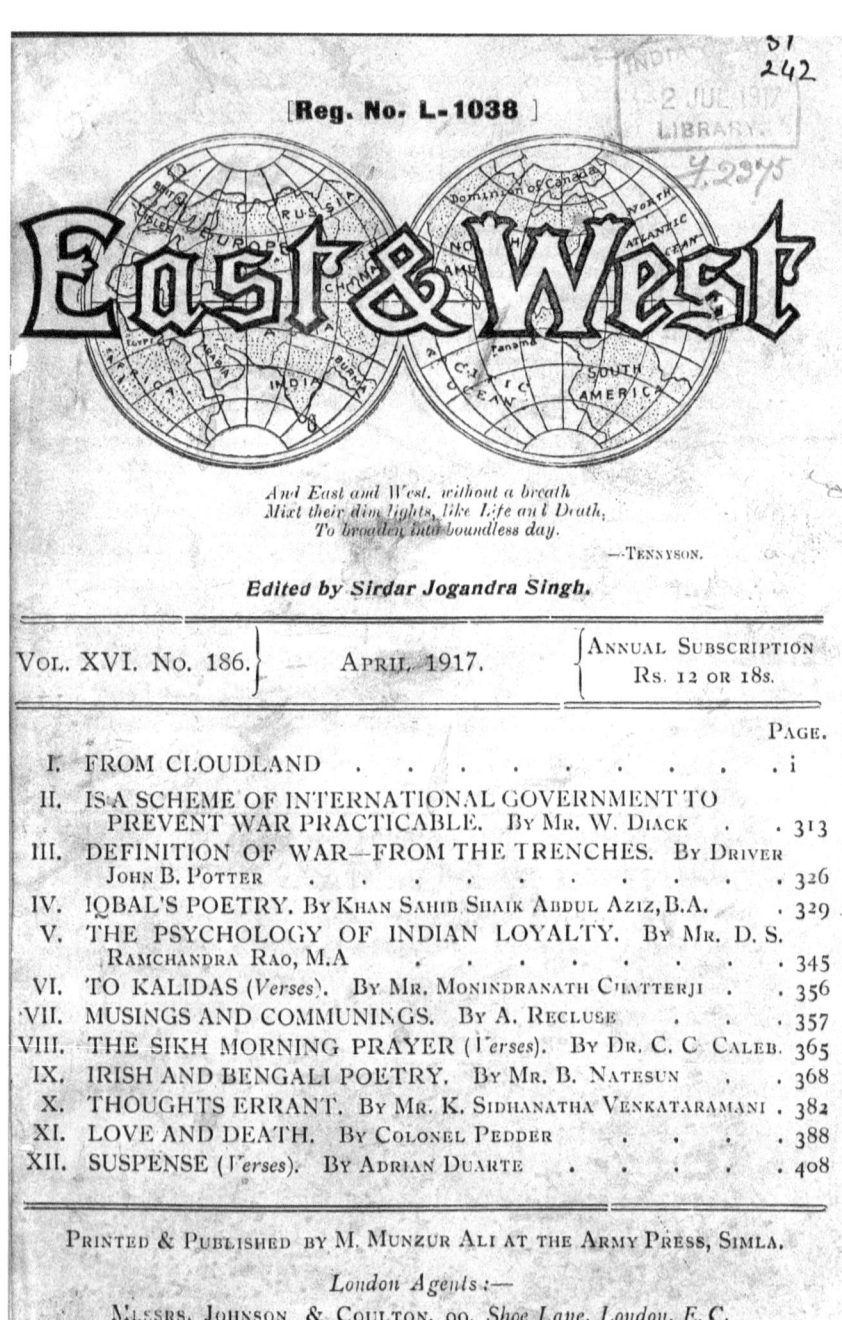

FIGURE 4.3 / Table of Contents from *East and West*, April 1917. Asia Pacific and Africa Holdings, British Library. Shelfmark SW 238, © British Library Board.

(among them Frances Power Cobbe, W. T. Stead, Sarojini Naidu, C. F. Andrews, and Gandhi) and its twenty-year run was unusual for an experimental periodical. A different notice to advertisers in later issues of *East and West* suggested that the journal had achieved its goal of speaking across the British-Indian divide by proclaiming it "the only review in Asia that can claim equal popularity among Europeans and Asiatics." We can deduce the relative success of the journal from the stature of many of its contributors and the fact that it was cited by other successful periodicals. In India it was repeatedly profiled in the *Indian World*, while in Britain it was cited in the *Asiatic Review* and its table of contents regularly summarized in W. T. Stead's *Review of Reviews*, along with those of other notable non-British periodicals.

East and West's utopian mission at a time of global conflict and nationalist unrest no doubt contributed to its broad appeal. In the earlier part of its run, the journal deployed the ideals of balance and critical distance that had been used as a rebuke to Indian emotionalism in the English-language public sphere (see introduction) to reenvision that sphere as a neutral space in which British and Indian writers conversed as equals. Thus, its issues always included both Indian and British writers as well as cultural perspectives clearly identified with each side—an article entitled "Oriental and Occidental Ideals," for example, stated that "the aim of the review is to get Britain and India to know each other and to see life through each other's eyes."[84] There were pieces by Indian writers reflecting on Western subjects (such as "An Eastern View of Western Science") as well as the more common spectacle of British writers commenting on Eastern subjects ("How Did Art Originate in the East?"). Other articles were comparative and analyzed both Indian and British culture or Asian and European cultures more broadly, dwelling upon cultural similarities ("The Traditional Mythic Histories of the Eastern and Western World") or differences: an article on "The Gulf between East and West" reflected on religious barriers to mutual understanding, for instance, whereas "The Great Separation" saw attitudes toward women and different culinary traditions as the chief impediments to friendship between British and Indian peoples. While British and Indian writers addressed both audiences across the journal, they spoke for their own cultures in doing so, making frequent use of the plural pronoun for themselves and the second person to address the other.

---

84. "Oriental and Occidental Ideas," *East and West* 1, no. 2 (December 1901): 151.

Yet, even at this early stage, when the journal tended to emphasize affection and rapprochement between Britain and India, the idea of disaffection and dissent was always present as well. If the Tennyson epigraph on its front page implied that *East and West*'s content represented a perfect synthesis of the two sides, Kipling's "The Ballad of East and West," which the journal's title would more readily have evoked for its readers, figured the space of the periodical as a battleground instead:

> Oh, East is East and West is West, and never the twain shall meet,
> Till Earth and Sky stand presently at God's great Judgment Seat;
> But there is neither East nor West, Border, nor Breed, nor Birth,
> When two strong men stand face to face, tho' they come from the ends of the earth!

Kipling's infamous vision of well-matched masculine rivalry is a significant intertext for the journal given the frequent association of the English-speaking Indian literary elite and its periodical culture with effeminacy and callowness. *East and West*'s global purview and the parallelism of its title imagined Britain and India as equal players, or combatants, on a world stage. Its dialogic structure, too, insisted on cultural parity and emphasized the antagonism implicit in the meeting of East and West.[85]

Over time, the journal began to use a comparative perspective that went beyond the East-West binary, connecting India to other colonies in the context of pressing social and political issues in order to "negotiate change and modifications for India's regional and parochial problems ([such as the] status of women, peasants, and education)."[86] By the 1910s, as the nationalist movement gathered momentum, *East and West* began to publish more inflammatory pieces that reflected both British and Indian perspectives on the viability of colonial rule. Each side used cosmopolitan rhetoric as the grounds for claims to civilizational superiority and to stage arguments for and against Indian nationalism.

A 1913 play *The Anarchist* by the British writer Edward E. Long, for example, constructed its critique of Indian nationalism around a story of failed cosmopolitanism. Long's play was one of many literary texts in this period to juxtapose violent nationalism with pacifist cosmopolitanism (the most famous being Tagore's 1916 *The Home and the World*), as a response to the more militant forms of anticolonialism that arose after the 1905 Partition of Bengal and the

---

85. On the feminization of the Indian literary elite, see Sinha, *Colonial Masculinity*.
86. Codell, "Getting the Twain to Meet," 215.

rise of the Swadeshi movement. Durba Ghosh's *Gentlemanly Terrorists of Bengal* describes how in this period an increasing number of "educated and predominantly Hindu men and women" took up internationalist revolutionary ideals and added violent tactics to the other forms of activism targeting colonial rule and economic exploitation: "As revolutionary terrorists organized violent attacks to draw attention to the swadeshi campaigns, the 'cult of the bomb' threatened to overtake the nonviolent project of boycotting foreign goods."[87]

Long's play responds directly to this threat. Its titular anarchist, Guru Das, is an Indian student who is pressured by his peers into throwing a bomb at a British administrator to whom he has privileged access, thanks to a letter of introduction from a man he once visited while studying in England. Before he gets a chance to do the deed, however, the administrator, presented as sympathetic and compassionate, enraptures Guru Das via reasoned debate, making him admit that he was treated kindly by his English hosts and must therefore not violate their trust.

In this exchange, cosmopolitanism—associated with an enlarged understanding of the other's point of view and the sanctity of guest-host relations—is depicted as a quality the British have mastered and that Indians have yet to learn. Convinced by the administrator's arguments, Das ends up extolling the cosmopolitan virtues of his English host: "I went to England a stranger: and he took me in. I was a raw youth, of narrow ideas and curious prejudices; he helped me to become enlightened—to know something of the larger world. He taught me to admire the free institutions of your country, to look upon it as the home of liberty—its people as just and kind, friends of the oppressed of every race, creed and caste. In mind and morals, he helped me to expand."[88] Overwhelmed by the moral superiority of both his erstwhile English host and his current interlocutor, Guru Das eventually kills *himself* with the bomb to spare the latter's life. The play's clumsy allegory thus reinforces the idea of cosmopolitanism as a proprietary British value. The revolutionary potential represented by Guru Das, identified by his name with the radical Hindu nationalism of the period, is violently erased by the story's end and the idea of India's political immaturity reestablished. Before the peculiar guest-host relation that is the imperial contest can come to a nonviolent end, the play implies, Indians must learn to be good hosts to their colonizers and capable, like the play's English characters, of transmitting enlightened values. Correlatively, *The*

---

87. D. Ghosh, *Gentlemanly Terrorists of Bengal*, 5–6.
88. Edward E. Long, *The Anarchist, East and West* 12, no. 139 (May 1913): 392.

Anarchist links political treason, or disaffection, to a failure of friendship and cosmopolitan ethics on the part of Guru Das. Because he comes to appreciate the friendship offered by his English host only after he has already committed to violence, he must turn that violence on himself in order to reciprocate affection, silencing himself forever in the process.

If the play most obviously functions as a thinly veiled critique of radical nationalism—indeed of any form of Indian nationalism, as it suggests that Indians are not enlightened enough to govern themselves peacefully—it might also be read as an allegory of the colonial public sphere, with British hospitality standing in for freedom of the press; Guru Das's bomb standing in for Indian critiques of colonial government; and his death serving as a grim warning that Indians will have only themselves to blame if they end up self-immolating, thereby eradicating themselves from rational debate (i.e., being censored). Through the very act of publishing *The Anarchist, East and West* was demonstrating its own cosmopolitan tolerance of varied viewpoints, for the piece was sure to rankle the journal's Indian readership. At the same time, however, in setting the play up as a dialectical contrast to the nationalist articles it was increasingly publishing, the journal was establishing disaffection, rivalry, and conflict rather than friendship and mutual understanding as the grounds for the East-West encounter.

An article published in the same year, "Tennyson in Light of Indian Thought," which touched off a debate between K. S. Ramaswamy Sastri, a scholar of Indian aesthetics, culture, and religion, and a British psychiatrist, Owen Berkeley Hill, similarly demonstrates the way the East-West relationship gradually became framed as a contest between different universalisms. Though he praises "In Memoriam" for its "glorious sincerity and melody" and insight into immortality, Ramaswamy Sastri argues that Tennyson lacks a fully transcendent vision because he is stymied by "the tangled labyrinth of modern views on life."[89] Tennyson, and the West as a whole, are connected with "democracy and science" in the article, but these characteristics of modernity are figured as liabilities as well as virtues, for they cast doubt on the eternal truths of religion revealed, the author argues, by the "deathless verse" of Hindu scriptures.[90] In citing scriptures from the Bhagavad Gita in support of his critique of Tennyson, Ramaswamy Sastri notably leaves them untranslated from Sanskrit, underscoring their inaccessibility to the Western reader.

---

89. K. S. Ramaswamy Sastri, "Tennyson's 'In Memoriam' in the Light of Indian Thought," *East and West* 12, no. 135 (January 1913): 63, 57.

90. Sastri, "Tennyson's 'In Memoriam,'" 60.

Responding to the article in a letter to the editor, Berkeley Hill objects to its critique of Tennyson and performs what he pointedly calls a "scientific and therefore utterly uncompromising examination" of its argument, in which he takes Ramaswamy Sastri to task for demonizing science and for not approaching "the so-called sacred writings of India in a critical spirit"—a claim that the Indian writer counters in another letter to the editor by arguing that "emotion, intuition, and spiritual vision are as good gateways to the shrine of Truth as pure logic and observation and experiment."[91] Though he appeals to public sphere norms of scientific detachment to discredit Ramaswamy Sastri, at this point in the journal's history the argument from inside another site of knowledge—Hindu scriptures—is situated as equally authoritative. Both letters and the original piece were published prominently (the letters were printed on the first page of the correspondence section within one issue of each other), suggesting that the editor wished to emphasize the dialectical and intractable nature of the conflict they embodied.

By rearticulating cosmopolitanism as an Eastern value, Indian writers in *East and West* drew on the discourse of Indian spirituality that had become central to the nationalist movement but focused on recruiting India's ancient religions to a new world-spirit that was at once anti-materialist, anticolonial, and antirational. In an article on "Irish and Bengali Poetry," for example, the pseudonymous author compares Yeats's Irish Renaissance to Tagore's Bengali revival and argues that both have had the effect of waking ancient peoples to a new self-consciousness but have also "(burst) asunder all shackles of race or language" to speak across cultures.[92] Another, entitled "Indian Nation—A Dream or a Reality?," stressed the affect rather than rationality of cosmopolitan sentiment, thus differentiating it from the Kantian cosmopolitanism of British print culture: "People have begun to *feel*, if they cannot argue, that there is an essential unity beyond and above the petty groups which we call Communities or nations—a brotherhood between the vast multitudes that inhabit the earth, and that the great purpose of religion is missed if it does not lead to harmony."[93]

In a recurrent editorial called "From Cloudland" that first appeared in 1920, the editor argued for a new dispensation that must come about in the aftermath of the war—one to which the journal was well-positioned to contribute: "All

---

91. Owen Berkeley Hill, "To the Editor," *East and West* 12, no. 137 (March 1913): 288, 289; K. S. Ramaswamy Sastri, "To the Editor," *East and West* 12, no. 139 (May 1913): 481.

92. B. Natesun, "Irish and Bengali Poetry," *East and West* 16, no. 186 (April 1917): 369.

93. Taher S. Mahomadi, "Indian Nation—A Dream or a Reality?," *East and West* 20 (January 1921), 38–39.

Governments stand discredited.... It is here that *East and West* comes with its message of symbiosis of mankind.... Our movement must succeed because it offers a permanent and abiding nucleus of universal brotherhood and universal peace.... The world is feeling for a unity which will shape itself and whose development will be very different from any conception of the present malignant contrivers."[94] Indian unrest and labor unrest on a worldwide scale, the editor goes on to argue, are part of the progress toward this world unity. References to the future economic unification of the world elsewhere in the piece point to the radical outcomes of globally dispersed labor movements which the journal champions and draws connections between. Rather than using older universalizing frameworks such as world literature or liberalism as the basis for claims to nationalism, the editor makes it a point to gesture toward new nonnational frameworks such as the global solidarity of labor—ones that might avoid the failures of Western modernity, or as he puts it, "the conception of the present malignant contrivers."

The "Cloudland" editorial, written by the journal's then-editor, Sardar Jogendra Singh, thus suggested a transcendence of the East-West divide through a form of solidarity that is felt rather than conceptualized. The title of the recurrent piece, with its reference to an impossible utopia, at once points to the fiction of the view from nowhere associated with public sphere cosmopolitanism and suggests a space beyond the East-West geopolitical frame in which a new politics might take shape. The perspective from "Cloudland" is, paradoxically, disembodied but visceral, universal but different. Shortly after the "Cloudland" editorial first appeared, however, *East and West* ceased publication (in 1921), most likely because of financial problems alluded to by Singh in its last issue. But its disappearance, like that of *Hindi Punch*, was appropriate given its growing insistence on the irrelevance of the East-West binary to its vision of the future. Staging and manipulating the ambivalent affective structures of the colonial relationship, the journal participated in a discursive shift from the notion of East-West dialogue and reconciliation to that of pan-Asian and nonaligned solidarities. In this way, it demonstrated over the course of its publication the kind of ambivalence about the possibility of rapprochement with the West also visible at the URC.

As we saw at the beginning of the chapter, Tagore and his poems were embraced by the West partly because his spiritualism, within the context of modernist syncretism, seemed complementary to Western aesthetics. After the war,

---

94. "From Cloudland," *East and West* 20 (January 1921): 1–5.

however, Tagore became more openly anti-Western in his public lectures and statements—reflecting the transformation in the colonial public sphere to which *East and West* had also contributed—and famously returned his British knighthood after the Amritsar Massacre of 1919. If World War I contributed immensely to the spread and urgency of both anticolonial nationalisms and internationalisms, it was not just because of the way it gave the lie to the West's "civilizing mission ideology" or because of the immense numbers of colonial subjects who had lost their lives defending it.[95] It was also because it helped bring Western global hegemony into view as such, accentuating the necessity of alternative visions of world order already in circulation: Pan-Asian, Afro-Asian, Pan-Islamic, socialist, and communist.[96]

As I have argued in this book, the form of the periodical, among other forms of discourse in the colonial public sphere, also participated in this visualization exercise. If the editorial vision of *East and West* was one of intercultural dialogue and mutual understanding, the journal also created a vivid portrait of the racialized and fragmentary nature of the colonial public sphere, making manifest the tension between public and counterpublic that operated in periodical culture at large by setting up the East-West binary as both a dialogue and a dialectic. By using the ambivalence written into the ideal of East-West union to mandate its critical perspective on culture and politics while circumventing censorship, it demonstrated the ways in which East-West exchange in the Indian context was structured by discord, rivalry, and disaffection as well as by professions of camaraderie and affection. Anticipating Forster's similar approach to syncretism in *Passage to India*, the journal demonstrated how the intimacy and mutual influence of East and West, framed as a romance by the law against disaffection but underwritten by colonial violence, was modernism's condition of possibility.

---

95. Michael Adas's term in "Contested Hegemony."
96. See Cemil Aydin, *The Politics of Anti-Westernism in Asia: Visions of World Order in Pan-Islamic and Pan-Asian Thought* (New York: Columbia University Press, 2007).

CONCLUSION

Appalled and outraged by the Amritsar massacre of 1919, Gandhi wrote a letter to the government renouncing three medals he had received for his humanitarian work and military service. He underscored his dissent with a speech act of noncooperation: "The attitude of the Imperial and Your Excellency's Government on the Punjab question has given me additional cause for grave dissatisfaction. . . . Your Excellency's light-hearted treatment of the official crime . . . and *callous disregard for the feelings of Indians* betrayed by the House of Lords, have filled me with the gravest misgivings regarding the future of the Empire, have *estranged me completely* from the present Government and have *disabled me from tendering, as I have hitherto tendered my loyal Cooperation*" (my emphasis).[1] The letter, like the sedition trial that was to follow two years later, demonstrates Gandhi's adeptness at enacting resistance not only politically but at the level of the sentence: "estranged," "disabled," and "filled . . . with the gravest misgivings," he is no longer able to provide cooperation, not because of his own feelings but because of those imposed upon him by the actions of "the present Government." Through this deft logic, Gandhi associates bad affect with the colonizers (not only those they have generated in him, but also their own "callous disregard" and "light-hearted treatment" of an egregious crime) and civility with the colonized (exemplified here by his polite yet unwavering renunciation of the regime—a particular version of civility that combined firm resistance with moral request that played a central role in the philosophy and praxis of nonviolent resistance he developed in this period).[2]

The 1922 trial of Gandhi for articles in his newspaper *Young India* gave him the opportunity to perform this reversal on a global stage and thus to transform the imperial public sphere more broadly. A turning point in the nationalist

---

1. Mahatma Gandhi, "Letter to Viceroy," August 4, 1920, in *Young India* (1922).
2. On the role of civility in Gandhi's philosophy and in his disagreements with Ambedkar, see Aishwary Kumar, *Radical Equality: Gandhi, Ambedkar, and the Risks of Democracy* (Stanford, CA: Stanford University Press, 2015).

movement from the standpoint of public culture and sedition legislation, the trial represents a departure from the print mimicry and double-coding upon which this book is focused because of the way Gandhi used the occasion, to brilliantly appropriate the discourse of disaffection for the nationalist cause, draw it out into the open, and reconfigure it as the very grounds of resistance.

As in the *Bangavasi* and Tilak cases, the government sought to make an example of the popular leader and turn the courtroom into a disciplinary spectacle, but Gandhi managed to steal the show by using the trial to stage a rousing critique of the depravities of British colonialism. While he nominally addressed this critique to those in the courtroom, his speech was also calculated to expose those depravities to the global audience who were following the trial in the press—in particular those in Britain who were already uneasy about colonialism's moral standing and its long-term viability.

Rather than denying his disaffection, Gandhi proudly laid claim to it, using a quietly ironic mode to hold the British position up to ridicule and underscore the justice of his cause; after the charges against him were read to the court, for instance, he asked if he could make a statement and, when asked for a record of this statement, said "I shall give it as soon as I finish reading it."[3] This understated resistance to the bureaucratic disciplines of the state exemplifies his stance throughout the trial and his philosophy of passive resistance. The statement that he read explained why he had become an "uncompromising disaffectionist and non-cooperator." He not only refused to contest the charges against him regarding the "preaching of disaffection" but wryly confessed that it was his "painful duty to admit before this Court that it commenced much earlier than the period stated by the Advocate-General."[4] In other words, he openly admitted to disaffection; made his accusers look weak by laying claim to greater amounts of it; *and* rearticulated it as loyalty and duty to his fellow Indians rather than to the British. He was forced to risk promoting violence, he argued, in the interests of speaking the truth: "I knew that I was playing with fire. . . . I know that I was feeling it so every day and I have felt it also this morning that I would have failed in my duty if I did not say what I said here just now. . . . I had either to submit to a system which I considered had done an irreparable harm to my country, or incur the risk of the mad fury of my people bursting forth when they understood the truth from my lips."[5] In listing the "irreparable harms" done to his people,

---

3. Cited in Noorani, *Indian Political Trials*, 232.
4. Noorani, *Indian Political Trials*, 232.
5. Noorani, *Indian Political Trials*, 232.

Gandhi honed in on the injustice of the legal system: "My experience of political cases in India leads one to the conclusion that in nine out of every ten cases the condemned men were totally innocent. Their crime consisted in the love of their country. In ninety-nine cases out of hundred, justice has been denied to Indians as against Europeans in the Courts of India. . . . In my opinion, the administration of the law is thus prostituted consciously or unconsciously for the benefit of the exploiter."[6]

Gandhi uses affect here in two key ways: first, he underscores his righteousness by suggesting that his sense of duty is something he *feels* "every day" and is compelled to respond to. Later in the trial, he also spoke of giving the judge "a glimpse of what is raging within my breast to run this maddest risk that a sane man can run." In drawing feeling, duty, and action together in his account of his behavior, Gandhi seeks to exemplify his integrity. Second, he conveys a not-so-subtle threat about the dangerous affective consequences of colonial exploitation by suggesting that "the mad fury" of his people, and the ensuing civil unrest that prompted the trial, was an inevitable consequence of their "learning the truth" about imperialism.

Employing the logic of the law against itself by arguing that if loyalty or affection was what was at stake, Indians were innocent because they had plenty of both, Gandhi suggested that disaffection for British rule was in fact evidence of the genuine, uncoerced affection one had for one's country. In one of the *Young India* articles used to accuse him of disaffection ("Tampering with Loyalty," September 29, 1921), he had urged his followers to "spread disaffection openly and systematically till it please the government to arrest us. And this we do, not by way of angry retaliation, but because it is our Dharma." In this article, as in the trial, he suggested that the cause of justice—in this case, speaking the truth about the evils of imperialism—was incompatible with the colonial rule of law, which he firmly resituated on the wrong side of history. That the judge was moved to commend him for his ethics and leadership at the end of the trial was a testament to the success of his strategy.

Gandhi's speech also tacitly addressed British people in Britain and India in order to provide them with face-saving language that might help them withdraw support for empire. After enumerating different ways imperialism had negatively affected India, such as famine, immiseration, and demoralization, he stated that "the greatest misfortune is that Englishmen and their Indian

---

6. Noorani, *Indian Political Trials*, 234.

associates in the administration of the country do not know that they are engaged in the crime I have attempted to describe.... They do not know that a subtle but effective system of terrorism and an organized display of force on the one hand, and the deprivation of all powers of retaliation or self-defense on the other, have emasculated the people and induced in them the habit of simulation. This awful habit has added to the ignorance and the self-deception of the administrators."[7] In this part of his statement, the law-and-order arm of the British government and its "terrorism" is sectioned off from the rest of the polity, which thus remains blameless. Gandhi notes that the state's disciplinary apparatus produces the culture of duplicity that allows Indians to escape charges of disaffection, while the Indian people, the "associates" he mentions (either Anglo-Indians or Indians who had government jobs, or both), and those in Britain are all simply victims of this duplicity. In depriving the people "of all powers of retaliation or self-defense," the disaffection law produces the emasculated, simulating babu who must hide his dissent—this figure in turn produces the ignorant, misguided administrator by masking the true disaffected nature of the colonized subject.

Gandhi's performance in the trial was designed to undo this vicious cycle of duplicity once and for all. Stating that "affection cannot be manufactured or regulated by law," he pointed to the coercion and violence that underlay Section 124a and flouted it, not only by embracing the role of seditionist, but by turning the trial itself into a large-scale act of sedition, in which the rousing nationalist rhetoric for which he was being tried was reenacted *and* guaranteed wider circulation, thanks to the international media coverage of the trial. He also reoriented the affection for the government required by law to the Indian people by demonstrating their allegiance to him (in responding affectively, or "with mad fury," to his leadership), his for them (by potentially sacrificing his freedom on their behalf), and theirs for each other (in acting out of love of country).

At the beginning of the trial, when nationalist leaders and other supporters rose to greet him, he announced that "this is like a family gathering and not a law court," thereby elevating volitional community over the nonconsensual imperial community that Section 124a was meant to suture together.[8] His statement

---

7. Noorani, *Indian Political Trials*, 234.

8. This quote is taken from Sarojini Naidu's account of the trial in her foreword to *The Great Trial of Mahatma Gandhi and Mr. Sankarlal Banker*, ed. Ke Pi Kēśavamēnōn (Madras: Ganesh, 1922), ix.

toward the end of the trial—"non-cooperation with evil is as much a duty as is cooperation with good"—with its notable emphasis on negation, accentuates the way disaffection with empire is at once a moral imperative and, according to the structure of the sentence, a precondition for good cooperation: the volitional community of the postcolony to come.[9] At least as rhetorical performance, Gandhi's trial marked the end of the tactics of evasion and transferred affect from coercive to consensual community. It also demonstrates the extent to which the law against disaffection galvanized the nationalist movement, shaped its rhetoric, and helped it gain an international profile.

My story of how the law against disaffection created a culture of subterfuge and print mimicry ends here, then, but some of its negative effects, as the preface notes, continue to play out in dispiriting and violent ways in contemporary India. While somewhat defanged in the postcolonial era, Section 124a continues to be used to quell dissent. More disturbing, though, is the way the law against disaffection helped shape the nationalist imagination. Framing community in affective and filial terms, as the law encouraged subjects, and then nationalists, to do, can contribute to solidarity, as Gandhi demonstrated. But it has also contributed to communal and gender-based violence and caste oppression because the filial community was from the start imagined and instantiated largely in Hindu, upper caste, and patriarchal terms. Meanwhile, as it did during British rule, Section 124a shapes the contours of the public sphere in restrictive ways. Because of the enduring practice of state censorship, Deepak Mehta maintains, Hindu and Muslim groups respond to various cultural texts by arguing "that religious sensibilities have been hurt. The group demands that state authorities censor the publication or performance. In the process a particular kind of seeing or viewing public is created, defined primarily through affect." Censorship thus circumscribes what can be said by "establishing in advance what will and will not be acceptable public discourse."[10]

In the United Kingdom and the United States, debates about free speech and censorship also flare up continually, reflecting deep anxieties about the breakdown of public discourse that recall those that shaped the period this book analyzes. At the end of 2017, a professor of theology at Oxford University, Nigel Biggar, published an article in the *Times* entitled "Don't Feel Guilty

---

9. Noorani, *Indian Political Trials*, 235.
10. Deepak Mehta, "Words That Wound: Archiving Hate in the Making of Hindu and Muslim Publics in Bombay," in *Beyond Crisis: Re-Evaluating Pakistan*, ed. Naveeda Khan (New Delhi: Routledge, 2010), 316.

about Our Colonial Past," which riffed on Bruce Gilley's now-infamous article on the benefits of colonialism in *Third World Quarterly*.[11] Arguing that "shame can stop us tackling the world's problems," Biggar insisted that Britain and its ex-colonies should recognize the benefits as well as evils of colonialism so that "pride can temper shame." Far from being the isolated opinion of a revisionist crank, Biggar's op-ed was attached to a larger project and bolstered by funding, in the form of a five-year interdisciplinary study of "Empire and Ethics" at the McDonald Centre at Oxford, with the goal of countering postcolonial critiques of empire via an exploration of its purported good deeds. Biggar's intervention prompted an immediate response from postcolonial scholars at the university in the form of an open letter asserting that many at Oxford did not support his project and found it intellectually bankrupt: "Good and evil may be meaningful terms of analysis for theologians. They are useless to historians. . . . There is no sense in which neutral 'historical data,' from any historical context, can simply be used to 'measure' the ethical appropriateness of either critiques of or apologia for empire, let alone sustain an 'ethic of empire' for today's world."[12]

In uncanny ways, Biggar's stance recapitulates the way the colonial government in India sought to consolidate power and defang political opposition by recasting critique in affective terms. He imagines himself the subject of injury and the target of anticolonial disaffection that "shames" him by making him feel evil as opposed to ethical. Just as the British required that Indian subjects admire their rulers by being affectionate, Biggar wants to create a public sphere—via op-eds and think tanks—in which a debate that considers "both sides" might restore his dignity by leveraging the kind of supposedly rational neutrality that prevailed in the British colonial press—a neutrality that refuses to hear critique that might undermine political and moral authority and turns it instead into emotion that wounds, thereby corralling it outside the pale. In their open letter, the Oxford postcolonialists noted that "neither we, nor Oxford's students in modern history will be engaging with the 'Ethics and Empire' programme, since it consists of closed, invitation-only seminars": in other words, Biggar's debate seeks "neutrality"—or positive affect (pride) as opposed to critique (shame)—through exclusion, just as the imperial public sphere did.

---

11. Nigel Biggar, "Don't Feel Guilty about Our Colonial Past," *Sunday Times*, November 30, 2007; Bruce Gilley, "The Case for Colonialism." Gilley's article was eventually withdrawn from *Third World Quarterly* and was republished in *Academic Questions* 31, no. 2 (2018): 167–85.

12. "Ethics and Empire: An Open Letter from Oxford Scholars," *Conversation*, n.d., http://theconversation.com/ethics-and-empire-an-open-letter-from-oxford-scholars-89333.

The way the term "ethics" is used in this debate is similar to the invocation of civility and incivility in political contexts in the contemporary United States. Like disaffection, "incivility" is a word loaded with underacknowledged historical baggage that makes it an unwieldy and double-edged rhetorical sword. On the one hand, it has been used to describe the uncensored racist, misogynist, and ad hominem attack politics of Trumpism that refuse the idea of shared norms and a common humanity; more frequently, however, it has been used to discredit politics and social justice movements that aim at radical inclusion rather than exclusion. Despite their profoundly antithetical motivations and ethical validity, both of these extremes are characterized as such from the perspective of the Enlightenment public sphere norms of reason, suspended judgment, and intercultural exchange that still, in theory, guide public debate. Yet together they make up the contradiction at the heart of these norms—the tension between the exclusion that has always existed in practice and the attempts to overturn it that must be made in the name of ideals supposedly already achieved (equality, free speech), and that are thus easy to brand as wrongheaded.

For example, in July 2020, following the explosive response to the murder of George Floyd, a "Letter on Justice and Open Debate" was published in *Harper's Magazine* that called for a return to civility and complained that the free exchange of ideas was being eroded by "cancel culture." The letter quickly elicited a response, "A More Specific Letter on Justice and Open Debate," that pointed out the myopism of the largely white and elite writers of the first letter: "the irony... is that nowhere... do the signatories mention how marginalized voices have been silenced for generations in journalism, academia, and publishing... in truth, Black, brown and LGBTQ+ people—particularly Black and trans people—can now critique elites publicly and hold them accountable socially; this seems to be the letter's greatest concern."[13] As the colonial history outlined here demonstrates, the use of fictions of civilizational difference, or incivility, to exclude nonwhite people demanding equality from public discourse in order to prolong their marginality was part and parcel of how civility worked as a norm, and how it continues to be leveraged.

In their "Eleven Theses on Civility," Tavia Nyong'o and Kyla Wazana Tompkins argue that "civility is the affective shape of administrative violence.... Civility discourse enforces a false equation between incivility and violence that works

---

13. "A More Specific Letter on Justice and Open Debate," *Objective*, July 10, 2020, https://theobjective.substack.com/p/a-more-specific-letter-on-justice.

to mask everyday violence as a civic norm."[14] Charges of incivility, as they suggest, have been used more effectively and for far longer to silence those who seek to oppose state violence and racism (such as the Palestinian-led Boycott, Divestment and Sanctions [BDS] movement) than those who support it (such as the many high-profile racists, including Anne Coulter, Milo Yiannopolis, Steve Bannon, and Charles Murray, invited to speak on college campuses and at other prestigious cultural venues in the wake of Trump's election despite their lack of intellectual credibility). If the way in which Section 124a aligned political critique with excessive affect during the colonial period informs the evocation of civility in contemporary political debates, its brand of exclusion also informs the correlative attempt, in writing from Franz Fanon to Nyong'o and Tompkins, to combat imperialism and its legacies by reclaiming anger as a spur to political change.

One way of identifying writerly critique with transformative affect that draws positively on the legacy of sedition law is suggested by Arundhati Roy, in the preface to her 2019 collection of nonfiction prose, *My Seditious Heart*. Roy's linking of sedition with the organ of feeling is based on her personal experience with Section 124a; as mentioned earlier, the law has been used in contemporary India by the conservative government against dissenting authors, politicians, students, and activists such as Roy, who was indicted for "anti-Indian" remarks in 2010. Though wearied by the constant public attacks she faces, Roy, like Gandhi, draws inspiration from the relationship between critique and affect articulated by colonial sedition law and uses it to reimagine critical writing as a collective enterprise in which everything, emotionally and politically, is at stake. Her essays, she writes in her preface, "opened doors for me to secret places where few are trusted, led me into the very heart of insurrections, into places of pain, rage, and ferocious irreverence. On these journeys, I found my dearest friends and my truest loves. . . . Although writers usually walk alone, most of what I wrote rose from the heart of a crowd. . . . It was never meant as neutral commentary. . . . It was just another stream that flowed into the quick, immense, rushing currents that I was writing about. My contribution to our collective refusal to obediently fade away."[15] Like Gandhi's speech in his trial, part of the force of this passage comes from negation, but also from a negation of that negation imagined in collective terms—a "refusal" to be obliterated that is also a movement, "quick, immense, rushing." This ardent and imperative dialectical vision, radically unfinished, is the legacy of colonial sedition law too.

---

14. Tavia Nyong'o and Kyla Wazana Tompkins, *Social Text Online*, July 11, 2018, https://socialtextjournal.org/eleven-theses-on-civility/.

15. Arundhati Roy, *My Seditious Heart*, 5.

BIBLIOGRAPHY

Abercrombie, Lascelles. "Poetry." *Blue Review* 1, no. 2 (June 1913): 117.
Abstract of the Proceedings of the Council of the Governor General of India, 9:446. 1870. Calcutta: Office of the Superintendent of Government Printing, India, 1906.
Adas, Michael. "Contested Hegemony: The Great War and the Afro-Asian Assault on the Civilizing Mission Ideology." *Journal of World History* 15, no. 1 (March 2004): 31–63.
Agamben, Giorgio. *Homo Sacer: Sovereign Power and Bare Life*. Palo Alto, CA: Stanford University Press, 1998.
Agathocleous, Tanya. *Urban Realism and the Cosmopolitan Imagination in the Nineteenth Century: Visible City, Invisible World*. Cambridge: Cambridge University Press, 2011.
Agathocleous, Tanya, and Janet Neary. "Before Bandung: Afro-Asian Cross-Referencing and Comparative Racialization." *Journal of Social History* 55, no. 2 (Winter 2021): 1–24.
Ahmad, Aijaz. "Jameson's Rhetoric of Otherness and the 'National Allegory.'" *Social Text*, no. 17 (Autumn 1987): 3–25.
Ahmed, Sara. *The Cultural Politics of Emotion*. 2nd ed. Edinburgh: Edinburgh University Press, 2014.
Ahmed, Siraj. *Archaeology of Babel: The Colonial Foundation of the Humanities*. Stanford, CA: Stanford University Press, 2018.
Aiyar, M. N. Rama. "The Prospects of an English Literature of Indian Growth." *Malabar Quarterly Review* 5 (1906–7): 280–83.
Aldrich, Robert. *Colonialism and Homosexuality*. New York: Routledge, 2002.
Anam, Nasia. "Can the Babu Speak (to the Dandy): A Study of the Nineteenth Century Literary Phenomenon of the Babu." Unpublished essay.
Anderson, Benedict. *Imagined Communities: Reflections on the Origins and Spread of Nationalism*. New York: Verso, 1983.
Arata, Stephen. *Fictions of Loss in the Fin de Siècle*. Cambridge: Cambridge University Press, 1996.
Aravamudan, Srinivas. *Guru English: South Asian Religion in a Cosmopolitan Language*. Princeton, NJ: Princeton University Press, 2006.
Arnold, David. *Colonizing the Body: State Medicine and Epidemic Disease in Nineteenth-Century India*. Berkeley: University of California Press, 1993.
Arnold, Matthew. "The Function of Criticism at the Present Time." In *Poetry and Criticism of Matthew Arnold*, edited by A. Dwight Culler, 237–59. Boston, MA: Houghton, 1961.
——. "Up to Easter." *Nineteenth Century* 73 (May 1887): 629–43.

Arondekar, Anjali. *For the Record: On Sexuality and the Colonial Archive in India.* Durham, NC: Duke University Press, 2009.
"Art I. The Nalodaya or History of King Nala, a Sanskrit Poem by Kálidàsa. Accompanied with a Metrical Translation, an Essay on Alliteration, an Account of Other Similar Works, and a Grammatical Analysis. By W. Yates." *Calcutta Review* 3, no. 5 (January 1845): 1–13.
Aydin, Cemil. *The Politics of Anti-Westernism in Asia: Visions of World Order in Pan-Islamic and Pan-Asian Thought.* New York: Columbia University Press, 2007.
Bakhle, Janaki. "Sarvarkar (1883–1966), Sedition and Surveillance: The Rule of Law in a Colonial Situation." *Social History* 35, no. 1 (February 2010): 51–75.
Bakhtin, Mikhail. *The Dialogic Imagination: Four Essays.* Edited by Michael Holquist. Austin: University of Texas Press, 1982.
Banerjee, Sikata. *Make Me a Man! Masculinity, Hinduism, and Nationalism in India.* Albany: State University of New York Press, 2005.
Banerjee, Sukanya. *Becoming Imperial Citizens: Indians in the Late-Victorian Empire.* Durham, NC: Duke University Press, 2011.
———. "Marriage, Modernity, and the Transimperial." In *Replotting Marriage in Nineteenth-Century British Literature*, edited by Jill Galvan and Elsie Michie, 145–67. Columbus: Ohio State University Press, 2018.
Barber, Karin. *The Anthropology of Texts, Persons, and Publics.* Cambridge: Cambridge University Press, 2007.
Barrier, Norman Gerald. *Banned: Controversial Literature and Political Control in British India, 1907–1947.* Columbia: University of Missouri Press, 1974.
Basker, James. "Criticism and the Rise of Periodical Literature." In *The Cambridge History of Literary Criticism*, vol. 4, *The Eighteenth Century*, edited by H. B. Nisbet and Claude Rawson, 316–34. Cambridge: Cambridge University Press, 2005.
Basu, Chaiti. "The *Punch* Tradition in Late Nineteenth Century Bengal: From Pulcinella to Basantak and Pācu." In Harder and Mittler, *Asian Punches*, 111–49.
Baylen, J. O. "Review of Reviews Office." In *Dictionary of Literary Biography*, vol. 112, *British Literary Publishing Houses 1881–1965*, edited by Jonathan Rose and Patricia J. Anderson, 266–68. Detroit, MI: Gale Research, 1994.
———. "W. T. Stead as Publisher and Editor of the '*Review of Reviews.*'" *Victorian Periodicals Review* 12, no. 2 (Summer 1979): 70–84.
Bayly, Christopher. *Empire and Information: Intelligence Gathering and Social Communication in India, 1780–1870.* Cambridge: Cambridge University Press, 1996.
Bell, Duncan. *The Idea of Greater Britain: Empire and the Future of World Order, 1860–1900.* Princeton, NJ: Princeton University Press, 2007.
Berlant, Lauren. *Cruel Optimism.* Durham, NC: Duke University Press, 2011.
———. "The Epistemology of State Emotion." In *Dissent in Dangerous Times*, edited by Austin Sarat, 46–78. Ann Arbor: University of Michigan Press, 2003.
———. "Intimacy: A Special Issue." *Critical Inquiry* 24, no. 2 (Winter 1998): 281–88.
Bhabha, Homi. *The Location of Culture.* New York: Routledge, 1994.
Bhattacharya, Baidik, and Sambudha Sen, eds. *Novel Formations: The Indian Beginnings of a European Genre.* Delhi: Permanent Black, 2018.
Boas, Franz. "Instability of Human Types." In Spiller, *Papers on Inter-Racial Problems* (1969), 99–104.

Boehmer, Elleke. *Empire, the National, and the Postcolonial, 1890–1920: Resistance in Interaction*. New York: Oxford University Press, 2002.
———. *Indian Arrivals, 1870–1915: Networks of British Empire*. Oxford: Oxford University Press, 2015.
———. "The Text in the World, the World through the Text: Robert Baden-Powell's *Scouting for Boys*." In Burton and Hofmeyer, *Ten Books*, 131–53.
Boone, Joseph. *The Homoerotics of Orientalism*. New York: Columbia University Press, 2014.
Bourdieu, Pierre. *Distinction: A Social Critique of the Judgement of Taste*. Translated by Richard Nice. Cambridge, MA: Harvard University Press, 1984.
———. *The Field of Cultural Production: Essays on Art and Literature*. New York: Columbia University Press, 1993.
Brake, Laurel. "Literary Criticism and the Victorian Periodicals." *Yearbook of English Studies* 16 (1986): 92–116.
———. "Stead Alone: Journalist, Proprietor, and Publisher 1890–1903." In Brake et al., *W. T. Stead*, 77–97.
Brake, Laurel, Ed King, Roger Luckhurst, and James Mussell, eds. *W. T. Stead: Newspaper Revolutionary*. London: British Library, 2012.
Brake, Laurel, and James Mussell. Introduction to *19: Interdisciplinary Studies in the Long Nineteenth Century* 16 (2013). http://doi.org/10.16995/ntn.669.
Brennan, Timothy. "Cosmopolitanism and Internationalism." In *Debating Cosmopolitics*, edited by Daniele Archibugi, 40–50. New York: Verso, 2008.
Brouillette, Sarah. "South Asian Literature and Global Publishing." *Wasafiri* 22, no. 3 (2007): 34–38.
Burton, Antoinette. *At the Heart of the Empire: Indians and the Colonial Encounter in Late-Victorian Britain*. Berkeley, CA: University of California Press, 1998.
Burton, Antoinette, and Isabel Hofmeyr. "Introduction: The Spine of Empire? Books and the Making of an Imperial Commons." In Burton and Hofmeyer, *Ten Books*, 1–29.
———, eds. *Ten Books That Shaped the British Empire: Creating an Imperial Commons*. Durham, NC: Duke University Press, 2014.
Butler, Judith. *Gender Trouble: Feminism and the Subversion of Identity*. New York: Routledge, 1990.
Chakrabarty, Dipesh. *Provincializing Europe: Postcolonial Thought and Historical Difference*. Princeton, NJ: Princeton University Press, 2008.
Chatman, Seymour. "Parody and Style." *Poetics Today* 22, no. 1 (Spring 2001): 25–39.
Chatterjee, Partha. *The Nation and Its Fragments: Colonial and Postcolonial Histories*. Princeton, NJ: Princeton University Press, 1993.
———. *Nationalist Thought and the Colonial World: A Derivative Discourse*. Minneapolis: University of Minnesota Press, 1993.
Chauduri, Supriya. "Modernist Literary Communities in 1930s Calcutta: The Politics of *Parichay*." In *Modernist Communities across Culture and Media*, edited by Caroline Pollentier and Sarah Wilson, 177–96. Gainesville: University Press of Florida, 2019.
Codell, Julie. "Getting the Twain to Meet: Global Regionalism in *East and West: A Monthly Review*." *Victorian Periodicals Review* 37, no. 2 (Summer 2004): 214–32.

Cohen, Ed. *Talk on the Wilde Side: Toward a Genealogy of a Discourse on Male Sexualities*. New York: Routledge, 1988.
Cohen, William. *Sex Scandal: The Private Parts of Victorian Fiction*. Durham, NC: Duke University Press, 1996.
Cohn, Bernard. *Colonialism and Its Forms of Knowledge: The British in India*. Princeton, NJ: Princeton University Press, 1994.
Cranmer-Byng, L. *The Classics of Confucius: Book of Odes (Shih-King)*. Wisdom of the East. London: John Murray, 1906.
Darnton, Robert. "Book Production in British India, 1850–1900." *Book History* 5 (2002): 239–62.
——. *Censors at Work: How States Shaped Literature*. New York: W. W. Norton, 2014.
——. "Literary Surveillance in the British Raj: The Contradictions of Liberal Imperialism." *Book History* 4 (2001): 133–76.
Das, Santanu. *India, Empire and First World War Culture: Writing, Images, and Songs*. Cambridge: Cambridge University Press, 2018.
Deleuze, Gilles, and Félix Guattari. *A Thousand Plateaus*. Minneapolis: University of Minnesota Press, 1987.
Denisoff, Denis. *Aestheticism and Sexual Parody, 1840–1940*. Cambridge: Cambridge University Press, 2001.
Devere, Heather, Simon Mark, and Jane Verbitsky. "A History of the Language of Friendship in International Treaties." *International Politics* 48, no. 5 (2010): 46–70.
Dirks, Nicholas B. *The Scandal of Empire: India and the Creation of Imperial Britain*. Cambridge, MA: Belknap Press, 2008.
Donogh, Walter Russell. *A Treatise on the Law of Sedition and Cognate Offences in British India*. Calcutta: Thacker, Spink, 1911.
Dorning, Mike. "Trump's Unthinkable Victory Is a Tonic for Disaffected Americans." *Bloomberg*, November 9, 2016, https://www.bloomberg.com/news/articles/2016-11-09/trump-s-unthinkable-victory-is-a-tonic-for-disaffected-americans.
Dowling, Linda. *Hellenism and Homosexuality in Victorian England*. Ithaca, NY: Cornell University Press, 1994.
DuBois, W. E. B. "The Negro Race in the United States of America." In Spiller, *Papers on Inter-Racial Problems* (1969), 348–64.
Dutta, Krishna. *Calcutta: A Cultural History*. Northampton, MA: Interlink Books, 2008.
Edgar, John. Letters from John Edgar, chief secretary to the Government of Bengal, to C. J. Lyall, secretary to the Government of India, April 20, June 13, and September 9, 1891. In *Proceedings of the Home Department*, P/3880, October 1891, 1501, 1507, 1615.
Eisenstein, Elizabeth. *The Printing Press as an Agent of Change: Communications and Cultural Transformations in Early Modern Europe*. Cambridge: Cambridge University Press, 1979.
Esty, Jed. *Unseasonable Youth: Modernism, Colonialism, and the Fiction of Development*. New York: Oxford University Press, 2011.
Fanon, Frantz. *Black Skin, White Masks*. New York: Grove Press, 1967.
Foldy, Michael S. *The Trials of Oscar Wilde: Deviance, Morality, and Late-Victorian Society*. New Haven, CT: Yale University Press, 1997.

Forster, E. M. *Passage to India.* London: Harcourt Brace, 1985.
——. *Two Cheers for Democracy.* New York: Harcourt Brace, 1951.
Fraser, Nancy. "Rethinking the Public Sphere: A Contribution to the Critique of Actually Existing Democracy." *Social Text* 25/26 (1990): 56–80.
Freitag, Sandria, ed. "Aspects of 'the Public' in Colonial South Asia." Special issue, *South Asia* 14, no. 1 (1991).
——. "Enactments of Ram's Story and the Changing Nature of 'the Public' in British India." *South Asia* 14, no. 1 (1991): 65–90.
——. "Introduction: The Public Eye and Its Meanings in Colonial South Asia." *South Asia* 14, no. 1 (1991): 1–13.
Friedman, Dustin. "E. M. Forster, the Clapham Sect, and the Secular Public Sphere." *Journal of Modern Literature* 39, no. 1 (2015): 19–37.
"From Cloudland." *East and West* 20 (January 1921): 1–5.
Gandhi, Mahatma, Ke Pi Kēśavamēnōn, and Shankarlal Banker. *The Great Trial of Mahatma Gandhi and Mr. Sankarlal Banker.* Madras: Ganesh, 1922.
Gandhi, Leela. *Affective Communities: Anticolonial Thought, Fin-de-Siècle Radicalism, and the Politics of Friendship.* Durham, NC: Duke University Press, 2006.
Gaonkar, Dilip Parameshwar, ed. *Alternative Modernities.* Durham, NC: Duke University Press, 2001.
Gasiorek, Andrzej. "War, 'Primitivism,' and the Future of 'the West': Reflections on D. H. Lawrence and Wyndham Lewis." In *Modernism and Colonialism: British and Irish Literature, 1899–1939,* edited by Richard Begam and Michael Valdez Moses, 91–111. Durham, NC: Duke University Press, 2007.
Gandhi, M. K. "Trial Statement." In *Collected Works of Mahatma Gandhi,* 26:377–86. New Delhi: Ministry of Information and Broadcasting, Government of India, 1958.
Ghosh, Amitav, and Dipesh Chakrabarty. "A Correspondence on Provincializing Europe." *Radical History Review* 83 (Spring 2002): 146–72.
Ghosh, Durba. *Gentlemanly Terrorists: Political Violence and the Colonial State in India, 1919–1947.* Cambridge: Cambridge University Press, 2017.
Ghosh, Durba, and Dane Kennedy, eds. *Decentring Empire: Britain, India and the Transcolonial World.* Hyderabad: Orient Blackswan, 2006.
Gibson, Mary Ellis. *Indian Angles: English Verse in Colonial India from Jones to Tagore.* Athens: Ohio University Press, 2011.
Gilley, Bruce. "The Case for Colonialism." *Academic Questions* 31, no. 2 (2018): 167–85.
Gilmartin, David. "Rethinking the Public through the Lens of Sovereignty." *South Asia* 38, no. 3 (2015): 371–86.
Gilmour, David. *The Long Recessional: The Imperial Life of Rudyard Kipling.* New York: Farrar, Straus and Giroux, 2002.
GoGwilt, Christopher. *The Invention of the West.* Palo Alto, CA: Stanford University Press, 1995.
Gokhale, G. K. "East and West in India." In Spiller, *Papers on Inter-Racial Problems* (1969), 157–67.
Goodlad, Lauren M. E. "Where Liberals Fear to Tread: E. M. Forster's Queer Internationalism and the Ethics of Care." *Novel: A Forum on Fiction* 39, no. 3 (2006): 307–36.

Goswami, Manu. "Imaginary Futures and Colonial Internationalisms." *American Historical Review* 117, no. 5 (2012): 1461–85.
Gramsci, Antonio. "Some Problems in the Study of the Philosophy of Praxis." In *Selections from the Prison Notebooks*, edited and translated by Quinton Hoare and Geoffrey Nowell Smith, 711. New York: International, 1985.
Greaves, Edwin. "The Universal Races Congress." *Hindustan Review* (September 1911): 327–30.
Griffin, Dustin. *Satire: A Critical Reintroduction*. Lexington: University Press of Kentucky, 1994.
Griffin, Lepel. "The Place of the Bengáli in Politics," *Fortnightly Review* 51, no. 306 (1892): 811–19.
Griffiths, Andrew. *The New Journalism, the New Imperialism and the Fiction of Empire, 1870–1900*. Houndsmills, Basingstoke: Palgrave, 2015.
Guerrini, Anita. "The Human Experimental Subject." In *A Companion to the History of Science*, edited by Bernard Lightman, 126–39. Hoboken, NJ: John Wiley, 2016.
Guha, Ranajit. *Dominance without Hegemony*. Cambridge, MA: Harvard University Press, 1998.
Gupta, Abhijit, and Swapan Charavorty. *Founts of Knowledge: Book History in India*. Hyderabad: Orient Blackswan, 2015.
———, eds. *Moveable Type*. Delhi: Permanent Black, 2008.
———. *Print Areas: Book History in India*. Delhi: Permanent Black, 2004.
Habermas, Jürgen. *The Structural Transformation of the Public Sphere*. Translated by Thomas Burger. Boston, MA: MIT Press, 1991.
Harder, Hans. "Prologue: Late Nineteenth and Twentieth Century Asian *Punch* Versions and Related Satirical Journals." In Harder and Mittler, *Asian Punches*, 1–11.
Harder, Hans, and Barbara Mittler, eds. *Asian Punches: A Transcultural Affair*. New York: Springer, 2013.
Hasan, Mushirul. *The Avadh Punch: Wit and Humour in Colonial North India*. New Delhi: Niyogi Books, 2007.
———. *Wit and Wisdom: Pickings from the Parsee Punch*. New Delhi: Niyogi Books, 2012.
Havard, John. *Disaffected Parties: Political Parties and the Making of English Literature, 1760–1830*. Oxford: Oxford University Press, 2019.
Hill, Owen Berkeley. "To the Editor." *East and West* 12, no. 137 (March 1913): 288–89.
Hindi Punch. "Preface to the Fourth Edition" (December 1902). In *Cartoons from the Hindi Punch*, edited by Barjorji Naoroji. Bombay: Hindi Punch Office, 1903–6.
Hofmeyr, Isabel. *Gandhi's Printing Press: Experiments in Slow Reading*. Cambridge, MA: Harvard University Press, 2013.
Hoggett, Paul, and Simon Thompson, eds. *Politics and the Emotions: The Affective Turn in Contemporary Political Studies*. London: Bloomsbury, 2012.
Holton, Robert John. "Cosmopolitanism or Cosmopolitanisms? The Universal Races Congress of 1911." *Global Networks* 2, no. 2 (2002): 153–70.
Hussain, Nasser. *The Jurisprudence of Emergency: Colonialism and the Rule of Law*. Ann Arbor: University of Michigan Press, 2003.
Hutcheon, Linda. "Parody without Ridicule: Observations on Modern Literary Parody." *Canadian Review of Comparative Literature* 5, no. 8 (Spring 1978): 201–11.
Hyam, Ronald. *Empire and Sexuality*. Manchester: Manchester University Press, 1991.

Hyde, H. Montgomery. *The Trials of Oscar Wilde*. New York: Dover, 1962.
The Indian Penal Code, 1860. Mumbai: Amit Nanda for Current Publications, 2016.
Jain, Anurag. "The Relationship between Ford, Kipling, Conan Doyle, Wells and British Propaganda of the First World War." Unpublished doctoral thesis, University of London, 2009.
Jain, Kajri. *Gods in the Bazaar: The Economies of Indian Calendar Art*. Durham, NC: Duke University Press, 2007.
Jameson, Fredric. "Third-World Literature in the Era of Multinational Capitalism." *Social Text* 15 (1986): 65–88.
Johnston, Harry H. "The World-Position of the Negro and the Negroid." In Spiller, *Papers on Inter-Racial Problems* (1969), 328–36.
Kalpagam, U. "Colonial Governmentality and the Public Sphere in India." *Journal of Historical Sociology* 14, no. 4 (December 2001): 418–40.
———. "Colonial Governmentality and the Public Sphere in India." *Journal of Historical Sociology* 15, no. 1 (December 2002): 35–58.
Kamra, Sukeshi. *The Indian Periodical Press and Nationalist Rhetoric*. New York: Palgrave Macmillan, 2011.
———. "Law and Radical Rhetoric in British India: The 1897 Trial of Bal Gangadhar Tilak." *South Asia* 39, no. 3 (2016): 546–59.
Kaur, Raminder, and William Mazzarella. "Between Sedition and Seduction: Thinking Censorship in South Asia." In *Censorship in South Asia: Cultural Regulation from Sedition to Seduction*, edited by Raminder Kaur and William Mazzarella, 1–29. Bloomington: Indiana University Press, 2009.
Kaur, Reetinder. "Representation of Crime against Women in Print Media: A Case Study of Delhi Gang Rape." *Anthropology* 2, no. 1 (2013). https://doi.org/10.4172/2332-0915.1000115.
Khanduri, Ritu Gairola. *Caricaturing Culture in India: Cartoons and History in the Modern World*. Cambridge: Cambridge University Press, 2014.
———. "Vernacular *Punch*es: Cartoons and Politics in Colonial India." *History and Anthropology* 20, no. 4 (2009): 459–86.
Kipling, Rudyard. *The Eyes of Asia*. New York: Doubleday, Page, 1918.
———. *Kim*. Edited by Paula M. Krebs and Tricia Lootens. 1901. New York: Pearsons, 2011.
Klancher, Jon. *The Making of English Reading Audiences, 1790–1832*. Madison: University of Wisconsin Press, 1987.
Kolsky, Elizabeth. *Colonial Justice in British India: White Violence and the Rule of Law*. Cambridge: Cambridge University Press, 2010.
Kosambi, Meera. "Girl-Brides and Socio-Legal Change: Age of Consent Bill (1891) Controversy." *Economic and Political Weekly* 26, nos. 31/32 (August 3–10, 1991), 1857–68.
Koven, Seth. *The Matchgirl and the Heiress*. Princeton, NJ: Princeton University Press, 2015.
Kumar, Aishwary. *Radical Equality: Gandhi, Ambedkar, and the Risks of Democracy*. Stanford, CA: Stanford University Press, 2015.
Law, Graham, and Matthew Sterenberg. "Old vs. New Journalism and the Public Sphere; or, Habermas Encounters Dallas and Stead." *19: Interdisciplinary Studies in the Long Nineteenth Century* 16 (2013). http://doi.org/10.16995/ntn.657.

Lazarus, Neil. *The Postcolonial Unconscious*. New York: Cambridge University Press, 2011.
Lee, Christopher J., ed. *Making a World after Empire: The Bandung Moment and Its Political Afterlives*. Athens: Ohio University Press, 2010.
Lelyveld, David. "Sir Sayyid's Public Sphere: Urdu Print and Oratory in Nineteenth Century India." In *Islamicate Traditions in South Asia: Themes from Culture and History*, edited by Agnieszka Kuczkiewicz-Fraś, 127–58. New Delhi: Manohar, 2009.
Levine, Caroline. *Forms: Whole, Rhythm, Hierarchy, Network*. Princeton, NJ: Princeton University Press, 2015.
Long, Edward E. *The Anarchist. East and West* 12, no. 139 (May 1913): 381–98.
Luschan, Felix von. "Anthropological View of Race." In Spiller, *Papers on Inter-Racial Problems* (1969), 13–24.
Macaulay, Thomas Babington. "Minute on Indian Education." Speech, February 2, 1835. In *Selected Writings*, edited by John Clive and Thomas Pinney, 237–51. Chicago: University of Chicago Press, 1972.
———. "Warren Hastings." *Edinburgh Review*, October 1841, 160–255.
Mahomadi, Taher S. "Indian Nation—A Dream or a Reality?" *East and West* 21 (January 1921): 38–39.
Maidment, Brian. *Comedy, Caricature and the Social Order, 1820–50*. Manchester: Manchester University Press, 2013.
———. "The Presence of *Punch* in the Nineteenth Century." In Harder and Mittler, *Asian Punches*, 15–44.
Makdisi, Saree. *Making England Western*. Chicago: University of Chicago Press, 2013.
Manalansan, Martin F., IV. "Servicing the World: Flexible Filipinos and the Unsecured Life." In *Political Emotions*, edited by Janet Staiger, Ann Cvetkovich, and Ann Reynolds, 215–228. New York: Routledge, 2010.
Manchester, Colin. "A History of the Crime of Obscene Libel." *Journal of Legal History* 12, no. 1 (1991): 36–57.
Manjapra, Kris. "From Imperial to International Horizons: A Hermeneutic Study of Bengali Modernism." *Modern Intellectual History* 8, no. 2 (August 2011): 327–59.
Marshall, A. *The Prince of Satire in England, 1658–1770*. Baltimore: Johns Hopkins University Press, 2013.
Martin, Amy. "Representing the 'Indian Revolution' of 1857: Towards a Genealogy of Irish Internationalist Anticolonialism." *Field Day Review* 8 (2012): 126–47.
Massumi, Brian. *Politics of Affect*. Cambridge: Polity Press, 2015.
McDonald, Peter. *The Literature Police: Apartheid Censorship and Its Cultural Consequences*. New York: Oxford University Press, 2009.
McGill, Meredith. "What Is a Ballad? Reading for Genre, Format, and Medium." *Nineteenth Century Literature* 71, no. 2 (2016): 156–75.
McKean, Lise. *Divine Enterprise: Gurus and the Hindu Nationalist Movement*. Chicago: University of Chicago Press, 1996.
Mehta, Deepak. "Words That Wound: Archiving Hate in the Making of Hindu and Muslim Publics in Bombay." In *Beyond Crisis: Re-Evaluating Pakistan*, edited by Naveeda Khan, 315–43. New Delhi: Routledge, 2010.
Mehta, Uday. *Liberalism and Empire: A Study in Nineteenth-Century British Liberal Thought*. Chicago: University of Chicago Press, 1999.

Menke, Richard. "Touchstones to Tit-Bits: Extracting Culture in the 1880s." *Victorian Periodicals Review* 47, no. 4 (Winter 2014): 559–76.
Metcalf, Thomas R. *Ideologies of the Raj*. Cambridge: Cambridge University Press, 1995.
Meyer, Moe. "Under the Sign of Wilde: An Archaeology of Posing." In *The Politics and Poetics of Camp*, edited by Moe Meyer, 75–110. London: Routledge, 1994.
Miller, Elizabeth Carolyn. *Slow Print*. Stanford, CA: Stanford University Press, 2013.
Miller, Henry J. "John Leech and the Shaping of the Victorian Cartoon: The Context of Respectability." *Victorian Periodicals Review* 42, no. 3 (Fall 2009): 267–91.
Mitter, Partha. *Art and Nationalism in Colonial India, 1850–1922: Occidental Orientations*. Cambridge: Cambridge University Press, 1994.
———. "Cartoons of the Raj." *History Today* 47, no. 9 (September 1997): 16–22.
———. "*Punch* and Indian Cartoons: The Reception of a Transnational Phenomenon." In Harder and Mittler, *Asian Punches*, 47–64.
Moffat, Wendy. *E. M. Forster: A New Life*. London: Bloomsbury, 2010.
Morley, John. *Sedition or No Sedition: The Situation in India; Official and Non-Official Views*. Madras: G. A. Nateson, 1907.
Morton, Stephen. *States of Emergency: Colonialism, Literature and Law*. Liverpool: Liverpool University Press, 2014.
———. "Terrorism, Sedition and Literature." In *Terrorism and the Postcolonial*, edited by Elleke Boehmer and Stephen Morton, 202–25. Chichester, West Sussex: Wiley Blackwell, 2010.
Mukherjee, Ankhi. "Introduction: Postcolonial Reading Publics." *Cambridge Journal of Postcolonial Literary Inquiry* 4, no. 1 (2017): 1–10.
Mullen, Patrick. *The Poor Bugger's Tool: Irish Modernism, Queer Labor, and Postcolonial History*. Oxford: Oxford University Press, 2012.
Muñoz, José. *Disidentifications: Queers of Color and the Performance of Politics*. Minneapolis: University of Minnesota Press, 1999.
Naidu, Sarojini. Foreword to *The Great Trial of Mahatma Gandhi and Mr. Sankarlal Banker*, edited by Ke Pi Kēśavamēnōn, ix–xi. Madras: Ganesh, 1922.
Nandy, Ashis. *The Intimate Enemy: Loss and Recovery of Self under Colonialism*. Delhi: Oxford India Paperbacks, 2009.
Naregal, Veena. *Language Politics, Elites, and the Public Sphere: Western India under Colonialism*. Delhi: Permanent Black, 2014.
Natesun, B. "Irish and Bengali Poetry." *East and West* 16, no. 186 (April 1917): 368–82.
Nath, Rai Bahadur Lala Baij. "Three Modern Indian Reformers." *East and West* 12, no. 137 (March 1913): 222–25.
Nechtman, Tillman. *Nabobs: Empire and Identity in Eighteenth-Century Britain*. Cambridge: Cambridge University Press, 2010.
Negri, Antonio, and Michael Hardt. "Value and Affect." *boundary 2* 26, no. 2 (Summer 1999): 77–88.
Nerlekar, Anjali. *Bombay Modern: Arun Kolatkar and Bilingual Literary Culture*. Chicago: Northwestern University Press, 2016.
Newell, Stephanie. "Local Cosmopolitans in Colonial West Africa." *Journal of Commonwealth Literature* 46, no. 1 (2011): 103–17.
Ngai, Sianne. *Ugly Feelings*. Cambridge, MA: Harvard University Press, 2007.

Noorani, A. G. *Indian Political Trials, 1775–1947*. New Delhi: Oxford University Press, 2005.
Nussbaum, Martha. *Political Emotions*. Cambridge, MA: Harvard University Press, 2013.
Nyong'o, Tavia, and Kyla Wazana Tompkins. "Eleven Theses on Civility." *Social Text Online*, July 11, 2018. https://socialtextjournal.org/eleven-theses-on-civility/.
"Opinions of the Press." In *Cartoons from the Hindi Punch* (1904 Annual). n.p.
"Oriental and Occidental Ideas." *East and West* 1, no. 2 (December 1901): 151.
Orsini, Francesca. *The Hindi Public Sphere 1920–1940: Language and Literature in the Age of Nationalism*. Delhi: Oxford University Press, 2009.
———. *Print and Pleasure: Popular Literature and Entertaining Fictions in Colonial North India*. Delhi: Permanent Black, 2010.
Oxford Scholars. "Ethics and Empire: An Open Letter from Oxford Scholars." *Conversation*, n.d. http://theconversation.com/ethics-and-empire-an-open-letter-from-oxford-scholars-89333.
Parashuram. "The Scripture Read Backward," translated by Sukanta Chaudhari. In *Words without Borders: The World through the Eyes of Writers*, edited by Samantha Schnee, Alane Salierno Mason, and Dedi Felman, 64–80. New York: Anchor Books, 2007.
Parry, Benita. "Signs of Our Times: Discussion of Homi Bhabha's *The Location of Culture*," *Third Text* 8, nos. 28–29 (1994): 5–24.
Pernau, Margrit, and Helge Jornheim. Introduction to *Civilizing Emotions: Concepts in Nineteenth Century Asia and Europe*, edited by Margrit Pernau and Helge Jornheim, 1–26. Oxford: Oxford University Press, 2019.
Peters, Julia Stone. "Theatricality, Legalism, and the Scenography of Suffering: The Trial of Warren Hastings and Richard Brinsley Sheridan's *Pizzaro*." *Law and Literature* 18, no. 1 (2006): 15–45.
Petitions to Charles A. Elliott, lieutenant-governor of Bengal, from *Bangavasi* editors and publishers (September 4, 1891). In *Proceedings of the Home Department*, P/3880, October 1891, 161.
Phillips, Richard. *Sex, Politics and Empire: A Postcolonial Geography*. Manchester: Manchester University Press, 2006.
Pinney, Christopher. *Photos of the Gods: The Printed Image and Political Struggle in India*. London: Reaktion Books, 2004.
Pinney, Thomas, ed. *The Letters of Rudyard Kipling*. Vol. 4, *1911–19*. Iowa City: University of Iowa Press, 1999.
Porterfield, Todd, ed. *The Efflorescence of Caricature, 1759–1838*. New York: Routledge, 2011.
Potter, Simon J. "W. T. Stead, Imperial Federation and the South African War." In Brake et al., *W. T. Stead*, 115–32.
Preface to Spiller, *Papers on Inter-Racial Problems* (1911), v–vi.
Proceedings of the Home Department, P/3880, October 1891.
Raman, Bhavani. *Document Raj*. Chicago: University of Chicago Press, 2012.
Raman, Geetika. "The 'Avenging Angel' and the 'Nurturing Mother': Women and Hindu Nationalism." *South Asianist* 4, no. 2 (2016): 165–71.
Rana, Preetika. "Cartoonist Faces Ban on Right to Poke Fun." *Wall Street Journal*, January 4, 2012. https://blogs.wsj.com/indiarealtime/2012/01/04/cartoonist-faces-ban-on-right-to-poke-fun/.

Rancière, Jacques. *Dissensus: On Politics and Aesthetics*. New York: Bloomsbury, 2013.
Record of the Proceedings of the Universal Races Congress. London: P. S. King and Son, 1911.
Rorty, Richard. *Achieving Our Country: Leftist Thought in Twentieth-Century America*. Cambridge, MA: Harvard University Press, 1999.
Rose, Margaret. *Parody: Ancient, Modern, and Postmodern*. Cambridge: Cambridge University Press, 1993.
Roy, Abhik, and Michele L. Hammers. "Swami Vivekananda's Rhetoric of Spiritual Masculinity: Transforming Effeminate Bengalis into Virile Men." *Western Journal of Communication* 78, no. 4 (July–September 2014): 545–62.
Roy, Arundhati. *My Seditious Heart: Collected Nonfiction*. Chicago: Haymarket Books, 2019.
Rudy, Jason. *Imagined Homelands: British Poetry in the Colonies*. Baltimore: Johns Hopkins University Press, 2017.
Said, Edward. *Culture and Imperialism*. New York: Knopf, 1993.
Sangari, Kumkum. "Politics of the Possible: Or the Perils of Reclassification." In *Politics of the Possible: Essays on Gender, History, Narratives, Colonial English*, 1–28. London: Anthem Press, 2002.
Sanos, Sandrine. "The Sex and Race of Satire: Charlie Hebdo and the Politics of Representation in Contemporary France." *Jewish History* 32, no. 1 (2018): 33–63.
Sarkar, Tanika. *Hindu Wife, Hindu Nation: Community, Religion, and Cultural Nationalism*. Delhi: Permanent Black, 2003.
Sartre, Jean-Paul. Introduction to *The Wretched of the Earth*, by Frantz Fanon, xliii–l. New York: Grove Press, 1968.
Sastri, K. S. Ramaswamy. "Tennyson's 'In Memoriam' in the Light of Indian Thought." *East and West* 12, no. 135 (January 1913): 56–63.
———. "To the Editor." *East and West* 12, no. 139 (May 1913): 481.
Sausman, Justin. "The Democratisation of the Spook: W. T. Stead and the Invention of Public Occultism." In Brake et al., *W. T. Stead*, 149–65.
Schmitt, Carl. *The Concept of the Political*. Chicago: University of Chicago Press, 1995.
———. *Political Theology: Four Chapters on the Concept of Sovereignty*. Chicago: University of Chicago Press, 2005. Originally published 1922.
Schneider, Wendie Ellen. *Engines of Truth: Producing Veracity in the Victorian Courtroom*. New Haven, CT: Yale University Press, 2016.
Schulz, David. "Redressing Oscar: Performance and the Trials of Oscar Wilde." *Drama Review* 40, no. 2 (Summer 1996): 37–59.
Schwarz, Henry. "Aesthetic Imperialism: Literature and the Conquest of India." *Modern Language Quarterly* 61, no. 4 (December 2000): 579–80.
———. *Constructing the Criminal Tribe in Colonial India*. Chichester, West Sussex: Wiley-Blackwell, 2010.
Scott, J. Barton. "A Commonwealth of Affection: Modern Hinduism and the Cultural History of Religion." In *Constructing Nineteenth-Century Religion*, edited by Joshua King and Winter Jade Werner, 57–61. Columbus: Ohio State University Press, 2019.
Scott, J. Barton, and Brannon D. Ingram. "What Is a Public? Notes from South Asia." In "Imagining the Public in Modern South Asia," edited by Brannon D. Ingram,

J. Barton Scott, and SherAli Tareen. Special issue, *South Asia* 38, no. 3 (2015): 357–70.
Sedgwick, Eve. *Touching Feeling: Affect, Pedagogy, Performativity*. Durham, NC: Duke University Press, 2003.
Sen, Guru Prosad. "An Introduction to the Study of Hinduism." *Calcutta Review* 91, no. 182 (October 1890): 226–55.
Sengoopta, Chandak. *Imprint of the Raj: How Fingerprinting Was Born in Colonial India*. London: Macmillan, 2003.
Shah, Svati P. "Sedition, Sexuality, Gender, and Gender Identity in South Asia." *South Asia* 20 (2019): 1–23.
Sharpe, Jenny. *Allegories of Empire: The Figure of Woman in the Colonial Text*. Minneapolis: University of Minnesota Press, 1993.
Shaw, Graham. "Lithography v. Letter-Press in India." *South Asian Library Notes and Queries* 29, no. 1 (1994): 988–98.
———. "On the Wrong End of the Raj: Some Aspects of Censorship in British India and Its Circumvention during the 1920s–1940s, Part 1." In *Moveable Type*, edited by Abhijit Gupta and Swapan Chakravorty, 94–172. Delhi: Permanent Black, 2008.
Sinfield, Alan. *The Wilde Century: Oscar Wilde, Effeminacy, and the Queer Moment*. New York: Columbia University Press, 1994.
Singh, Gajendra. *The Testimonies of Indian Soldiers and the Two World Wars: Between Self and Sepoy*. London: Bloomsbury Academic, 2014.
Sinha, Mrinalini. "Britishness, Clubbability, and the Colonial Public Sphere: The Genealogy of an Imperial Institution in Colonial India." *Journal of British Studies* 40, no. 4 (2001): 489–521.
———. *Colonial Masculinity: The 'Manly Englishman' and the 'Effeminate Bengali' in the Late Nineteenth Century*. Manchester: Manchester University Press, 1995.
Slate, Nico. *Colored Cosmopolitanism: The Shared Struggle for Freedom in the United States and India*. Cambridge, MA: Harvard University Press, 2012.
Slaughter, Joseph. *Human Rights, Inc.: The World Novel, Narrative Form, and International Law*. New York: Fordham University Press, 2007.
Smith, Caleb. *The Oracle and the Curse: A Poetics of Justice from the Revolution to the Civil War*. Cambridge, MA: Harvard University Press, 2016.
Spiller, Gustav, ed. *Papers on Inter-Racial Problems*. New York: Arno Press, 1969.
———, ed. *Papers on Inter-Racial Problems: A Record of the Proceedings of the First Universal Races Congress Held at the University of London, July 26 to 29, 1911*. London: P. S. King and Son, 1911.
Stark, Ulrike. *An Empire of Books*. Delhi: Permanent Black, 2007.
Stead, W. T. *The Americanization of the World, or the Trend of the Twentieth Century*. London: Review of Reviews Office, 1902.
———. "Freedom of the Press in India: A Typical Instance of Repression." *Review of Reviews* 40, no. 238 (October 1909): 348.
———. "The Future of Journalism." *Contemporary Review* 50 (November 1886): 663–70.
———. "Government by Journalism." *Contemporary Review* 49 (May 1888): 653–74.
———. "A Plea for a Censorship on the English Press Circulating in India: An Open Letter to Lord Morley." *Review of Reviews* 40, no. 240 (December 1909): 542.
———. "Programme." *Review of Reviews* 1, no. 1 (January 1890): 14.
———. "The Reviews Reviewed: *The Indian World*." *Review of Reviews* 32, no. 187 (July 1905): 83.

———. "To All English-Speaking Folk." *Review of Reviews* 1, no. 1 (January 1890): 15.
———. "What Is My Duty to the People of India." *East and West* 1 (November 1901): 70.
Stephen, James Fitzjames. *Liberty, Equality, Fraternity.* Edited by Stuart D. Warner. Indianapolis, IN: Liberty Fund Press, 1993.
Stephens, Julia. "The Phantom Wahhabi: Liberalism and the Muslim Fanatic in Mid-Victorian India." *Modern Asian Studies* 47, no. 1 (2013): 22–52.
Suleri, Sara. *The Rhetoric of English India.* Chicago: University of Chicago Press, 1992.
Sundar, Pushpa. *Patrons and Philistines: Arts and the State in British India, 1773–1947.* Delhi: Oxford University Press, 1995.
Szeman, Imre. "Who's Afraid of National Allegory? Jameson, Literary Criticism, Globalization." *South Atlantic Quarterly* 100, no. 3 (2001): 803–27.
"Transition States of the Hindu Mind." *Calcutta Review* 3, no. 5 (January 1845): 102–47.
van der Veer, Peter. "Colonial Cosmopolitanism." In *Conceiving Cosmopolitanism: Theory, Context, and Practice,* edited by Steven Vertovec and Robin Cohen, 165–79. Oxford: Oxford University Press, 2002.
———. *Imperial Encounters: Religion and Modernity in India and Britain.* Princeton, NJ: Princeton University Press, 2001.
Venkatachalapathy, A. R. *Scholars, Scribes and Scribblers in Colonial Tamilnadu.* Delhi: Permanent Black, 2011.
Viswanathan, Gauri. "Beyond Orientalism: Syncretism and the Politics of Knowledge." *Stanford Humanities Review* 5, no. 1 (1995), https://web.stanford.edu/group/SHR/5-1/text/viswanathan.html.
———. *Masks of Conquest: Literary Study and British Rule in India.* New York: Columbia University Press, 1989.
———. *Outside the Fold: Conversion, Modernity, and Belief.* Princeton, NJ: Princeton University Press, 1998.
Vivekananda, Swami. "Vedanta in Its Application to Indian Life." In *The Complete Works of Swami Vivekananda,* 3:110–19. New York: Discovery, 2018.
Vucetic, Srdjan. *The Anglosphere: A Genealogy of a Racialized Identity in International Relations.* Stanford: Stanford University Press, 2011.
Warner, Michael. *Publics and Counterpublics.* New York: Zone Books, 2002.
Weardale, Lord. Introduction to Spiller, *Papers on Inter-Racial Problems* (1911), vii–viii.
Weeks, Jeffrey. *Sex, Politics and Society: The Regulation of Sexuality since 1800.* New York: Routledge, 2014. First published 1981.
White, Daniel E. *From Little London to Little Bengal: Religion, Print, and Modernity in Early British India, 1793–1835.* Baltimore: Johns Hopkins University Press, 2013.
Wilder, Gary. *Freedom Time: Negritude, Decolonization, and the Future of the World.* Durham, NC: Duke University Press, 2015.
Williams, Carolyn. *Gilbert and Sullivan: Gender, Genre and Parody.* New York: Columbia University Press, 2011.
Yule, Henry, and A. C. Burnell. *Hobson-Jobson: The Definitive Glossary of British India.* Edited by Kate Teltscher. Oxford: Oxford University Press, 2016.
Yuval-Davis, Nira. *Gender and Nation.* London: Sage, 1997.
Zecchini, Laetitia. *Arun Kolatkar and Literary Modernism in India: Moving Lines.* London: Bloomsbury, 2016.

INDEX

Page numbers in bold refer to figures.

1857 Rebellion, viii, x, 1, 42, 85, 93, 102, 158

Adas, Michael, 147, 170, 183
affect, ix, x, xi, xii, 2, 4–12, 25, 29, 34, 36, 42, 51, 54, 55, 56, 59–73, 102, 107, 156, 158, 170, 178–183, 187–92
   "affective communities," 30, 151, 152
   and emotion, 10
   negative, xi, xii, 8, 26, 32, 34, 56, 59, 139, 185
   see also: friendship
Africa, 44, 134, 154, 171
   African, 107, 124, 126
   African American, 164
   Pan-African Congress, 160
   Scramble for Africa, 125
   South Africa, 17, 32, 90, 134, 165, 174
Agamben, Giorgio, 23, 26
Age of Consent Act, 36, 40, 51–55, 63, 64,
   see also: sexual violence
   controversy, 34, 39–56, 63, 119
agency, 20, 74, 169
Ahmad, Aijaz, xiii, 130
Ahmad, Sarah, 9, 11, 27, 35
Ahmad, Siraj, 27
Aldrich, Robert, 66
ambivalence, xiii, 28, 76, 162, 169, 170, 182, 183
America, 46, 112, 118, 120, 124–30, 142, 152, 153, 165, 175
Anam, Nasia, 43
Anderson, Benedict, 4, 111
Anglosphere
   colonial, 20
   imperial, 150
   Indian, x, 12, 13, 16–20, 32, 73, 78, 82, 97, 106, 107, 115, 131, 133, 150, 172
anticapitalist, 174
anticolonialism x, xii, xiv, 4, 10, 12, 19, 40, 42, 45, 51, 61, 63, 67–69, 75, 99, 109, 111, 113, 131, 133, 134, 144, 146, 149–52, 156–62, 172, 175, 178, 181, 183, 190
apartheid, ix, 32

Aravamudan, Srinivas, 173, 174
Arnold, Matthew, 119, 120, 128

Babu, 12, 25, 35, 36, 42, 43, 44–46, 51, 56–62, 63, 66–69, 76, **77, 78,** 97, **100,** 134, 156, 157, 188
   Babu English, 43
   see also: caricature
Bakhle, Janaki, 12
Bakhtin, Mikhail, 80, 93
bande mataram, 29, 45, 99
   see also: Chattopadhyay, Bankim Chandra
Banerjee, Sukanya, 30, 35, 45, 89, 117
Bangavasi,
   periodical, 21, 34–36, 53, 55, 59–61, 63
   trial, xi, 3, 6, 8, 32–40, 51–69, 186
Barber, Karin, 128
Barrier, Gerald, 5
Basker, James, 113
Basu, Rajshekhar, 81–83
   see also: Parashuram
Bayly, Christopher, 1, 14
Bengal, 1, 13, 15, 19, 23, 40, 43, 44, 45, 53–67, 81, 82, 86–89, 97–99, 102, 115, 133, 148, 172, 178–81
Bengali, 1, 15, 40, 43–45, 53, 57, 59–62, 66, 67, 81, 82, 97, 99, 172, 181
   partition of, 92–102, 133, 178
   tiger, 86–89
   see also: caricature
Berlant, Lauren, 9, 11
Bhaba, Homi, x, 12, 27–29, 74–78
   see also: mimicry, sly civility
Biggar, Nigel, 189, 190
Boehmer, Elleke, 18, 152, 173
Bombay, xi, 13, 14, 51, 72, 74, 83, 91, 141, 150, 151, 170, 172, 175, 189
Bose, Chunder Nath, **57,** 59
Bourdieu, Pierre, 78–81, 114
Brake, Laurel, 121, 143
Brennan, Timothy, 20

207

INDEX

Brouillette, Sarah, 131
Burton, Antoinette, 131

Calcutta, xi, 1, 3, 13, 14, 33–35, 38, 55, 56, 74, 112, 116, 117, 129, 138, 151, 175, 175
caricature, 12, 14, 45, 45, 46, 72, 73, 74, 75, 76, 85, 89, 90, 91, 92, 93, 97, 107, 109, 111, 134
caste, 83, 133, 153, 155, 165, 179, 189
censorship, vii, 4, 5, 7, 10–12, 17, 18, 26–32, 40, 51, 71–73, 92, 97, 102, 113, 130, 140–42, 150, 151, 154, 155, 156, 174, 180, 183, 189, 191, 196
Chakrabarty, Dipesh, 39
Chatman, Seymour, 79, 80, 107
Chatterjee, Partha, 4, 14, 22, 52
Cholera, 41
Christianity, 13, 83, 115, 116, 147, 148, 164, 169, 170
civility, 16, 28, 46, 191, 192
  incivility, 191, 192, *see also:* sly civility
class, vii, ix, 2, 3, 19, 20, 39, 45, 60, 62, 76, 85, 91, 111, 113, 119, 124, 148, 149, 152, 164, 166
  middle class, vii, ix, 2, 3, 19, 20, 39, 45, 60, 62, 76, 85, 91, 111, 113, 119, 124, 148, 149, 152, 164, 166
  working class, 41, 63, 64, 65, 14, *see also:* caste
Codell, Julie, 175
Cohen, Ed, 65
communism, 183
  see also: socialism
conspiracy, 38, 67, 140
Contagious Diseases Act, 63–65
cosmopolitanism, 20, 30, 113, 114, 117, 120, 130–33, 147–50, 157, 161, 166, 169, 172–75
Criminal Law Amendment Act, 20, 30, 113, 114, 117, 120, 130, 131

Devere, Heather, 165
Dirks, Nicholas, 36–38
dissent, viii, ix, xi, 8, 12, 22, 32, 35, 44, 45, 73, 86, 107, 130, 133, 156, 178, 185, 188, 189
Donogh, Walter Russell, 2, 3, 7
Dutta, Krishna, 46

East and West, see: periodicals
East India Company, 13, 37, 56, 93, 115
Edgar, John, 56, **58,** 59, 60, 61, 66
Elgin, Lord Thomas Bruce, 6, 7
effeminacy, 39, 42, 44, 45, 46, 62, 66, 67, 69, 178
  see also: masculinity
Enlightenment, 10, 13, 22, 28, 75, 113, 114, 120, 172, 174, 175, 191

English-Speaking
  folk, 112, 124, 125, 130
  Indians, 19, 20, 93, 178
  Races, 124–27
  World, 13, 128

Fanon, Frantz, 191
Floyd, George, 191
Forster, E. M., xi, 146, 152, 156–58, 171, 183
  Passage to India, 152, 157, 158, 183
Fraser, Nancy, 15, 16, 61
Freitag, Sandria, 14, 16
friendship, 75, 150–52, 156–58, 162, 165–68, 174, 177, 180
  see also: Civility

Gandhi, Leela, 18, 30, 151, 173
Gandhi, Mahatma, xii, 4, 12, 17, 21, 32, 40, 67–69, 134, 158, 165, 166, 170, 174, 177, 185–89, 192
  trial for sedition, xii, 4, 12, 21, 32, 67, 68, 185
gender, 20, 34, 40, 51, 54, 68, 69, 71, 72, 82, 102, 119, 162, 163, 189
Ghosh, Amitav, 5
Ghosh, Durba, 20, 23, 179
Gibson, Mary Ellis, 18, 30
Gilmartin, David, 33
GoGwilt, Christopher, 148, 149
Gokhale, G. K., 165–70
  see also: Universal Races Congress (URC)
Goswami, Manu, 149
Gramsci, Antonio, 149
Griffiths, Andrew, 128
Guha, Ranajit, 5, 26
Gujarati, 15, 74, 89, 90, 91, 92, 94, 97

Habermas, Jürgen, x, 11, 15, 16
Hastings, Warren, 36, 37, 38, 39
Hindi, 43, 90, 91
Hindi Punch, see: periodicals
Hinduism, 13, 21, 34, 44, 46, 53–55, 71, 83, 89, 98, 102, 116, 117, 146, 147, 154, 159, 173, 174, 179, 180, 181, 189
Hindustan Review, 138, 169
Hofmeyr, Isabel, 18, 11, 112, 172
Hoggett, Paul, 9
Hussain, Nasser, 22, 23

incivility, x, 191, 192
  see: Civility
Indian Charivari, see: periodicals
Indian Opinion, see: periodicals

Indian Penal Code, viii, 2, 21, 22, 34, 153
  Section 124a, vii, ix, 2, 3, 5, 6, 9, 13, 21–26, 34, 38, 40, 53–56, 60–64, 67, 68, 71, 79, 92, 102, 109, 153, 165, 166, 188–92
  Section 153a, 2
Indian World, see: periodicals
  see also: Review of Reviews
Ingram, Brannon D., 14, 15
internationalism, 120, 124, 149, 172
Irish nationalism, 41, 42, 65, 97, 126, 133, 181
Islam, 37, 98, 102, 117, 154, 183, 189

Jain, Anurag, 153
Jameson, Fredric, xiii, xiv
Jones, William, 27

Kalighat
  Temple, 14, 46, 89
  paintings, 46, 76, 89
  see also: caricature
Kamra, Sukeshi, xiii, 2, 4, 12, 36, 61, 73
Kannada, 15
Kaur, Raminder, 25, 26
Kennedy, Dane, 20
Khanduri, Ritu, 85, 86–91
Kipling, Rudyard, xi, 45, 46, 152–58, 171, 178
  The Eyes of Asia, 152–56
  Kim, **47**, 76, 152, 155, 156
  Mookerjee, Hureee Chunder, 45, **47,** 155
Klancher, Jon, 113
Kolsky, Elizabeth, ix
Koven, Seth, 151

Lelyveld, David, 14
lithography, 91, 92
Locke, John, 24
Long, James, 1, 25
Lyall, C. J., 56, 60, 61, 66

Macaulay, Thomas Babington, 24, 27, 62, 130, 147–49, 167, 173, 174
Makdisi, Saree, 149
Malabari, Behramji, 51, 52, 156, 172, 173
  see also: East and West
Manalansan IV, Martin F., xii, xiii
Marathi, 29
Mark, Simon, 165
Martin, Amy, 42
masculinity, 35, 36, 44–46, 53, 55, 63–69, 111, 178, 188
  see also: effeminacy
Mayhew, Henry, 85

Mazzarella, William, 25, 26
McDonald, Peter, 32
Mehta, Deepak, 189
Mehta, Uday, 24
Menke, Richard, 120
Meyer, Moe, 65, 66
Mill, John Stuart, 21, 24
Miller, Elizabeth, 175
mimicry, x, 12, 17, 27–32, 51, 72–82, 105, 107, 141, 142, 155, 156, 171
  colonial, 17, 27, 28, 74, 75
  print, x, 17, 27, 28, 74, 142, 186, 189
  see also: Bhaba, Homi
Mitter, Partha, 86, 92, 109
Mookerjee, Hurree Chunder, *see:* Kipling, Rudyard
Morley, Lord John, 73, 107, 134, 140
Morris, William, 114, 174
Morton, Stephen, 3, 23, 97, 98
Mother India, 13, 42, 54, 71, **72**, 89, 102, 119, 155
  see also: Bande Mataram, caricature, swadeshi
Mullen, Patrick, 41
Muñoz, José, 17
Mussel, James, 143

Nandy, Ashis, 68, 74, 75
Naregal, Veena, 19, 20
Native Newspaper Report (NNR), 2
New Imperialism, 128
Newell Stephanie, 44, 45
Newnes, George, 119, 120, 127
  Tit-Bits, 119, 120, 127
  see also: Stead, W. T.
Ngai, Sianne, 5, 6, 11
Nussbaum, Martha, 9
Nyong'o, Tavia, 191, 192

obscenity, 24, 25
O'Donnell, F. Hugh, 41, 42
Orientalism, 147, 149, 167
  see also: Said, Edward
Orsini, Francesca, 14

Pall Mall Gazette, see: periodicals
Panchoba, 93, 102
  see also: Hindi Punch
Parashuram, 81–82
  see: Basu, Rajshekhar
parody, xi, 30, 73, 66, 74, 75–86, 93, 90, 93, 97, 98, 102, 107, 109, 117
  see also: satire, mimicry

Partition (of Bengal), 92–102, 133, 178
Passage to India, see: Forster, E. M.
Periodicals, 1, 2, 12, 13, 16–21, 27–32, 36–40, 42, 51, 55–62, 72, 74, 82–86, 90–93, 97, 109–23, 126, 129–33, 139–43, 148, 151, 165, 169–78, 183
  Bangavasi, 21, 34–36, 53, 55, 59–61, 63
  Calcutta Review, 13, 34, 112, 116, 117, 129, 138, 175
  East and West, xi, 20, 32, 51, 117, 126, 138, 142, 145–51, 157–83, *see also:* Malabari, Behramji
  Friend of Indian and Statesman, 40
  Hindi Punch, xi, 83, 84, 87–99, 102–09, 118, 133, **138**, 182, *see also:* Panchoba
  Indian Charivari, xi, 74, 76, **78**, 84, 85, 97, **98**, **100**, **101**
  Indian Opinion, 17, 90, 134, 165, 174, 175, *see also:* Gandhi, Mahatma xi, 74, 76, 78, 83–93, **96**, 97, **99**, 107, 134, **137**
  Indian World, xi, 2, 21, 22, 34, **132**, **135**, **136**, 153
  Irish Freeman's Journal and Daily Commercial Advertiser, 41
  Liverpool Mercury, 41
  Nation, 42
  Northern Echo, 41
  Pall Mall Gazette, 118, 119, 140, *see also:* Stead, W. T.
  Review of Reviews, xi, 17, 18, 40, 52, 90, 112, 118, 119, 121–26, 128–31, **138–42**, 159, 177
  see also: Stead, W. T.
  Standard, 41
  Times of India, 40, 61
Postcolonial
  era, 189
  literature, xiii, xiv, 141
  publics, x, 14, 15
  studies, 27, 150, 190
  subjectivity, 20
Punch (British), *see:* periodicals
Punjabi, 89

race, 66, 73, 97, 124, 160–65, 169, 175, 179, 181
  "English Speaking Races," 124–27
Raman, Bhavani, 43
Rancière, Jacques, 16
Ray, Prithwis Chandra, 129–31, 141, 142
review, xi, 30, 40, 111–18, 129–33
Review of Reviews, see: periodicals

Rose, Margaret, 80
Roy, Arundhati, viii, 192
Rudy, Jason, 18

Sagar, Rahul, 19
Said, Edward, 18, 149
  see also: Orientalism
Sangari, Kumkum, 16
Sanskrit, 55, 68, 89, 116, 180
Sarkar, Tanika, 54
Sastri, Ramaswamy, 180, 181
  see also: East and West
satire, 74, 79, 81, 84–87, 89, 92, 97, 133, 134, 157
  see also: mimicry, parody
Schneider, Wendie Ellen, 56
Schwarz, Henry, 115
Scott, J. Barton, 14, 15
Section 124a, *see*: Indian Penal Code
Sedgwick, Eve, 31, 51
sedition, vii, viii, 3–9, 24–35, 38–42, 53, 54, 60–69, 73, 98, 107, 133, 134, 139, 140, 185–88
sexuality, xi, 17, 34, 40, 51, 53, 65–69
  homosexuality, 33, 36, 41, 51, 52, 63–69, 119
  queer, 17, 34, 36
sexual violence, 71, 102, 158, 169
  rape, 28, 53, 56, 71, **72**, 102
Shah, Svati, 34, 35
Shaw, Graha, 18, 91
Singh, Gujendra, 154
Sinha, Mrinalini, 18, 20, 63, 64
Slate, Nico, 173
sly civility, 12, 16, 21, 28–32, 62
  see also: Bhaba, Homi, civility
socialism, 65, 183d
  see also: communism
Spiller, Gustav, 159–64
  see also: Universal Races Congress (UCR)
Stead, W. T., xi, 17, 18, 40, 52, 64, 90, 112, 113, 118, 118, 119, 120, 121–31, 136, **138–43**, 159
  see also: Review of Reviews
Stephen, James Fitzjames, 7, 21, 23, 166
Stephens, Julia, 14, 38
Suleri, Sara, 39
Swadeshi, 53, 99, 131, 179
syncretism, xi, 30, 32, 146–51, 158, 159, 171, 172, 175
  see also: Viswanathan, Gauri

Tagore, Rabindranath, 45, 145–47, 152, 157, 178, 181–83
  Gitanjali, 145
Tamil, 15, 90
Thompson, Simon, 9
Tilak, Bal Gangadhar, 5, 6, 29, 31, 40, 53, 60, 99, 139, 167, 186
  see also: sedition, trials
Tit-Bits, see: Newnes, George
Tompkins, Kyla Wazana, 191, 192
trials
  1922 trial for sedition, xii, 4, 12, 21, 32, 67, 68, 185, 186, *see also:* Gandhi, Mahatma
  1987 trial for sedition, 5, 6, 31, 40, 53, 60, *see also:* Tilak, Bal Gangadhar
  Bangavasi, 3, 6, 8, 32–40, 51–69, 186, *see also:* Age of Consent Act
  Great Wahabi Case, 38
  Hastings, 37–39
  Regina v. Hicklin, 25, *see also:* obscenity

Trivedi, Assem, 71, **72,** 73
  See also: Mother India

Universal Races Congress (URC), xii, 150, 158–67, 170, 172
Urdu, 89

van der Veer, Peter, 12, 116, 173
Vande Mataram, *see:* Bande Mataram
Verbitsky, Jane, 165
Viswanathan, Gauri, 18, 124, 147, 148, 173
Vivekenanda, Swami, 45, 46, **48, 49,** 51, 68, 146, 157, 173

Warner, Michael, 15, 16
Wilde, Oscar, xi, 33–46, **50,** 51, 52, 55, 62, 63–69, 159
  The Portrait of Dorian Gray, 33
  see also: trials
Wilder, Gary, 159
Williams, Carolyn, 82–83

www.ingramcontent.com/pod-product-compliance
Lightning Source LLC
Chambersburg PA
CBHW030735250426
43671CB00035B/396